The Dynamics of Knowledge

Recent Titles in
Contributions in Philosophy

Ethics of Withdrawal of Life-Support Systems: Case Studies on Decision Making in Intensive Care
Douglas N. Walton

Insight-Imagination: The Emancipation of Thought and the Modern World
Douglas Sloan

Making Believe: Philosophical Reflections on Fiction
C. G. Prado

Arguer's Position: A Pragmatic Study of *Ad Hominem* Attack, Criticism, Refutation, and Fallacy
Douglas N. Walton

Physician-Patient Decision-Making: A Study in Medical Ethics
Douglas N. Walton

Rethinking How We Age: A New View of the Aging Mind
C. G. Prado

Rationality in Thought and Action
Martin Tamny and K. D. Irani, editors

The Logic of Liberty
G. B. Madison

Coercion and Autonomy: Philosophical Foundations, Issues, and Practices
Alan S. Rosenbaum

Einstein and the Humanities
Dennis P. Ryan, editor

From Science to Subjectivity: An Interpretation of Descartes' *Meditations*
Walter Soffer

José Ortega y Gasset: Proceedings of the *Espectador universal* International Interdisciplinary Conference
Nora de Marval-McNair, editor

The DYNAMICS of KNOWLEDGE

A CONTEMPORARY VIEW

David Z. Rich

Contributions in Philosophy, Number 36

GREENWOOD PRESS

New York · Westport, Connecticut · London

Library of Congress Cataloging-in-Publication Data

Rich, David Z.
The dynamics of knowledge : a contemporary view / David Z. Rich.
p. cm.— (Contributions in philosophy, ISSN 0084-926X : no. 36.)
Bibliography: p.
Includes index.
ISBN 0-313-26102-4 (lib. bdg. : alk. paper)
1. Knowledge, Theory of. I. Title. II. Series.
BD161.R49 1988 87-36100
121—dc19

British Library Cataloguing in Publication Data is available.

Library of Congress Catalog Card Number: 87-36100
ISBN: 0-313-26102-4
ISSN: 0084-926X

First published in 1988

Greenwood Press, Inc.
88 Post Road West, Westport, Connecticut 06881

Printed in the United States of America

The paper used in this book complies with the Permanent Paper Standard issued by the National Information Standards Organization (Z39.48–1984).

10 9 8 7 6 5 4 3 2 1

This work is dedicated to my mother, Vanessa, to the memory of my father, to my sisters, family and friends, and to my Beautiful Diana Lerner, who keeps the salt on my bread.

Outstanding unsolved problems demand new methods for their solution, while powerful new methods beget new problems to be solved. But, as Poincaré observed, it is the man, not the method, that solves a problem.

E. T. Bell, *Men of Mathematics*

Contents

Preface ix

Part I. On Our Era of Knowledge—I

1. General Comments 3
2. Comments on Social Time 19

Part II. On Our Era of Knowledge—II

3. General Comments 41
4. On the Dynamics of Creativity 47
5. The Dynamics of Creativity—I 57
6. The Dynamics of Creativity—II: A Theory of Creativity in Our Contemporary Era of Knowledge 79
7. On Acceptance and Rejection in Our Era of Knowledge 105

Part III. The Dynamics of Our Era of Knowledge

8. Further Comments on Anti-Realism and Social Time 131
9. Some Consequences of Our Era of Knowledge 147
10. Further Remarks 185

11. Coda 203
Notes 209
Selected Bibliography 219
Index 223

Preface

This work is a culmination of study, research, and debate over twenty-three years, from its original statement while I was an undergraduate at Florida State University, through its variations while I attended the London School of Economics as a post-graduate student, to its present form, finalized in its argument in Tel Aviv.

I owe a debt to all those bright, sensitive people who listened to me, who debated my ideas and helped sharpen them. I hope this work will be a form of repayment.

The ideas expressed here are original in their usage. The terms "past-, present-, and future-oriented societies or countries" stated in the last part are those of the writer, as are the understanding and interpretations of the societies and countries I have designated them to represent.

I wish to express my thanks and gratitude to Diana Lerner for her unselfish help and devotion; without her, these ideas would never have been put on paper.

PART I

ON OUR ERA OF KNOWLEDGE—I

1

General Comments

> As soon as you leave the beaten track of vague clarity, and trust to exactness, you will meet difficulties.
>
> Alfred North Whitehead, *Science and Philosophy*, 1984

Is there a conflict between vague clarity and exactness where truth is concerned? Indeed, truth is what is, and what is is true; there can be no more exactness than that. Indeed, there is no conflict here. The conflict does exist, however, on another plane, one more interesting than the tautological statement that "Truth is true and what is true is truth." For example, consider an accident to which there are three witnesses: the accident happened and the three witnesses are joined by the accident's victim in providing the details. The vague clarity of the truth will be extrapolated from the witnesses' testimonies together with the victim's report (assuming the victim survived), but the details will differ, no matter how slightly. Exactness is elusive, indeed unobtainable, but truth can be gained by combining those parts of the description that are held in common by the witnesses' testimonies together with the victim's, while those points of difference are held in question. In this example there is no conflict between vague clarity and exactness concerning truth because truth does not require exactness at the expense of clarity to be obtained.

However, consider another example, one of great depth and expanse: what can be said about both the vagueness and clarity of Universal Truth, the religious and mystical Truth that binds all humans together in their search for understanding of their predicament? Certainly, if such a truth exists it must be absolute and certain, clear in its statement and meaning, although throughout history it has been most vague, to the extent that it has generated differences of such intensity that blood has been shed for it. Can this be one of the paradoxes of the human condition—Truth, Absolute and Unchanging, so real to its believers that they will kill and die for it?

For this situation, Alfred North Whitehead's comment is appropriate, for our human predicament is such that this Absolute Truth, be it vague and lacking in clarity and exactness, and held by those privileged to have achieved the highest levels of comprehension and awareness of this Truth, has led and will continue to lead to difficulties. Religious truth has led to great ideological and physical clashes, often with the majority of cultures called to bear arms for the truth of which they have no real understanding of the points of issue. Philosophical truths have caused the followers of one school to disassociate themselves from those schools of differing views. Often in economics, the holders of one doctrine that has been incorporated in a political system have little or nothing to do with the proponents of differing schools of thought. Hence, all too often in the history of humanity the search for Absolute Truth and its attainment by the privileged classes of intellectuals and mystics has resulted in the negation of what this Truth is claimed to possess, this being the wisdom of the universe and the peace for all mankind.

There is another, counteracting, factor of our social inheritance manifested in the cultures of mankind as they have developed. Regardless of the cultural differences that often lead to strained relations, it is the distinctions of each particular culture that set it apart from all others, and this is the idea of history as expressed in the scientific and artistic contributions of each of our cultures. For history is not only a diversifier as it relates to the uniqueness of each people and tells of the conditions and events in each culture that sets it apart from others; history is also the story of humanity and is thus a unifying discipline, for it tells of our common inheritance, our collective contributions and ideas, our local and global conflicts, and our coming together in times of crisis and joy.

History can thus be broken down into subelements, each with its own unique system of conflicts and unions, each with forces that bring the subsystem into a working pattern and demonstrate its effects on other such systems, as well as indicating the inputs from other systems and the influences these exert in turn.

There are, however, two fields in the history of mankind that seek to unify the various and diversified cultures rather than generate friction among them; these two fields are the sciences and arts. This is so because on the common level, at least, the sciences—as applied by technology—are useful in making our lives easier, and the arts bring out the feelings in us that the burdens of everyday living require we keep held inside. The sciences unlock our private and public awareness as they are applied to the problems that confront us, providing products that enhance our material and physical well-being. The arts allow us to express our private personal emotions, either in groups, as spectators listening to a concert or watching a performance portrayed with great sensitivity and skill, or alone, as when reading a great and uplifting work of emotional or intellectual depth. The need for public and private expression of feelings seems to be an integral part of the human condition, and the constraints of daily life prevent these feelings from being expressed. Artistic contributions are made within the cultural conceptualizations of the artist, and it is often the case that the wider traveled the artist, whatever his or her medium of expression, the more universal is the artistic message and the greater the appeal of the work, as he or she acquires the influences of different cultures and conceptualizations and interprets these influences within the mode of the chosen artistic activity. There is another factor with which the artist has to work, this being the coming together of our world through the conditions of travel and the information media, which bring our attention to different cultures to a greater extent than ever before; different events and contributions throughout the world are now exposed to us for our scrutiny and understanding. Hence, while the East and West are in a seemingly perpetual state of military, economic, and political conflict, they share the music and literature and paintings of the other's cultures. The boundaries of artistic freedom are very weakly drawn, and in those societies where officialdom seeks to limit artistic expression and the movement of ideas across geopolitical boundaries, there are always networks of "underground" couriers to make these works known to the rest of mankind.

While the arts have been individualistic expressions within cultural orientations, the sciences have their origins within the mass acculturations of early societies. In the history of mankind the advent of science is relatively new, to the extent that Sir Isaac Newton called his monumental work *The Mathematical Principles of the Philosophy of Nature*; although the linguistic and intellectual concept of "science" was already established by that time (the term and approach had been used even before Galileo by such thinkers as Jean Buridan), it was philosophy that stirred Newton to use that title.

"Philosophy" comes from the ancient Greek, meaning 'the love of wisdom.' The purpose of philosophical inquiry is to discover wisdom. Wisdom is eternal, unchanging, established. The various deities of the ancient peoples, which were worshipped as the creators and rulers of the world, were considered the possessors and propagators of this wisdom.

This conceptualization of deity, of a supreme being as the ruler of the universe because of his or her all-powering superior wisdom, has throughout the ages been the cause of most good in the world. Systems of ethics were derived from codes associated with various deities. Obeisance to deities has also been the source of much conflict and bloodshed; throughout history, war and crimes against humanity in general and individuals in particular have been committed willingly and officially in the names of such deities.

This is, of course, not the place to argue the merits of religion or of the superiority of one religious attitude over another. What must be said here is that science—knowledge and its systematic classification—is the direct offspring of philosophy and developed through the need to de-emotionalize the pursuit of wisdom. Whereas wisdom is eternal, permanent, and never changing, knowledge is never steady and is in fluctuation. It is altered as different and more diversified information infiltrates these knowledge systems, rendering them antiquated and no longer pertinent or relevant. It may have been historically true that science was considered a means of reaching the ultimate, that being wisdom; throughout the centuries, science has been demonstrated as a powerful instrument for understanding the universe and working with it. As a result the umbilical cord has been cut and a new relationship formed: that of philosophy working together with science to help mankind to live in a better world.

While religious conflict has not ceased completely it has definitely subsided as a major source of tension. The current revival of fundamentalist movements has largely been localized, and while these movements' members are often extreme and vocal, their influence in the contemporary world (the term "contemporary" is used to contrast with the fantastic world these people claim to desire) is marginal compared with the big power potential for confrontation.

The consequence of the decline of religion as a source of conflict is that ideology has replaced religion as the cause of confrontation. In this sense, World War I can be considered as a sort of watershed, with the Imperialist powers of Germany and the Austro-Hungarian Empire fighting the powers of the British and Russian Empires and France, Italy, and the United States. After World War I and the signing of the Treaty of Versailles, ideology as the cause of confrontation had become firmly established as the source of conflict, with technology serving as the handmaiden in the pursuit of geopolitical power. The Communist movement had been transformed from an economic and political ideology into the government of the Soviet Union. In contrast was the Nazi movement in Germany which seized control in 1933, even though it began as an ideological movement in 1919. Allied in ideology to suppress the Axis powers, the countries that joined forces in World War I were again on the same side in World War II. The Westernized countries involved had the loosest ideology, that of democracy, with each country manifesting this system of government according to the historical workings of its political processes throughout its development.

Regardless of the influence of ideology on the political processes, most practitioners of science sought to avoid the difficulties of ideologies and personal perspectives, which philosophy and religion have provided as intellectual and emotional inheritance. The theories of science could be tested, proven or refuted in all parts of the world where people were sufficiently educated and trained. The language of science was mathematics, the objective and universal language that knew no national or geographical barriers, so that science could expand without political restrictions. Moreover, mathematics was developed on its own as a unique discipline and became the queen of intellectual activity, second only to the physical and biological sciences. It seemed, therefore, that the ties between philosophy and science were cut permanently. The philosophers continued their speculations, and religion still played a major role in philosophy. Though many scientists were religious, when practicing their disciplines they remained true to their code that science should be detached from human emotion as much as humanly possible, that all speculation be objective in nature and that all experimentation be conducted without bias.[1]

Perhaps the first big rift between religion and science was initiated by the Church when the confrontation with Galileo took place. One of the most influential thinkers of his time (and indeed of all time), Galileo argued the Copernican teaching that the sun is the center of the solar system. Reacting in fear, the Church declared that the doctrine of the heliocentric system was in complete conflict with its teachings. Their response was an expression of the uncertainties that the new science had to offer for both that time and the future. Yet as time passed and more progress was made in science, especially with the powerful tools of Newtonian physics and the reasoning that followed, there was again accord between the Church and the men of science. For one aspect of the conflict was indeed significant: that the realm of learning, as it had developed through the Dark and Middle Ages, was no longer the sole property of the religious institutions, that the sciences opened a revolution in education, which threatened the intellectual elite at the established centers of learning. These centers were primarily religious oriented. Even the impact of Aristotelianism, reintroduced by the writings of St. Thomas Aquinas, remained in the hands of the elite, albeit it was this development, perhaps more than any other, that turned the religious thinkers from the Platonic "other world" to the Aristotelian "this world" and restored the intellectual elite's interest in their fellow men.

There were at least two other great shocks to religion that the philosophers of religion still must come to grips with: the Darwinian approach to the development of life and the Freudian contributions to understanding human behavior. The religious institutions are based philosophically and mystically on the conceptualization that humanity is created in the image of the deity of their professed persuasions; if this is so and if this is their reason for their existence, then how could they comprehend the hard scientific reasoning of Darwin and his followers that mankind evolved from the lower animal species, which are life-forms without souls, and hence lacking responsibility for their actions, neither subject to the beauty of a promised heaven nor to the condemnation of a threatened hell. Moreover, the concept of the "missing link," a primate evolved from the ape, proved so absurd to religious authorities that the clash Galileo started with his advocating the heliocentric system of planetary motion—a revised version of the ancient Aristarchus's contribution but one of greater accuracy—was again revised. The domain of science, it was rebutted, should remain in the fields of science, while that of religion should pertain to matters of religion; never the twain were to meet. But they did meet and clashed openly in the universities, in the popular press, and in the courtrooms.

Mankind's position was reduced from the center of the universe, with the planets and sun revolving around the earth, to a satellite of the sun, subject to Galilean-Newtonian relativity. Mankind's unique position on this traveling planet was further diminished by being evolved from lower life-forms and being a not-too-distant relative of the lower primates. Freud further reduced mankind's status as thinking and productive creatures. He argued that many human motivations are based on factors outside the range of immediate awareness, that we are constantly at war on the level below conscious awareness with issues we dare not face openly, and that this subconscious war affects life in ways of which people have no comprehension. Religion, presenting humanity with the freedom of choice, was unable to struggle with this argument of subconscious motivation, which entailed humanity's not having the ability to choose freely in decisions of ethics, of good and evil, and being submitted to a complex entity of unconscious struggling forces manifesting themselves in subtle ways of human behavior. Science and philosophy, each as an expression of inquiry, parted ways for a while. Science stayed with the real world, a tradition re-established by the Aristotelian St. Thomas Aquinas, while philosophy retained its Platonic roots and searched for religious ideas to strengthen the fight against the inroads made by the works of all-powerful science.

Of course, there was not such a clear-cut dichotomy as many of the practitioners of philosophy and science maintained. There was a fusion of both Platonic and Aristotelian roots in the contributions of several philosophers, together with the influences of other earlier and later Greek thinkers. This issue cannot be explored in depth here, but to mention Arthur Schopenhauer and Friedrich Nietzsche as two examples may perhaps suffice. Schopenhauer was an idealist with a small "i," in contrast to the Platonists, among them Bishop George Berkeley in Britain at an earlier period. For the German Schopenhauer, the world is will and representation (*vorstellung*, sometimes translated in the Platonic esprit as "Idea"), but the significant difference between his teachings and that of the Platonists is that Schopenhauer maintained that only mankind can bring this representation into living reality through their actions. Schopenhauer thus rejected the movement of ideas, the dialectical mechanism expounded by his contemporary and intellectual rival Georg Hegel. Schopenhauer was a philosopher with a neo-Aristotelian scientific leaning; he maintained that changes come about by people working with the materials of the world, thinking of new forms, new methods, and new concepts, and bringing them into reality. There was, for Schopenhauer, no automatic movement of ideas. He did not accept the Hegelian cycle: the synthesis of a paradigmatic concept is created by the clash of opposing ideas and then their fusion, and then the synthetic concept eventually generates its opposite concept and results in a further clash and fusion.

Schopenhauer placed mankind once again in the center of the universe, a position somewhat weakened by the Copernican-Galilean revolution, which removed the planet earth from the center to revolve around the sun and obey the physics of the subservient position. For Schopenhauer, not the forces of nature nor the laws of physics ruled mankind, but these were forces and laws at mankind's disposal to be used in the shaping of the world. Hence, philosophy, the love of wisdom, was restored in Schopenhauer's argument to its earlier status, as it joined with science to become mankind's instrument for working with the world and for shaping it according to mankind's representative conceptualizations.

Nietzsche went further, proclaiming that only mankind was of value, that all the forces that tied mankind to the laws of nature or science were to be broken; that all the scientific, religious, mental, and physical restraints were to be cast off so that complete moral, political, and emotional freedom could be established. This is not anarchy, not a philosophy of egotism nor of solipsism, for there is no reason why a working social system cannot be established according to the esprit of Nietzsche, one that would allow human relations and individual expression to be formed and stated. Nietzsche rejected the levelling down of mankind that the quasi-theories of socialism had advocated, as well as the mental restrictions that religion imposed, with its forbiddings that confine the human spirit and dull the senses.

This brief description cannot but fail to do justice to the ideas of these two German thinkers and to the currents of scientific and philosophical thought that were stirring imaginations during that time. The ideas these theories posited and the backlashes that resulted, however, established new dogmas that would be exploited and then cast aside after their usefulness had ceased. In the United States, for example, the pragmatic school of thought proclaimed that if an idea, machine, or system worked, that is, if it fulfilled the purpose for which it was designed, then it was true for that purpose. In Britain, the use of models for explaining ideas had taken hold, especially in light of the two great British thinkers, the skeptical and economics-oriented David Hume and the strict religious idealist Bishop Berkeley. Models served to demonstrate the theories that were being developed: by experimenting with models of ideas or systems, philosophers could demonstrate their benefits and flaws; then the models could be cast aside after serving their purposes. In France and on the Continent in general—apart from the rumblings coming from Germany—the concept of reason in the esprit of René Descartes held sway; logic and strong premises could describe ideas that could be tested according to the rigors of intellectual activity to be cast aside if shown to be defective and to be kept for further use if demonstrated to be sound.

Stirring among these movements was the spirit of the Renaissance, the revival of inquiry that unleashed the scientific and artistic revolutions, which in the spirit of Aristotelian philosophy, revived by St. Thomas Aquinas, placed mankind and its environment in the center of inquiry along with matters of religious consideration. Hence, a new relationship was established: Mankind serving the Creator through worship and deeds, but the Creator providing mankind with new tools and conceptions for exploring the world, thereby enabling mankind to realize the second part of the first commandment in the Bible, of not only being fruitful and multiplying on the earth, but of conquering it.

Still, with all the new philosophies, their practitioners sought to replace the influence of religious institutions and make these philosophies domains in their own right. Schools of thought were established and their proponents sought to do intellectual battle with those who did not accept their proclaimed "true" teachings. In the course of the intellectual debates, the strengths and weaknesses of the various approaches were brought to the fore, with the true believers either not noticing their weaknesses or arguing them away with trivial explanations, yet emphasizing their strengths as significant points to be reckoned with. To those who were already ideologically committed, these arguments were merely exercises in intellectual sophistry—a fallback to one of those less desirable aspects of ancient Greek thinkers; to those who were not committed but still searching, these ideas provided intellectual stimulation and aided in the formulation of new ideas.

In the spirit of the renewal of inquiry, two aspects came to the fore that perhaps caused the greatest stir among the intellectual community. One was the reconsideration of the basic building material of the universe, the atom. As a particle, the atom was considered to be solid and hence not subject to further reduction into parts; when it was smashed, broken down to even smaller particles and when the relationships among these particles were explained and constructed as models, the entire scientific community was amazed. Moreover, the great intellectual structure formulated first by the ancient Greek Democritus (c. 460–c. 370 B.C.) and argued for by the Roman Lucretius (c. 96–c. 55 B.C.) and expounded by Sir Isaac Newton and Gottfried Leibniz and their followers—that matter was composed of the basic substance of particles—was brought into question by field theories and wave phenomena. The movement of genuine inquiry was well underway when the scientists, the seekers after knowledge, began breaking down ideological dogmas that philosophers, in their search for permanent wisdom, sought to construct.

In light of the breakthroughs in science, two philosophical systems were initiated, one claiming to be based in the spirit of scientific inquiry, the other reflecting the breakdown of previously held institutional values and again placing mankind in the center of the universe. Each system offered much benefit to the intellectual and emotional development of inquiry in the twentieth century; each had in its characteristics the making of its own demise.

Logical positivism developed as a form of inquiry in light of the contributions made in science and mathematics. The logic of Aristotle, as expounded and developed by the schoolmen down to the eighteenth century, was demonstrated to be antiquated with respect to the problems arising in mathematics, such as attempting to prove the derivation and logical validity of Euclid's fifth axiom of parallels. This axiom appealed more to intuition than to sound mathematical reasoning, and in the spirit of inquiry mathematicians sought to base their discipline not on intuition but on logical sound reasoning. The fifth axiom defied their attempts; moreover geometrical theories, such as those posited by Bernhard Riemann and Janos Bolyai, sought to reconstruct Euclid's axiom to develop other possible geometries where the axiom holds and that are mathematically interesting.[2] How was mathematics, in which this classic geometry and other difficulties, such as the continuum problem of functions and the theories and paradoxes of sets, to be logically valid? What of logic itself?

The position of logical positivism stated that propositions that were to be considered seriously, as intellectual statements asserting some point about a subject, had to be established within a formal context, such as a scientific theory. As these statements had to be theoretically derivable, they had to be affirmable, both by corresponding to their expressed domain, and by being derived without contradiction. This derivation was through the application of logic, with the validity of the statements determined by the logical referral to their domains, which expressed their positivistic aspects. Hence, in the determination of validity for this approach, logic ruled supreme.

The other system of thought that developed during this period was an expression of the breakdown of all respectable systems, first in science and philosophy and then in the real world of politics, exemplified in the world chaos and useless slaughter of World War I. This was a movement that was to be known as existentialism. This movement expressed development of the human being and psyche through the accumulation of experiences. Moreover, when mature people make a decision they enter into an emotional and psychological "contract" with their decision and must existentially accept the consequences of their actions, even though they may not accept the action, the decision they made, as the very best possible decision they could have taken given the unique circumstances. Existentialism removed the system from its imposition on mankind and placed mankind in the center, free to choose the system and its restrictions, free to reject the system and perhaps establish a new one on its own terms. Whatever the choice, the consequences or the decision must be accepted and borne with integrity.

Interestingly, an existentialist could become a logical positivist by accepting the rationale of the positivist approach and the significance of its requiring that statements be logically derivable and affirmable. But existentialism cannot be logically verifiable, for it is a philosophy and not a system of knowledge, which has testable statements.

The positivist teachings sought to give the inquiring person the opportunity to come to grips with the world. Statements thus logically derived and affirmed could be considered true, especially if they had been derived from theories. The greater proportion of a theory's statements so affirmed, the closer the theory came to representing the true world as delineated by the theory's range and domain. Affirmation was sought in light of the revolutions in physics, chemistry, and mathematics.

There is another reason why affirmation was so important, and here the logical positivists and the existentialists share, in a sense, common ground. This reason is the political upheaval that resulted from World War I, which that war had fought to put an end to. The economic fluctuations, the standoff in the political sphere, the fall of democracy and rise of Nazism in Germany, and the Japanese ventures in Asia, demonstrated that the immediate postwar optimism, furthered by the establishment of the League of Nations, was merely an illusion. The positivists sought affirmation, which could guide them securely in their inquiries and bolster themselves against the instability all around them. On the other hand, the existentialists sought to explore life to its fullest, to live for the moment in the moment's given conditions, and to affirm life through this living and experiencing. The world was in turmoil, with the great economies at a near standstill, with the world's governments threatening or being invaded, with promises of stability by leaders who could establish political systems to endure for a thousand years. The only outcome from this chaos and confusion was another attempt to sort out the difficulties and to achieve stability for political development and economic growth. The forces of contrast had become so intense and uncompromising that war was again proclaimed. The decline of the search for certainty was immediate and the positivist and existentialist movements, in the aftermath of the war, survived primarily as college adventures and experiments.

TRUTH AND ANTI-REALISM

The spirit of inquiry was not stilled after World War II. Indeed, a new optimism set in, for the United Nations served as a forum for world opinions and provided policing forces when necessary to reduce world tensions. With Keynesian reasoning it appeared that the problems of severe economic depression had been solved, and idle capital and heavy unemployment would be only memories and material for historians interested in the period. These impressions were soon altered by the postwar recession and the world conflicts, which resumed after a brief hiatus.

However, as a consequence of the prewar scientific developments and because of the technology developed during the war, coupled with a strong desire on the part of humanity to build a better world, finally, we have entered a new historical era, the era of knowledge. This era will be discussed in detail in Chapter 3; what must be mentioned here is that for all historical areas, the past is not eliminated immediately and a new set of dynamics established, unique to the era. On the contrary, the social and political development of mankind, as expressed in the various societies, are so often unnoticed over short periods of historical time that revolutions, be they political or technical, seem to be the most outstanding generators of short-run change. What then is our era of knowledge, and how is it apart from all other historical eras? The answers to these questions rest largely on the function of social time, which will be discussed in the next chapter. What must be considered here is that one unique aspect of our era of knowledge is our use and conceptualization of truth.

In prior historical eras, truth was considered absolute, unchanging, permanent; the task of the philosopher was to search out this truth as truth is wisdom. As was stated in the previous section, the difference between truth and knowledge was that truth is enduring and knowledge is changing; according to the philosophers and scientists, therefore, knowledge was subject to error and hence potentially wrong, while truth belonged to a category not touchable by error and hence permanently correct.

The doctrine that truth is permanent, unchanging, absolute is called the realistic theory of truth. It is realistic because it describes truth as representing the real world in the sense that the world is objective, with a truth-value independent of our means of knowing it. In other words, conditions and situations are true without our subjective influence on them, but our describing them as true means that our statements correspond to the truth-value of these conditions or situations. These events possess a reality independent of our subjective interpretations, and although for whatever reasons we may reject them as being false, the error lies in our subjectivity and not in the reality. Truth, for the realist, is independent of human observation and consideration, which means that we cannot affect its value in any way.[3]

The anti-realist argument to be presented here is not a counter argument but a variation of the realist argument for truth. For what are the realists describing, if not situations and conditions that exist at the time of their descriptions of events that they have witnessed or were informed about by sources they consider reliable. In previous historical eras all attempts to posit anti-realist approaches to truth would have been criticized, indeed perhaps dismissed out of hand. In our era of knowledge, however, this cannot be the case. The situation in our era is such that the dynamics of knowledge render conditions or events true for one defined period of time and circumstances, while false during others. Truth has become enduring so long as the conditions remain so; there is no Greek wisdom in contemporary truth, no absolute permanent set of circumstances that are hidden from the philosopher's comprehension and that can be understood only by the way of the search for truth. If the social philosopher has any role to play in contemporary society, it is to look at this era of knowledge and seek to understand its dynamics. The relevance of the anti-realist truth—a truth that is relevant so long as the conditions and circumstances for truth are viable—will then be made plain. This does not mean that there is no Greater Truth in the sense of the Supreme Being; it does mean that this aspect of truth, the religious Truth as is sought be people in their hours of trouble or amazement or deep emotion, is outside the dynamics of contemporary society. Our era of knowledge is historical and not religious. Truth, therefore, is also defined within the confines of this historical era and not by the religious experience.

Of course, all this has to be demonstrated. This anti-realistic approach to truth, together with the function of social time in our era, will be treated together in the context of the historical era of knowledge in order to accomplish what this philosopher seeks, to shed light on our era.

2

Comments on Social Time

> The notion that each subsequent generation would necessarily know more than its predecessor and that this progressing would never be completed—a conviction that only in our time has found challengers—was important enough; but for our context, even more important is the simple, matter-of-fact perception that "scientific knowledge" has been and can be attained only "step by step through contributions of *generations* of explorers building upon and gradually amending the findings of their predecessors."
>
> Hannah Arendt, *The Life of the Mind*, 1981

CHRONOLOGICAL TIME

Can one generation know more than its predecessor? Can this progressing of knowledge ever be completed? Moreover, is there a period in time that offers unique conditions for completing one progression of knowledge and opening others?

These three questions are the themes of this chapter. It can be seen that time in its general form is directly related to history, and it will be shown for the argument of this work that two types of time are important. Historical time is calculable, measurable by events according to our understanding. Social time, however, is more evasive, harder to penetrate, and indeed may contain information that the following period lacks or is unable to expand upon.

First, the idea that one generation can know more than its predecessor is debatable. If this idea is to be taken in its strict meaning, then "more" is a quantifiable relationship, measurable and comparable. One can think of such diverse historical periods as the ancient Greek culture and compare it to Europe as the inheritor of this culture, but as it was in its historical era of the Dark Ages. When wisdom was considered to be at the disposal of the religious authorities and the mystics, who had vested interests in maintaining their positions of authority during the Dark Ages, could the amount of knowledge be considered greater than when Socrates debated in the Athenian marketplace and Plato listened, or when Aristotle studied with Plato at the Greek Academy? The question takes on a slightly different nuance when it is considered that the knowledge of Plato existed to some extent but was employed primarily in support of the religious and mystical authorities. Indeed, much of Greek philosophy and culture was dormant, to be revived during the period of the Renaissance, the rebirth of knowledge. Hence, as the knowledge of the ancient Greeks existed but largely in a dormant state during the Dark Ages, because it was not used, did the people of the period of the Dark Ages have more knowledge than the ancient Greeks?

If knowledge and information are to be weighed and measured with the consideration of their mere existence, then the answer must be that knowledge and information were greater in the Dark Ages than during the times of ancient Greece, when Athens was the center of intellectual and artistic activity. As far as generating more wisdom and knowledge based on the measurement and weight of content, the Dark Ages are self-defining: a historical era of little creative activity, where art works followed certain patterns and molds—mainly religious—where music was little developed, and literature dealt mainly with the world of the angels.

Can this process of knowledge ever be completed? It depends on what type of knowledge is being considered. Consider, for example, the knowledge that prevailed before Nicholaus Copernicus and held by many that the earth is flat—a conception that was dominant even though Aristarchus and other ancient Greeks maintained that the planet is round and revolves around the sun. It is now merely an intellectual exercise to hold the flat-earth position, in spite of its weighty history, but the knowledge gained about the cosmos for this position is far from complete. The steady-state theory of cosmic creation, for example, holds its own unique dynamics for a flat earth, and perhaps is the only cosmological theory which offers some consistency with this approach, and this is a highly respected theory. The big-bang theory, with an expanding universe, depends largely on an Einsteinian relativistic conceptualization, with the consequence that, in an expanding universe, the flat earth per se could not exist but would be saddle-shaped but still with edges. The knowledge gained from the flat-earth concept may never be complete, no matter the cosmic dynamics. The real question here, however, is: Should such an approach even be considered, given our present state of knowledge? The question about whether the progress of knowledge can be completed depends on what knowledge is being considered and whether it is important for the current state of the arts to deal with it.

In general, however, the progress of knowledge in its aggregate can never be completed. That is the definition of knowledge, that it is temporary, changing, and ever dynamic. Knowledge is subject to the requirements of truth and falsity, to the extent that knowledge considered true in one time period, may be brought into question in another such period and demonstrated to be false in still a latter period. This is the advancement of ideas, of the arts and sciences, and it is based on the correction of ideas that are questionable and the rejection of those that are no longer relevant.

Hence, the question about the completion of one progression of knowledge and the opening of other such progressions is significant. This is the entire issue of chronological and historical time, with the further refinement of the latter into social time.

Chronological time is the indication of our human history as signified by events that have generated change. Our history stands as the inheritance of all mankind, whether we are aware of it through our cultures and no matter how diversified these events are. We learn of such time in our schools, by our own unique social and cultural functions, and by our holidays and ceremonial events, which are based on our ancient and modern collective histories that we consider significant enough to be remembered.

Chronological time allows for the world's great events to become part of collective and national-social histories. This time is shared by all peoples, all nations, and it is the conceptualization of time that binds all mankind. Tribes of humanity, having little or no contact with the mainstream of civilization, share with all humankind the measurement of the days, the calculation of the seasons, the counting of years. Indeed, calendars can be transposed, so that common time can be derived, no matter how diversified the methods of computation may be. The cultural and historical events celebrated by these peoples can also be interpreted in the mainstream conceptualization. Appointments of leaders, of ministers, the ceremonies of obtaining and maintaining offices of authority, these are common to all societies; their dates, their periods of reign, are determined by chronological time, which signifies an event in the historical social fabric requiring celebrations with such honor. As these types of events are common to all societies, the socioreligious aspects of these ceremonies can be readily understood for their particular and universal significance.

Because of its particular and universal dual aspects, chronological time is all-encompassing, extending with human history. Contrasted to this time is *era* time, signifying the representative stages in human development. For example, the prehistoric era represents that part of human history not known but conjectured. The prehistorical Stone Age, and the historical Bronze Age, the Golden Age of Greece, each of these periods is known—if not entirely known, then at least for the main contributions made during their eras. We possess enough information so that historians and archeologists can do valid research into these eras and formulate hypotheses about them which have greater import than mere historical conjecture.

Era time is both historically unique and represents the continuum of human history. No era is begun in isolation of the past and ends its uniqueness regardless of the future. Each era carries with it the dynamics of the past, the contributions of the previous era, its values and difficulties. Hence, two questions must be raised. First, what are the factors that bring about the demise of an era and the beginnings of another? Second, what is the uniqueness of our era and how are these factors to work for us? These questions will be treated with respect to social dynamics.

It must be considered that there are universalities concerning social dynamics, regardless of the era under discussion. This is because all humans have common traits that unite them in humanity for all the good and bad that this entails. But it must be understood that the differences among people—partly due to genetic make-up and partly due to environment—are the generators of social specifics that determine (the term is used here loosely) the dynamics of social interaction, the duration of these dynamics, and, most important, the directions they take.

Up until the Industrial Revolution, the dynamics that generated the delineation of an era were those brought to the fore by the gentry and the artists, musicians, and people of letters who associated with them, as well as the military leaders who shaped national boundaries and allowed for people and material to be employed and worked and converted into economic prosperity. Going back to the earliest history, the strongest ruled and to these rulers artists and musicians turned. For group leaders needed the artists and musicians to uplift them from the mundane and often nasty chores of ruling. It can be assumed that this was so during prehistoric times, when the human psyche came into its own with the enlargement and development of the brain. The Bronze Age offered no difference in this respect. Indeed, as societies became more complex, with tribes being replaced by nations, artists and musicians and scribes occupied special places in the royal courts, and these professions were to glorify these peoples' gods and praise and at times deify the rulers. The period of the ancient Israelites also illustrates the roles of the artists, musicians, and scribes. The building of the Tabernacle in the wilderness was most certainly a work requiring great thought and artistic abilities, which later were to be recognized in the Temple of Solomon in the holy city of Jerusalem. Moreover, the Psalms—written in part by Moses, and attributed in part to the first man Adam, added to by David, his son Solomon, and the Levites who served the priests in the temple—indicate the great abilities of this ancient people. However, these abilities were directed primarily to religious and political matters (a distinction not often clear during that period), related primarily to the service in the Temple.

The period of the empire in Rome was similar in the respect that the artists and musicians were at the service of the emperors and the ruling class, and the scribes came mainly from that class. With the decline and fall of Rome and the establishment of the Holy Roman Empire, music and painting took on an extremely religious aura, portraying the story of Christ and varying little from this theme. The only exception was the folk arts, which permitted self-expression on themes not accepted by the authorities; they may have been the first real rumblings of social (as contrasted to political) rebellion. Social rebellion was manifested when the Dark Ages thawed and Renaissance Man entered the world picture. This all-around person, versed in the academic literature of the time and extremely curious as to the applications of renewed knowledge to the artistic and scientific issues of the day, brought about an open intellectual rebellion, which is still prevalent today. The patterns of established forms and concepts and fixed and reliable methods of thought and procedure certainly are important, but their results are predictable, hence they remain valid for only those problems and procedures for which they were formulated. Other issues that have since arisen cannot be resolved using these established methods, so that other approaches must be formulated that will have validity for these issues, in spite of the vested political, artistic, and scientific interests maintaining the established methods and approaches. Rebellion as expressed in the arts and intellectual activity became partly defused as a cause for social unrest, as the experimentations of artists, musicians, writers, and scientists became acceptable to the current vested interests, who, in turn, had their attitudes and concepts influenced by the artists and intellectuals.

It must be noted that in the earliest of historical times when people were engaged in commerce, most of the men of commerce were literate, those who developed existing markets and explored new ones. The development of writing aided commerce, and only after the period of the Israelite Exodus from Egypt did literature expand and diversify into other forms. Hence, in Imperial Rome, the writers were lawgivers and historians and to some extent philosophers; in the time of the ancient Greeks, they were philosophers, conjecturalists, and historians who were storytellers in their own right, basing their history on the prevailing mythologies. The people of letters in the period of the Dark Ages were scholastic philosophers, and except for such thinkers as John Duns Scotus and Buridan, who lived during the decline of the Dark Ages and on the threshold of the rebirth of knowledge, men of letters were concerned primarily with heaven and its hierarchies.

ERA TIME

Each historical era carries in it the past and its own unique present. In the beginning of the Industrial Revolution, certain forces aspired to the dark ages of economic and spiritual control. Together with the changes in the methods of production which led to changes in the style of clothing due to the textile factories of Rochdale in England and the centers of manufacturing which were being formed in the United States and the other countries influenced by industrialization, religion was still very strong in its hold and the newly formed industrial wealthy classes which controlled business and banking controlled the peoples' buying habits, their credit-worthiness, and their abilities to improve their situations. This situation was, however, due to the fact that in the early stages in this era the entrepreneurs did not understand the very dynamics of industrialization that would develop, nor had they the knowledge sufficient to fully comprehend their newly acquired means of production and economic activity; therefore, it was somewhat natural that they revert to the patterns already established with historical validity, that is, the patterns of widening the control and power over the people. Hence, the development of city slums as workers sought employment in the new system. Hence the subsistence wages, the absence of worker (and child) protection, and the nonexistence of another historical establishment, the guild, as a form of protection.

It did not take very long in the development of industrialization for entrepreneurs and workers alike to realize that for the first time in history a paradoxical situation existed. Workers with low pay will purchase only subsistence goods and services, while industrialists vie with each other to gain the consumers' money. Hence, the social conditions evolving with industrialization had to be treated in a manner unique to the era. The power of applying the science of mechanics to the means of production, the application of imagination to opening new markets and creating demand, the ability of firms to adapt to the newly formed competitive situations, only demonstrated that social legislation had to be enacted to provide more than a living wage. Hence, as part of the revolution in industry, there was another revolution taking place, that of the laborer speaking out for his and her rights for the first time in history within a mass workers' movement.

This was certainly one of the many unique contributions of the Industrial Revolution. Like every innovation in an historical era, this too had its roots in history, only to gain full expression in the latter part of industrialization. In the Dark Ages, for example, people engaged in subsistence living, primarily working the land, consuming what they could of their products, and seeking to trade off the surpluses. Specialization of labor did exist, of course; tailors then produced their goods and services in exchange for their own needs, and so did the medical professions and all other forms of livelihood. The conception of national currencies was far from developed, and the functions of the banking system were nonexistent. All real control was at the disposal of the religious authorities together with the political rulers; it was not uncommon for religious leaders to be the real politicians or the politicians to be wielding the power behind the religious authorities. This system prospered during the Middle Ages, but during the Renaissance, both religious and secular learning had spread, especially with the aid of the printing press.

The spread of education helped the laboring classes to cope with the changing world, and when entrepreneurs began to apply the methods of science to the means of production, local and national economies developed the means of commerce to deal with the new production techniques, means such as marketing and sales and the development of international exchange. Labor was no longer engaged in the same types of production as in the earlier periods, for there was great migration from the rural areas to the centers of commercial and business activity. Machinery was brought to the farms, which resulted in more output for less work, releasing more people for industrial production. With the development of commerce, banks became more sophisticated, handling the greater amount of paper currencies being used as means of payment for business transactions. But to whom was this production geared ultimately, if not for those very same people who worked in the industries that produced the goods and services? This point was not lost on the industrialists, who sought both foreign and domestic markets.

In order to export, prices must be competitive; to achieve this, production costs as well as profit margins must be kept at an accepted ratio, which allows for profitable exporting. In this sector workers' wages were low, and profits were reasonably high, a situation that acted as a sort of trade-off, keeping costs within an acceptable level with revenues. For domestic markets, the emphasis was on expansion, so that no matter how low wages were, new sales due to an increasing absorption of people in the labor force would offset the lack of steady purchases from a committed buying public.[1] Together with increased advertising, employing ever greater sophistication, the producers sought to obtain sufficient sales to make their remaining in business worth their efforts.

Of course this could not last for long, as the industrialists were dependent on the workers for using their purchasing power, as much as the workers were on the industrialists for employment. If left alone this situation would have eventually straightened itself out, and in the long run a reasonable aggregate wage schedule, commensurate with what the economy could produce and move as goods and services, would have been obtained. But as John Maynard Keynes once remarked, in the long run we are all dead. The action that was taken was a throwback to the old guild concept of artisans, this time as workers guilds or unions to define and protect workers' rights. This is certainly a movement unique to the Industrial Revolution.

Still two more factors are unique to the period of industrialization, each of which applied sciences to the demands required by them. One, very costly and whose affects are still very much with us today, is the concept of world war for domination. Of course, war is as old as mankind's claim for territorial integrity, with the means by which wars have been fought determined by the sizes of the opposing forces and the ingenuity of the military planners. Single innovations, however, such as the incorporation of explosive power into weaponery, changed the manner by which wars have since been fought. For example, with the development of gun powder and rifling gun barrels, the old fighting positions of standing line by line guarded by shields and shooting arrows had to be altered—although in their campaign against the American colonials the British still employed this fighting stance and suffered great losses—so that the necessity to take sufficient cover for protection resulted, changing the entire strategy for waging battles.

The same is true of industrial techniques applied to waging war. Mobile vehicles, better and more accurate means for discharging projectiles, and (as applied in the two world wars) aviation and aerial bombing also changed the shape of military strategy. Without the motor, there would have been neither mobile vehicles nor aircraft; without industrialization, there would have been no motor, no means of gasoline-propelled motion.

Of course this position can be criticized as discussing the situation from the vantage of hindsight, that this is a historical tautology. This, however, is far from the case. It merely indicates the historical fact that each area delineates and is delineated by the very contributions made and their applications. As soon as these contributions become obsolete as the full focal issues and become secondary to other contributions, then the era has come to an end and another era begins. Social time depicts the contributions made in each era as the era is developed and as the contributions are applied and generate further contributions within the same contextual conception.

Just as the means of waging war had altered during the Industrial Revolution due to the concepts of industry applied to strategy, so in the sciences did such radical changes occur that it is possible to conceive that the amount of pure theoretical scientific development that occurred during the period of industrialization outweighs all the scientific contributions that went before. Of course this approach is somewhat improper, for scientists during this period, to paraphrase Newton, stood on the shoulders of giants who went before them, to gain their insights and visions. Science for the sake of science as well as for technology, then, was developed during this period, and this was due in part to the problems of industrialization and to the solutions of which the sciences most certainly contributed.

Nor was the very conception of science limited to the physical and biological realms, as it had traditionally been. New sciences developed, applying as well as possible the scientific methods of investigation. Economics is but one example. Indeed, Adam Smith's great work, *The Wealth of Nations*, can be said to have heralded in the Industrial Revolution. It is no wonder that his main contribution was in the fields of production and the theory of competition. Such economists as David Ricardo, J.-B. Say, and, along a more sociological line, William Thompson, followed the esprit of Smith, while Karl Marx, following Thompson, challenged the very health of the theory and practice of capitalistic economics that had then developed, with the social distortions and class realignments that were occurring at the time that he and Friedrich Engels wrote.

Partly because of the socio-economic problems that Marx brought to the fore and partly independent of Marx's influence,[2] the science of sociology developed, with such writers as Max Weber and

Gustave Le Bon making their contributions to the understanding of humanity in their socioeconomic-political ambience. These social sciences developed, moreover, because of the impact of industrialization on life styles, as these styles affected the influence of wealth on production and on the shifting living patterns and labor mobility due to the requirements of both employment and industrialization.

Consider economics, for example. With the early users of applied science to technology, the problems of efficient production relative to potential markets arose, and economists sought prescriptive-descriptive theories to explain these difficulties and provide guidelines for dealing with them. Production methods improved, and consumers gained greater market sophistication and discrimination. The uses of mathematics for determining cost and production curves, for linear and nonlinear programming, for nonstandard analysis of economic planning and costing had to be extremely sophisticated in order to cope with the problems of contemporary production and decision making at the management levels. Hence, mathematics, in itself the queen of the sciences, became the handmaiden of the economic thinkers, who related their ideas to the entrepreneurs, who in turn moved the wheels of industry for their own financial advantages; increasing consumer choice and the wealth of the nations were the consequence.

Each era is broken down into its levels of social time. For example, the era of the Industrial Revolution began approximately in 1776—interestingly enough when the American colonists proclaimed their independence and when Adam Smith's work, *The Wealth of Nations*, appeared—and ended with the breakdown of the capitalistic system as it then existed with the Great Depression of 1929. By the beginning of World War II, the processes of industrialization had been completed within the conceptual framework of the era; in the aftermath of the war, a new era had begun, built on the contributions of previous eras but more specifically on the contributions made in the Industrial Revolution.

Social time in an era is delineated by the specific universal contributions made in the era. For example, the development of the steel industry can be interpreted as occurring during the social timespan that existed from the time the Bessemer process was developed to convert iron ore into steel for industrial use and the spread of competitive companies among the industrial countries, with the consequent improvement in the techniques of iron-ore processing.

This is, of course, only a single development, albeit one of great importance in the era of industrialization. This one single social time is, moreover, congruent with other social times equally important in the era of industrialization.

Hence, an era is defined by the many social times within it, the events of each time having a common property uniting them with the era. We would certainly not treat history seriously if we considered the age of electronics as occurring in the Renaissance or the computer age coming to the fore in the 1930s. While the nature of the atom was considered since the time of the ancient Greeks, to be more modern we would not say that the atomic age began in the 1930s, even though attempts to smash the atom were seriously considered then. We would be treating history seriously, however, if we considered the relationship between the Renaissance and electronics, for the rebirth of knowledge opened a period of contemplation and exploration never before undertaken by humanity, with one of the areas of exploration being the magnet and electric current.

The question that must now be raised is: How can we determine which ages or social times are part of our unique era?[3] Indeed, does the movement of historical events indicate a cyclical periodicity yet to be calculated, in which circumstances are similar so that eras can be delineated by the similarity of events? For example, the intellectual inquiry of the ancient Greeks resulted in many questions being raised that are relevant today, among them being the problems of mathematical infinity and the basic structural material of the universe. With the combined contributions of the Greek and Roman civilizations, we should have flourished, and our cultures should have developed at an enormous rate. Then came the destruction of the library in Alexandria and with it the decline of learning, plunging the world into darkness. With the Renaissance, the world reawoke to the traditions of the ancient civilizations and began to expound on their artistic and intellectual contributions, bringing these contributions into new areas and conceptualizations. Then came a period of relative intellectual calm, not darkness, of course, for the civilized world was no longer prepared to destroy or abandon what had already been accomplished.

But there was no historical legacy for the applications of the ideas of the ancient civilizations and this threw the world into patterns of searching, with such distortions as the aftermath of the French Revolution, the incongruity of American democracy during the process of actual industrialization, the paradox of the necessity of wealth for purchasing the goods and services resulting from production, the actual poverty that existed in the newly formed slums, and the inability to distribute wealth according to the economic forces that were imposing themselves on industry and society.

All this resulted in the situation in society in which intellectual processes were still developing while social inabilities to cope with intellectual progress resulted in social conflicts and finally in two world wars. Can these events be interpreted in a cyclical framework? Are we not engaging in a period of intellectual activity never to have been experienced since the ancient library in Alexandria flourished or since the other historical peak, the Renaissance, broke loose on the world?

This is certainly a tempting thesis; with all the certainty of mathematical mechanics and with the proper conceptualizations, a cyclical approach to history can be constructed. But perhaps such a construct depends on the intentional misinterpretation of history or on the ignoring of events that lack the conformity to the demands of the construct. Such a construct would require that eras are of sufficient similarity to be accepted as historical repetitions, albeit with different personalities but with events so similar as to give credence to George Santayana's warning in *Dominions and Powers* that those who forget history are bound to repeat it.

SOCIAL TIME

If eras are so similar as to be treated exactly in the same manner, then so must the specific social times in each era. As to whether a distinct social time belongs to an era, this question must be answered within the context of the era considered. The example of the Bessemer process can serve this purpose, for it further expanded the processes of industrialization. It could have been developed during the Iron Age, but there would have been little or no use for steel then, for there were no industrial demands for the product; steel would have been a side product with no market.

The problems of industrialization indeed gave rise to the Bessemer process for hardening iron in order to increase its utility in building and in machinery. Such equipment was most certainly lacking in all previous ages, and architecture—domestic or public—required no steel reinforcements or decorations. The requirements placed on society by industrialization led to the use of steel in building to house the masses that came to live in the industrialized areas, as well as for constructing the factories required by industry, which was expanding due to its own dynamic processes.

Social time is thus delineated by the events, processes, and circumstances that impress utility on the eras in which they occur. There may be individual social times occurring in the era, or several such times may be occurring more or less congruently, depending on the contributions made and the dynamics generated by each contribution. Likewise, there may be only one contribution of such significance to occupy the interests and efforts of those working in the field so as to overshadow all other contributions, thereby diminishing their significance and perhaps ultimately depriving the era of their benefits. Charles Darwin's theory of evolution is such an example; its influence was so great that the social sciences could not release themselves from its grip. All of biology came into its sphere, and despite the significance of Lamarckian evolution, it was greatly overshadowed and reduced—wrongly—into insignificance, a factor that contributed to its near-demise with its misadoption by T. D. Lysenko in the Soviet Union as official policy on sociobiological evolution.[4]

It may appear to be a tautology to say that social time is dependent on the era in which it occurs because only the events in that era have value in the specific era alone. This, however, is not a tautology, for on closer inspection it reveals itself as a historical truth. Just as an era is delineated by the demise of its predecessor, being formed by the events of the past and crystallized into a set of unique circumstances, these circumstances are the manifestations of events, of social times, which impart to the era its uniqueness. Wars have been fought throughout history, but with the coming together of the nations because of the ideology of unity (a concept advocated by Immanuel Kant and given expression in the League of Nations and later in the United Nations) and the improvements of transportation (specific to the Industrial Revolution with the advances in rail and seagoing transportation) the methods of war were able to engulf the world, bringing the combatants of many countries to face each other in destruction. World War I was such an example and the attempt at world unity made with the formation of the League of Nations failed because of the misapplications of the fruits of industrialization to alleviate the difficulties that resulted from the outcome of the terms of the armistice. The conditions imposed on Germany became intolerable, and the failure to understand the difficulties of neoclassical economics, such as the assumption presented most eloquently by A. C. Pigou of full employment, also hindered economic revitalization.[5] Indeed, Germany's economic condition (hyperinflation, declining industrialization, and declining industrial output as the Industrial Revolution drew to a close) resulted in several paradoxes that Germany attempted to resolve by the age-old political reaction of war.

One such paradox was the fantastic industrial ability and potential built up over the duration of the Industrial Revolution, existing idle alongside a work force that sought employment but was unable to find it. It was as if there existed a total saturation of demand so that no new demand existed to stimulate retooling and production. Some economists and politicians blamed the union movement for generating unemployment by excluding from the workers' ranks people who were nonunion members and by keeping wages artificially high so that the demand for increased labor and consequent increased potential production was nonexistent.

On this point it can be argued that the development of the union movement occurred independently of the world depression. The labor movement had its beginnings in the early days of industrialization, although its successes then were very limited. In fact, the wage scales were what the markets could afford according to those seeking work and those supplying it. The investors and speculators in both property and in paper shares lost confidence when the levels of profits were too high for the banks and other lending institutions to keep control over them. When the crash came, the lack of confidence was almost immediate and people began panic selling and attempting to rescue their money from the rapidly declining values of stocks.

The uniqueness of this great economic crash was in its extent and duration. Capital markets have always been subject to speculation and fluctuations in the values of their shares. But in the Great Depression, the crash that signaled this period of stagnation was so swift and deep, the only way revolution could have been prevented was the way taken, once the shock had eased and people began to see their lives and the general situation in somewhat proper perspective: the government underwrote the banks and regulated the stock market through legislation. The uncontrolled growth of the economies during the period of industrialization had finally ended, and a new era was in the offing. Unfortunately, the dawning of this era had to wait until the sociopolitical disorientations of the depression, manifesting themselves in the age-old remedy of military conflict, this time on a world scale with the power of destruction outshadowing that of the previous world war.

Necessity is the mother of invention, especially when lives are at stake. World War II, with all its wasted lives and destroyed productive capacity, did result in some interesting contributions. One, of course, was the successful explosion of the atomic bomb, achieved by the United States in the deadly race with the Nazi regime. This gave the era to come a unique complexion, an advantage which had never existed before in history, the unleashing of energy—albeit this time for destruction—realizing the dreams of the ancient Greek and Roman atomists, the particle physicists such as Newton and Leibniz, and forerunners of Einstein and his contemporaries. Another unique invention was the development of the computer, which today is an integral tool in industry, education, and medicine.

When the smoke of the war had cleared and the newly established governments in Europe and Asia began reconstruction, it had become clear that the period known as the Industrial Revolution had come to an end. This does not mean that there was no longer a need for industrialization, for the war-torn countries most certainly had to re-industrialize, often implementing new concepts of production and management. Also, the countries emerging from nondevelopment and underdevelopment had to undergo their own basic industrializations. This was not the revolution of industry, however; it was the application and adaptation of processes that had been developed through industrialization and were being applied to the specific conditions and situations of each of these countries as it evolved.

The economic system which brought about industrialization and which thrived in its climate was no longer operable, as the Great Depression had given witness. Keynes questioned Pigou's assumption of classical and neoclassical full employment, and indeed the invalidity of this assumption in the economic reality was most certainly the case during the Depression. This full-employment assumption was abandoned in the postwar period as recession set in, brought about by the retooling of industry from wartime to peacetime production. In the shadow of the atomic age and the computer technology, education was emphasized. The collective memory of the aftermath of World War I was still fresh; demobilized servicemen had been unemployed and contributing nothing to their own welfare and to that of society. The mistakes of that period were to be avoided again. The opportunity to study, to learn to cope and prosper in the new era, was provided by several governments, the ones that had achieved the highest levels of industrialization. They thereby averted the danger of a postwar backlash and possible revolution by the most sophisticated of publics, those of the industrial countries.

Moreover, the specter of great unemployment, a natural response to the period before the war, was avoided by the massive efforts at postwar reconstruction. Even in Britain, one of the victors, a massive effort was made to reconstruct the social and economic basis on which the country had flourished for so long. In the postwar elections, the Conservatives headed by the wartime prime minister Winston Churchill were deposed, and the Labour Party given a new mandate.

This does not mean that there were not postwar economic fluctuations, but they differed from those that occurred in the Industrial Revolution because they were brought about by the changeover from massive wartime production to the production of peacetime goods. People who worked in the factories had to be laid off or retrained; demobilized soldiers had to find employment, and while there was a decline in de facto aggregate demand, the potential aggregate demand was at a level never before experienced. It took only the retooling process and the reinstatement of the demobilized military into the production process for this aggregate demand to become de facto. The Industrial Revolution had ceased to exist for industry, and this was well established. In the unleashing of new hopes and aspirations, in the attempt to build better lives and to avoid nuclear confrontation, new approaches to research were made. New products were presented to the public; academic centers were also becoming oriented to an extent greater than ever toward social problems and international relations. Education began to take on an ever-increasing importance for the building of one's career, and with the continuing developments in the sciences and technologies, the emphasis was being placed on these aspects of education, so that there was knowledge explosion never experienced since the Renaissance. But there is one important difference: the Renaissance was an era of refinding knowledge, rediscovering what had already existed and expanding upon it. In the beginning of our era of knowledge, new forms of knowledge were brought to the fore. Granted that atomic energy had been unleashed during the war, but in the aftermath of the confrontation the problems of using atomic energy for peaceful causes were raised, along with potential hazards of applying atomic energy to such uses as generating power for domestic and industrial consumption. Granted, computers existed in crude forms prior to the war, but after the programs for peace had been established, methods for handling the transfer of vast amounts of funds and their applications had to be established, and the computer was an effective tool for dealing with this problem.

Moreover, television, a British invention in the 1920s, was not really exploited until after the war. Transistors and microchips are among the contributions of postwar research and development. These developments occurred after the war, not before or during it, because the requirements of industrialization had changed along with the era of industrialization itself. There was no longer a need for massive industrialization, for this had already been established and had come to an end with the Great Depression and the Keynesian approach. While industrialization had, of course, not ceased, the necessary patterns and socioeconomic infrastructures had been established and accepted. Indeed, cities had risen around industries, the health and education systems had adapted to the requirements of industrialization, and social legislation had been enacted to ensure the rights of the citizenry in light of the increasing political power of industry. Unions had been somewhat effective as a counter to industrial power, patterns of employment had been established, and the knowledge of new and sophisticated industrial equipment had been gained.

Because of the tremendous potential aggregate demand in the postwar period, industry was ready and able to absorb the newly released soldiers. The questions confronting both government authorities and industrialists, as well as the civilian population expanded by demobilization, were: What should be produced, how to underwrite the economy to prevent another depression, and how could the newly demobilized soldiers best prepare themselves for the new era after being so long in uniform.

The answers to these questions were provided by the new social dynamic then being formed and developed. With industrialization and unions already established, with social legislation enacted for the protection of the consumers and producers alike, the potential of both industry and the labor force lay open for exploitation. The form of exploitation was in product research, in the development of new commodities to stimulate demand, thereby opening markets that hitherto did not exist. The standard products, such as automobiles and refrigerators and the like, were of course continued. But with computers and television coming into their own, the new electronics, the use of atomic power, and new medicines to fight disease, our era of knowledge came into existence, exploiting research and development and basing consumer production on their findings. Moreover, with the increasing complexities of international relations, especially with isolationist United States becoming the dominant world power and competing for markets and spheres of influence with its previous ally-in-arms, the Soviet Union, another form of industry was developed, that being industry of knowledge. Think tanks, as they have come to be called, were formed to provide scenarios of possible cold-war situations and the viable actions and reactions which these scenarios could project and analyze. Hence, on the basis of industrialization and the emphasis on knowledge, in the postwar period the era of knowledge began and has since been flourishing.

Chronologically, our time is a progression, an addition of years calculated according to the various traditions based on religious considerations and astronomical computations. In the known history of humanity, from the beginning of history to the present, humanity has not changed much over the years. The great ancient centers of civilization have yielded impressive humanistic contributions in the arts and in philosophy; they have also been breeding grounds for poverty, jealousy, and civil strife. But history is past, open for understanding and speculation, for interpretation and debate. One of history's tasks is to allow us to reflect on our past in order to understand our present and to project into our possible futures. Here, however, three forms of time are being discussed. Chronological time, of course, is the times of the past, present, and future; as such, these times are without content. Historical time is chronological time with content, that is, with the events of human history. It is social time which is of significance for us now, for this is the time in our contemporary era of knowledge and represents the various stages it has undergone: from the applications of wartime techniques to peacetime production in the immediate postwar period, to the reactionism of those who sought the status quo, and the potential and actual threats to the new seekers of knowledge who were exploring the first grounds of the new era, to our present social time with its emphasis on knowledge forms and the potential threats to intellectual development posed by those still uncertain of our era and its dynamics. The era of knowledge and our social time within a context of anti-realism will be explored in the next part. It remains to be mentioned here, however, that our era provides humanity a chance to be different from our historical ancestors, to place our era on the continuum of chronological time as a milestone in the historical time-evolution.

In our era there are two basically opposing opportunities: to begin to achieve greatness for humanity or to end it all, to destroy our existence, its history, and its bloody but necessary inheritance. The choice is ours, and the opportunities, mutually exclusive as they are, exist side by side. Our era of knowledge will now be explored.

PART II

ON OUR ERA OF KNOWLEDGE—II

3

General Comments

While every historical era is unique, delineated by the circumstances that bring it about and defined by the activities that occur in it and that generate further activities, our era of knowledge is perhaps the most dynamic in the chronological-historical existence of humanity. This is because the opportunities available for us for our own personal exploitation and the possibilities provided by societies, opportunities that have never existed before, can, if properly used, lift humanity out of the difficult conditions that have existed, bringing us into another dimension of living, into an era in which knowledge is exploited for the benefit of mankind. In a way, then, this era has for us both a promise of a better future and a choice in the way we make our future collectively and personally. It also holds for us a caveat, a warning that our basic humanism should not be lost in the wonderment of knowledge, that the ancient Greek philosophers who sought wisdom should not be ignored and should serve as an ideal while the dazzle of the search for and the development of knowledge tantalizes us in its pursuit.

While studying the contemporary period, we see that conditions have remained more or less as they have always been throughout history: we see rich and prosperous nations and nations plagued with poverty, we see an ever-continuing situation in which nations confront each other in battle and in which internal rebellion results in the taking up of arms to defend principles. We deal with economic crises, with diseases, with poorly educated peoples, with the socially exploited and those who exploit. Despite the advances made in chemistry and physics in the Industrial Revolution, and despite the great industrial progress made during this era, there were still two world wars fought with untold losses for the past, present, and future of humanity. How does our contemporary era differ from the historical past? In our era of knowledge, the world has been plunged into a major recession, the developing countries have suffered setbacks in their advancements due to the oil power game, regions which once flourished have become deserts, leaving proud peoples to the mercies of the rest of the world to keep them from perishing. Where are the benefits of our era of knowledge?

The validity of these points cannot be dismissed; the philosophical assumption on which they are based can, however, be questioned. These points are descriptions of events that have occurred and are occurring in our time, events that are part of our social time and contemporary historical era and cannot be denied. Our era is only in its early stages, however, and has to be understood so that its benefits can be realized. An era is not isolated from its past and its roots; it does not make previous conditions irrelevant. The grip of darkness was very strong in the early stages of the Renaissance, so much so that a backlash took place in Spain and other countries in the form of the Inquisition. The influences of feudalism were so ingrained that during the early stages of American political and industrial development, the Civil War was fought in which the industrialized North was victorious. The outstanding conditions of historical eras are often passed onto the eras that follow, to be cultivated by the receiving eras and altered accordingly as the receiving eras exert their influence.

What we see, therefore, is a clash of concepts, of our past with the present and the potentialities our era offers, of systems established in previous eras with those that exist today, even to the extent that our contemporary contributions, so significant in our era of knowledge, have also been turned into weapons systems for the destruction of civilization. Throughout history, knowledge that has existed for the betterment of humanity has also been employed for war and destruction. Fire, for warmth and heating food, has been used for burning homes and persons. The wheel, vital for transportation and later for production, carried chariots of war and later mechanized weapons for defence and destruction. Where, then, is the uniqueness of our era? Are we not merely in possession of extremely sophisticated instruments that can be employed for peaceful purposes as well as for aggression and destruction? If so, then how does our contemporary era of knowledge provide us with opportunities never existing before to cope with these difficulties?

While the validity of these points cannot be denied nor their weights in this present discussion be ignored, they must be placed in proper perspective with respect to our circumstances and to the potentialities of our era. Indeed, these very arguments with respect to our present potential for destruction place us in a social paradox. These conditions have existed throughout recorded history and are certainly part of our contemporary existence; the difference is that now we have the intellectual ability and indeed the moral imperative to act on these circumstances and to remove their threats forever from mankind. We must use knowledge for the social benefit of humanity, for these contributions place on us a moral dictate for our present survival and for the future of all humanity. Under these circumstances, there can no longer be inactivity, as was possible in previous historical eras; we must be active in the removal of the threat of technology, concentrating on its peaceful applications. In the search for knowledge, technology carries a momentum of its own. Research into further uses and control systems for weapons as well as their limitations will only result in their greater sophistication, with the result being even greater destructive power and the diverting of scientific and technical talent into weapons development when it could be otherwise employed solving the scientific and social problems that are part of our contemporary existence.

We now possess the means for removing poverty from our midst, for eliminating diseases that have afflicted us, and for raising the levels of education throughout the world so that people can partake in our era, contribute to it, and enjoy its benefits. We also possess the means for destroying all that has evolved and that which we have constructed. This opportunity is certainly unique, for it has never existed in any other era of history. The League of Nations, for example, was formed to settle international differences, to prevent war, to eliminate those very problems which bring nations into combat. Now, with the weaponry we have developed in our era of knowledge, war has become an impossibility, for no great power seeks to achieve the consequences of war. Battles are still fought, but they are localized and indeed manipulated to a large extent by the great powers. These surrogate combatants are controlled in their methods and in the areas they dominate by the possessors of universal destruction. Moreover, when the great powers deploy their troops, this is to exert leverage on their international political rivals or to protect their tacitly agreed-upon spheres of political interests. These confrontations are the allowed remnants of what would have been world conflict had the weapons of such destruction not been in existence.[1]

Nevertheless, this type of battle is also becoming obsolete as the combatants and their supporters are finding it increasingly worth their while to devote their resources and abilities to dealing with their problems, the social, economic and educational difficulties, rather than maintaining the archaic and really stupid and horrifying approach of seeking solutions on the battlefields. It is as if our present era of knowledge is serving as a step in the evolution of mankind, placing the greater emphasis on the higher parts of the brain and hence enabling us to turn from animalistic instincts and actions/reactions to stimuli to generate conceptualizations and activities in keeping with the new sociological environment of increasing and using knowledge.

However, humanity has not yet reached the level of psychic integration that will enable us to do away with our destructive tendencies; thus our era of knowledge has acquired the dualistic characteristics already indicated. Atomic energy can be used for medicinal purposes, for providing fuel for domestic and industrial consumption, and for eliminating mankind from our planet. Computers can provide calculations that allow us to comprehend somewhat the origins of the cosmos; they are used in medical research, in education, for banking and the sending and paying of bills, and for targeting atomic missiles for destruction. Hence, with such great stores of knowledge available to us, we must also know where we are going and therefore which paths should be avoided and which should be approached with great suspicion.

These difficulties will be explored in this work, for they are necessary, integral parts of our contemporary era of knowledge. They are incorporated in our era and are real situational examples of the dangers and benefits which our era provides. Before this can be undertaken, however, further comments are in order.

Our era has been called the computer age and the atomic age, but these terms are not accurate, for they refer to different aspects of the greater historical era, that of our era of knowledge. These developments, mostly conducted in the postwar period, have certainly had great impacts on our lives. No doubt that over the next few years, given intensive research, clean atomic energy plants could be developed to either reduce significantly or eliminate completely the reliance on fossil fuels for supplying energy. No doubt this development would rid the threat of the politicization of energy supplies; it would also provide cheap and endless supplies of energy and expand technologies for industrial production and domestic consumption.

Computers provide great efficiency in calculation, and their applications in science and industry are still being explored. The field of artificial intelligence is not only providing more efficient methods of production and at lower costs than had existed previously; it also supplies models for living organisms and establishes alternative methods for understanding biological operations.[2] Computers are necessary for controlling energy, and this energy may well be applied to power computer systems.

These "ages" are, however, incorporated into a greater and certainly more encompassing historical era, that of the era of knowledge. The expansion and control of atomic energy requires ever-increasing sophisticated knowledge, and to this end much research is directed. The development and expansion of computers, from computer toys to controlling industrial production in the form of robotics, necessitates increasing research into their manufacture and their programs. The silicon chip, once considered the highest degree of microproduction, is itself becoming more complex and sophisticated, especially as the competition among the various firms drives intensive research and greater understanding of the possibilities for theoretical and practical expansion into the future.

Hence, the computer age and the atomic age rely on knowledge, on the accumulation of comprehension and utility of information pertinent to the problem at hand. Knowledge, however, is far from stable, for what we comprehend and understand to be valid now, of working utility, will most likely be shown to be inadequate at a future date, as problems shift and the means for dealing with these problems are revised. The growth and developemnt of knowledge most certainly depend on human ingenuity—witness the development of atomic physics and its expansion into microbiology as well as cosmology; witness the rapid turnover of the generations of computers and the formulation of new computer languages, as well as the development of new fields to which computers are applicable.

Our era is one of change, at a pace more rapid than at any other time in history. Knowledge systems are rendered obsolete, in part or total, at rates never before experienced. The absolutes of truth and falsehood most certainly retain their importance for issues of morals and personal conduct, but in our era they have been replaced within working systems of knowledge by the concepts of utility and entropy. All is relative to the information of knowledge systems, and the same concept takes on different nuances within the contexts of its various systems. We often employ more than one system of knowledge as our problem areas become diversified; often the languages of one system becomes incorporated into another, thereby altering its direction and relevance. Utility is sought, entropy is to be repaired if possible, or if not—if the system is beyond alteration, to the extent that none of its original purpose can be retained—then it is to be abandoned.

Our era of knowledge is still in its infancy. From the dust and ashes of World War II it developed, and in its wake there have formed three types of social structures, three forms of society. The future-oriented society is working fully within the dynamics of knowledge. The present-oriented society is the society in its developing stages, and its direction is still uncertain. The past-oriented society primarily formulates its present and future conceptualizations and directions on the basis of its foundations and historical roots. This last society represents the established, authoritarian social structure in which the regime determines the materials to be studied, the economic system to be followed, and the types of consumer and industrial products to be manufactured. These three societies will be discussed in Part III of this work, and the consequences of our contemporary era of knowledge for these societies will be examined and analyzed. But first, the dynamics of knowledge in our contemporary era must be explained.

4

On the Dynamics of Creativity

> Human creative energy, like nothing, isn't anything if it isn't potential. It is also an indomitable part of being alive, as countless experiments have documented. People who are deprived of their senses by being floated in silent, dark tanks of water warmed to body temperature will hallucinate. It is as though the human mind will not be stilled of its propensity to make something of nothing even, or especially, when immersed in nothingness.
>
> Michael Guillen, *Bridges to Infinity*, 1984

Human creative *energy* is indeed potential, unmeasurable and unexpressed. Human creative *activity*, however, is subjective to measurement, is expressed, and its results are either incorporated into the mainstream of knowledge or rejected as being inadequate. Moreover, there exist objective criteria for the acceptance and rejection of a contribution, even though the subjective personal aspect may at times determine the contribution's fate. There are also occasions in which the contribution is controversial, to the extent that some people may accept it, while others dismiss it out of hand or reject it after criticial evaluation.

There is no objection to the concept that the human mind cannot be stilled, especially when the body is subjected to the types of experiments Michael Guillen discusses. An active mind, compensating for deprived senses, does not necessarily mean that creative activity is occurring. Creativity pertains to a specific set of circumstances and now occurs at levels never before experienced in history; consequently, development of knowledge occurs at rates unique to our contemporary era.

Creativity has been a part of our historical development. The works of art and writings of the ancient Greeks, and indeed the civilizations prior to the development of philosophy in Greece, attest to this. The monuments in Egypt, bearing witness to its long-past glorious civilization, are reminders that their planners and executers overcame obstacles in engineering and construction in ways unique to that society and that, while feats of engineering in our time are truly wonderous and testify to contemporary ability and imagination, the ancient civilizations were not lacking in their skills. The endurance of these monuments throughout the travails of time give witness to the abilities of the builders of long ago.

Works of art in the Renaissance are most certainly wonderful and are studied by the artists, musicians, and builders of our time. The sciences of the Enlightenment provide the basis for much of our contemporary investigations; the music of the classical composers still serves to instruct us in structuring harmony and developing progressions.[1]

Creativity in our era differs from that of the past, however, in a significant way. In our era creativity can relate to a change in the system, or a singular contribution never experienced before (this latter being the type in previous historical eras). In our time, most creativity depends on the groundwork prepared by those using an existing system, bringing its elements into question, and perhaps subjecting the entire system to scrutiny, planning renovation. Often the rate of creativity is such that it results in whole systems being eliminated and others being formed to replace them, others that have greater utility in dealing with the problems, such as the introduction of computerized flight in air navigation, thereby eliminating the third person in the cockpit. This system requires the revision of flight communications, and it will eventually replace the conventional navigation system still predominant and based on a somewhat obsolete state of the art.

The level of creativity in our era is higher than at any other time in history; this is due to the prevalence of knowledge incorporated into working systems and the availability of this knowledge to a wider range of the world's population. In the area of international commerce, for example, the manufacture of goods requires the latest state of the technical arts, and the application of these technologies to the various fields of production requires levels of knowledge not existing in any other period.[2] Agricultural produce, for example, is watered according to computerized systems; nourishment provided to produce is dispensed according to computerized instructions; and the packaging, refrigerating, and shipping of the produce are processes calculated according to market forces and price ranges, again evaluated by computers. Packaging must help the produce retain its freshness, and this requires the latest state of the packaging art, together with refrigeration, which must be of sufficient strength to preserve the freshness but must be regulated for the various types of produce. Shipping, market distribution, and selling have also become very technical, and all these processes rely on the uses of technology and the ability to adapt them to the specific products and markets. This is knowledge and it is formulated into working systems.[3]

Moreover, the very uses of computers and the construction of the technologies involved in their development, require knowledge and linguistic metaknowledge as formulated in knowledge systems. The formulation of these linguistic systems into computer operations to cope with and perform according to the problems for which they are developed as high-powered instruments to deal with problems unique to our times, illustrates the dynamics of creativity.

Thus, creative activity in our era differs significantly from that of the previous eras of history, because of the forces of human energy unleashed in the aftermath of World War II, the competition between the great superpowers, and the economic competition among the world's countries. There are still great innovators, the artists and scientists who make unique contributions; the majority of creative activity, however, occurs within established systems, in altering them and thereby producing greater efficiency and utility.

In a sense, the second type of creativity, to be called here *initiation*, is derived from the first type, termed here *innovation*, for innovation was the prevalent form of creativity and reigned supreme until our era. It was Copernicus, for example, who innovated a heliocentric theory of astronomy, employing the Ptolemaic epicycles, but placing the sun at the center of our universe. Johannes Kepler described the motion of the planets around the sun in elliptical orbits, and Newton, the great synthesizer, joined the Galilean earth physics with Kepler's contribution and developed a unique system of theoretical and practical physics. Leonardo Da Vinci explored artistic techniques and developed his own unique style of expression; he also set the patterns for classical training and conceptualization in painting and drawing, the techniques that are still taught to inspiring artists. Compared to our present era, these contributions were few and far between and thus served as the main bodies of knowledge by those who explored them.

Today, the levels of innovation are still somewhat sparse, with great singular contributions being as rare as they were in the previous historical eras. Most of the creative activity pertains to initiation, the changing of elements within established systems; on the basis of these changes, knowledge develops and expands. While the great quantity of knowledge is gained within these systems, with their respective elements being altered as they become faulty (entropic), it is through the efforts of innovation that these systems are originally established, so that initiation occurs because of the problems arising within innovated systems. The structure of these systems must now be discussed, after which the dynamics of creativity will be treated.

THE SCHEMATIC OF THE SYSTEM

Each system of knowledge is composed of two interrelated languages. One language is that which defines the area of concern for which the system deals; the other defines the working operations of this area. The area language, as it is constructed according to the designs of its formulator and those who employ it, tends to be complete, as the area defined is to be restricted according to the problem for which it was formulated. Hence, the operative language also tends to be restricted, as the types and forms of operations allowed by the innovator and those who work with the construction are determined by the area language. The schematic for a knowledge system S therefore takes the form: $S_t = \Sigma(O_d A)$, where O is the operative language as it works on A, the area language. The d stands for the delineating operative relationships allowed by the system. The t subscript indicates the time period of the system; the sigma sign is the summation operator of the total area and operative elements in the system. The time-signature, t, shows that the system itself is not static but dynamic, with no guarantee that S_{t1} will be of the same content and structure, that is, will pertain to the exact same problem area and contain the exact same operative relationships as S in time period 2. The reasons for the differing time periods are that the impacts of different contributions may induce changes within a specific S system and that competing systems may render one or the other of lesser value or entropic.

Hence, for S_t, if there are n-statements for A, there will be, originally, a corresponding number of statements for O, so that the a elements that compose A are matched isomorphically with their o elements in O. This is a static picture of a knowledge system; as knowledge is far from static but either changing or being considered with respect to changes, S is a highly dynamic system, the viability of which depends on the conceptualizations of those who work with the system. Their terms may be taken from other languages, but as soon as they are incorporated into a system, these terms take on the specific nuances attributed to the system. The term "optical," for instance, has many meanings, and no doubt the first that one thinks about is the study of the eye and the fitting of lenses. Optical art (better known as Op art), however, was a movement in the contemporary art field that relied on the use of certain types of illusions and images to make the message of the artists. Hence the term has itself become a system; the definitions of the subjects and the messages desired to be conveyed by the practitioners of this artistic form are delineated by the A and O elements as they are incorporated within the Op-Art system. The Big Bang theory of cosmology is also a system, the terms of which describe a very likely scenario for the origins of the universe. The terms of reference are the A statements and the procedures for working with these statements are incorporated within the O. A describes the predicament of an initial big explosion, spewing cosmic dust in all directions, dust that, after a great length of time, fell into gravitational relationships and began to form galaxies, with their solar systems and all that we know about the dynamics of the universe. On the basis of this A and its statements, O is employed to build models, construct computerized languages that are able to handle stellar observations based on the Big Bang theory, and offer explanations for observed and predicted phenomena.

A system remains static for the duration that it handles the situation for which it was formulated. The area described remains fixed according to the understanding of those who work with the system, and the operative terms are fully competent to handle the area language. There is no difficulty considered, nor are any conceived. The system functions smoothly, as it should, as it was initially designed to function.

Difficulties do arise, however, when either one or another situation occurs. Either the language of the area becomes ambiguous and therefore loses some of its relevance for the real area it describes, or the operative language is no longer completely relevant due to the ambiguity of its terms. The other situation is one in which the area itself has been altered, so that the languages are no longer appropriate for dealing with the area. In the latter case the change is often small and thus has no affect on the total *S*, except that the defective elements are brought into question.

Of course there is no reason why both occurrences cannot exist for the same system. In this case, the difficulty is compounded by the complications, and chances are that the degree of damage done to the system will be extensive. In both cases, however, the system may be salvaged and the damages repaired. The occurrences will be discussed in order.

The ambiguity of system languages arises because of terms of other systems being incorporated into the languages. As languages are tools for communication and expression in general, this generality applies also to the specific realm of systems. Languages not only delineate; they also allow for operations to be performed according to the system's requirements. They are employed by people who cannot close themselves off from the rest of the world, nor prohibit their own intellectual and emotional pursuits. These people often borrow words or concepts from regular vocabularies or from systemic constructions that interest them; because of the explanatory power of these words, or because of the imagery they evoke, they are incorporated into the system, perhaps as assisting words, perhaps as additional or substitutive terms.

These words have an impact on the system in which they are incorporated. They provide a different approach—no matter how slight the difference—to the system and result in an entropic situation that requires repair. The conceptions of utility and entropy are extemely important, but clarification of them must wait until the next chapter: it is utility that provides the system with its working ability, and entropy determines its malfunction or complete demise, depending on its extent. New words introduced into the system alter it, bringing about deviations from its area description and corresponding operations. These problems are corrected through creativity; the corrections may leave the system as it was, thereby bringing about an identity between the new terms and the others already existing in the system, so that their incorporation has no influence and their impact is insignificant, or the system is changed correspondingly and according to the influence these terms exert. As these terms may relate to either the operative or area language, or both, where the change is made in one language—aside from the identity of the terms—then there has to be a corresponding alteration in the other language to account for the change.

The languages become ambiguous because of the incorporation of other terms, thereby providing meanings that may pertain directly to the existing terms of the languages as well as conceptualizations not really relevant to the system. These semantic difficulties can be overcome leaving the system intact, providing they are not intensive to the point of bringing about real damage.

The second occurrence, that of a shift in the area for which the language was constructed, has its own set of difficulties. As the area language was established to define the area, and as the operative language was formulated to work with the area language on the area, then an event or situation for which the area language cannot handle must require a shift in the language and a resultant alteration of the system in general. This situation does not pertain to the case where there are circumstances within the area that are not understood. The lack of knowledge of the physics within the black holes in space does not invalidate the relativity theory of Albert Einstein nor the quantum physics of Werner Heisenberg and the other microphysicists; the laws of physics may be the same for the entire universe, or they may differ according to circumstances. Until this is known, physical theories and laws remain intact.

The type of situation being discussed is when the area is altered, either because of new technology or new observations. For example, with heart difficulties, the advent of transplanting hearts changed the entire field of immunology and the methods for treating circulatory difficulties, such as the fatigue or failure of the heart muscle. With further advances made in technology, the construction of artificial hearts is coming into its own; the artificial heart may soon be a viable alternative to transplants and a solution for the complications related to immune systems, as the body attacks foreign organs and rejects the alien heart.

In response to these developments, the entire system of immunology knowledge has been revised, and the introduction of this knowledge into areas such as cancer treatment and infectious diseases is being studied and, where successful, applied. The techniques of medical knowledge directed to organ construction, using computer-based models and the latest in chemistry to make plastics and other materials for the construction of artificial organs and relating them to functioning bodily parts, have resulted in both the understanding of the body at levels never before obtained and to the ability of the medical profession to advance in organ replacement, thereby making life more bearable to those who would have had to remain handicapped. Moreover, the development of immunology has resulted in systems of knowledge and theories of the body and its responses to disease that shed more light on our bodies and their responses to environmental and infectious hazards in situations of industrialization and economic development.

Shifts in industrialization have brought about changes in our biological responses and hence in our understanding of our bodies in light of these circumstances. Systems of knowledge have had to be revised and in cases reformulated to deal with these problems; hence the innovations in medicine and in theories pertaining to drug reactions and to the physical and chemical functions of the human organism. Economic development has resulted in changes in the life styles of those peoples undergoing economic vitalization, with corresponding changes in knowledge and knowledge systems to cope with these environmental and social alterations.

This situation of changing areas thus requires necessary and corresponding changes in the knowledge systems. In extreme cases, where the alterations are radical—radical being defined as not within the realm of the knowledge system—the system has to be replaced or at least stand in competition with alternative systems formulated to cope with the situation.

Hence the significance of creativity in our era of knowledge; for only through creativity can the alterations within a system be made and new systems formulated when existing systems are demonstrated as inadequate. It must be understood that these alterations result from the introduction of knowledge derived from interdisciplinary information—from terms and concepts of other systems, no matter how closely related or conceptually different—with the adaptation of this information according to the system's requirements, that is, its unique problem area and its operational knowledge.

5

The Dynamics of Creativity—I

Corruption. The surest way to corrupt a youth is to instruct him to hold in higher esteem those who think alike than those who think differently.

Friedrich Nietzsche, *The Dawn of Day*, 1974

ON THE UTILITY OF A SYSTEM

A system of knowledge is established to work with a specific problem area, and the operational language of the system pertains directly to the usefulness of the area language in relation to the area for which the system is formed. Hence, a difficulty in such a construction can already be detected, for while the general area may be very broad, encompassing the activities of several disciplines, a system seeks to limit the range by its rigorous definitions, thereby attempting to remove or lessen as much as possible the influences of those parts of the general area that are not considered to be within the system's realm. The system's construction must be such that all extraneous influences are eliminated or kept to a minimum, so as to allow for the maximum effect of the utility prescribed to the system.

Utility, therefore, is a measure of a system's effectiveness, as determined by the system's objectives within the delineated problem area and its ability to incorporate influences not part of the original construction. A system S is constructed to be measured between two limits. The lower limit, zero, is a boundary that is never reached, for the system breaks down before and is not subject to resuscitation; its elements are incapable of reaching this limit because of the information which has entered into *S*, thereby rendering it of no workable utility, hence it is abandoned.

The system's languages comprise its elements that contain and convey information. The area language describes the range and contents of the system, while the operative language determines the working of the area. When these languages perform as they are supposed to, the upper boundary, 1, is approached. Like the lower limit, this upper limit is never reached. The quantity and content of information within the general area is in a continuous state of movement, increasing and altering with new contributions, changing and being reformulated as systems fade out and others enter the area. Full and maximum utility therefore can never be reached because the languages are changing, and the area is in a state of flux. This maximum level can be approached, however, as is the intention of those who work with the system and indeed, that of its innovator.

These boundaries are thus determinants, indicating the relative health of the system at any specific period of time. Thus, $0<S<1$ is the general position of a working system; the nearness to the limits determines its state of viability. As *S* approaches 0, the system is becoming entropic; as it approaches 1, its utility is gaining in strength.

Utility is assessed in accordance with the aims of the system, its problem area, and its operability and ability to cope with the area. The system's innovator states the position, presents the system, and demonstrates its workability. The system's languages contain information, and the viability of the system is determined by the ability of its languages to influence the area as stated by the system's construction. This is a probabilistic determination, because complete maximum utility is unachievable. Utility tends toward the maximum limit when the system functions according to its requirements, so that it works with the area in a given time as stated and its operative language in turn deals with the area as stated. The system's languages function according to their information content; hence, the area language must be so formulated as to have information pertinent and relating directly to the area and the operational language must be so constructed to work with the area language. The area language of a school of art, a systematic approach to art, must have the language of the subjects and concepts considered appropriate to that school, as well as the operational language, those techniques allowed for expressing the concepts and asserting the specific artist's identity within the system. Thus, the area and operational languages contain information relevant to the system's functioning. All other information is for either clarification of the languages or for embellishment, thus rendering this information metalanguage, relevant in that it relates to the working languages and seeks to improve on them conceptually. The metalanguages cannot, however, assist in the working of the operational and area languages.

A system's utility is therefore assessed according to how well it achieves its aims, as set out in its languages. As maximum utility is impossible to reach, so that the system functions according to a probabilistic relationship between the workings of the languages and the actual designated areas, utility can be stated thus: $U_t \equiv [P(O_dA = I(O_dA)]_t$, that is, the system's utility at a specific time period is identical to the equality between the system's probability measure and its information content with "d" being the defining or delineating operator of O on *A*. The probability measures the information of *O* and *A* as they relate to the area and hence measures every *o* in O and *a* in *A* of the system. As these languages contain information, the probabilistic measure determines the validity of the statements, that is, their information, *I*, as they relate to the area, so that the closer these statements relate the greater their probabilities and hence the greater the utility measurement for *S*. Of course, the innovator seeks to formulate a system whose utility approaches the maximum 1, while both the innovator and the system's followers, imitators, seek to maintain the high level by attempting to reconstruct whichever elements are reduced in their utilities, due to area shifts or language changes. The lack of treatment in these circumstances results in further erosion of *S*'s utility, which may eventually bring the system into a condition of entropy.

COMMENTS ON ENTROPY

Utility is a measurement of the system's ability to perform as it is supposed to, to yield results according to its stated terms in its area and operational languages. Utility, then, is a measurement of how well the system achieves its purpose, how significant its information content is with respect to its delineated problem area, and how effective its operational language is on its area language.

Entropy, on the other hand, is both a measurement and a condition of the system's decline, as assessed by its inability to perform according to its languages and objectives. As a measurement, it indicates just how far the system has deviated from its original position with respect to utility, that is, from the original problem area it delineated and hence from its operational abilities. Usually, this entropic condition can be removed or at least be alleviated, thereby restoring utility, perhaps not to its former level but to the extent that the system can be employed without too much difficulty.

The general definition for entropy is

$$\mathrm{H}S_{\mathrm{t}} = -\left[\sum_{1}^{\mathrm{n}} o,\ a \supset \mathrm{I}(A_o,\ O_a)\right]$$

which reads that the entropy of system S at time t is the negation of the elements o and a as they are included in A and O during this time period. Those elements not included in this summation are not entropic, so that this equation pertains to defective area statements affected by the operational language. Thus, the minus sign indicates that these statements are negated with respect to the system. The number of statements affected indicates the extent of the entropic condition and hence the system's general viability.

As with utility, the determination of entropy relies on the system's information content; this is assessed with respect to the information's probability as its operational elements relate to its area. The decline in information content is the direct result of the lack of effectiveness of the system's elements, so that the probability measurements of these statements tend toward the lower limit. Altering these defective statements changes the content and may affect the original intentions of the system as it was originally constructed, but if this change is not too extensive, the system retains its utility and continues to be used as a working formulation for the area it delineates. Should such reconstruction not be undertaken, then the system in its original form would most certainly decline further until the extent of entropy becomes so pervasive that the system cannot be saved.

One way this decline occurs is that alternative systems are introduced as competitors, systems that, under competition, maintain their utility. People then abandon the entropic system and work with its competitors, thereby rendering the weakened system of little or no utility, hence nearly totally entropic.

However, should alterations be initiated because of the lack of solutions for the entropic statements, then the system will most likely be continued, but restricted in its uses because of its defective statements. This situation will exist until there are finally changes made in the area not dealt with by the corresponding alterations in the statements until the extent is reached where the entire system will be brought into decline. Entropy will be approaching the lower limit, and the system will either be replaced by one of vastly higher utility, or it will fall into disuse and be abandoned.

One further point has to be made and this pertains to the use of the thermodynamic term, "entropy." Sadi Carnot, Rudolf Clausius, Ludwig von Boltzmann, and the others who worked on the principle of entropy in physical systems were not concerned with information per se, but with the functioning of these physical systems and their eventual breaking down. Since the pioneering work done on this second law of thermodynamics, the law has attracted attention in other fields of inquiry. Systems do not have to be physical, and entropy does not have to relate specifically to the decline of physical energy. Systems are also abstractions—formulations and conventional methods for dealing with problems. As they are valid, they have utility; they are used and examined, accepted and applied, until better systems replace them, or until new information pertaining to the areas for which these systems were devised renders the accepted systems inadequate. Entropy is thus an internal condition determined by the inability of the system's information to relate to its designated area, rendering it inappropriate in its diminished utility. The extent of this diminution depends on available and better alternatives. A surgeon today would not perform an operation according to the medical knowledge of Francis Galton's time; yet the surgeon may apply techniques that differ from those of a contemporary who may approach the operation from a different conceptual viewpoint and a different procedural system. In this example, entropy would become relevant only in the case where one technique proved far superior to the other, independent of the individual surgeon's skills.

All systems of knowledge eventually decline, become entropic, and are abandoned. All systems have utility; otherwise they would not retain any semblance of a working body of knowledge. Systems encounter entropy in small amounts, as their elements lose their utility due to area shifts or to changes in their languages. The correction of this entropy is the task of contemporary creative activity but this activity depends on bringing the statements into entropic conditions. In the case of initiation, creativity relies on entropy; in our era of knowledge, the changes in knowledge systems are very rapid in comparison to any other historical era.

These systems need their original constructions: that organization into working operational and area languages that viably delineates a problem area. This formulation of knowledge systems is also creativity, and in those situations in which such construction is undertaken because of the inadequacies of other and competing systems, it is entropy that spurs on the innovator to construct a viable alternative system. There is another form of innovation, however, that does not rely on entropy: the construction of a system out of isolation, from the personal perspective of a problem area and the positing of a knowledge system that defines the problem and poses methods for dealing with it through the operational and area languages. These are the dynamics of creativity, and in the broader case of initiation it is the role of the imitator that is emphasized, for the imitator brings the system's elements into entropic conditions by seeking to draw out their fullest consequences. These points will be discussed, but first, two views of creativity must be treated and then critiqued, so that a formulation appropriate to our contemporary era can be stated, in which the strengths of the opposing theories are included, while the weaknesses are avoided.

THE CONVERGENCE ARGUMENT

" 'And yet,' said Legrand, 'the solution is by no means so difficult as you might be led to imagine from the first hasty inspection of the characters.' " In Edgar Allan Poe's *The Gold Bug*, a treasure is revealed by the correct interpretation of the symbols on a scarabaeus, through convergent reasoning. The deciphering of the code, reinterpreting the symbolic language into a familiar and workable form of communication, led to the finding of the treasure.

Creativity is the activity of problem solving. Problems may be fairly well defined, as in the case with the sciences, or they may be somewhat loosely defined or oriented toward the personality of the individual who constructs the problem, as is the case with most artists. Alternatively, problems that may be in cryptic form, in which clues have to be interpreted in a manner that leads to the solution, as is the case with crime detection and the type of problem expressed in Poe's story.

While both convergent and divergent reasoning are applied to problem solving, the difference between them is that the convergent approach stresses the existence of a solution in a subjective-objective relationship, while divergence is strictly a subjective approach and is imposed on the problem as a solution.

Convergent reasoning is therefore concerned with the manipulation of the terms and conditions of the problem, its symbols and operators, to yield the solution. It is based on the assumption that the solution is stated somehow within the problem's boundaries or is derivable from the conditions set by the problem.[1]

Convergence is divided into two categories. One category is primary convergence, in which the problem is well-defined and the solution is sought within the context of the problem, to be derived from the information that the problem contains. For this category, the limits of the problem area are set by the language in which the problem is expressed and the specific nuances of the terminology employed. The process of convergence is thus the manipulation of the problem's linguistics to find the phrasing that will yield the correct answer, correctness in this case being that answer which has the highest utility.

This type of convergent reasoning is used in crime detection, in which a number of clues exist and a specific number of people are suspected. The detective seeks to unravel the meanings of these clues to ascertain which suspect is most likely to be the culprit. Primary convergence is also employed in simple intelligence testing of the sort where a person is given a word and has to provide its opposite; for example, when the word "hot" is given, the word "cold" is the correct response. The terms of the problem for primary convergent reasoning are stated in such a manner that the solution tends to lie hidden in the contextual framework, so that convergent reasoning requires the manipulation of the terms to uncover, i.e., discover, its solution.

This category of convergence is primary because it relies upon behavior patterns and situations that are defined linguistically by the problem's language. The detective, for example, would not search out information considered irrelevant to the case; nor would the mathematician look for the solution to a symbolic puzzle by manipulating terms not stated in the problem or not brought into the problem as valid substitutes.

Secondary convergence does not rely on patterns and information established by the problem's formulation or linguistic construction, but depends on the discovery (uncovering) of information implied by the problem's language. Secondary convergence relies on the observation of events and on gathering of information not hitherto considered relevant and relating it to these events. This category takes two forms: purposeful and unintentional. The history of science contains many examples of each, but only one example of each will be given here.

As an example of purposeful convergent reasoning, consider William Harvey's discovery of the heart's chambers and the circulation of blood. The basis of his finding was already formulated by the Roman physician Galen, whose dissections of the human body and his anatomical studies were milestones in the science of medicine. Galen lived during the post-Hellenic period, when the human form was considered the highest expression of beauty. During the Dark Ages, which followed the Fall of Rome, little progress was made in medicine, and the human body was relegated to a far lower status, with the arts representing the human form primarily as a means of religious expression. The Middle Ages were little better in their approach to the human body, and medicine consisted largely of witchcraft and home remedies.

It was only when the spirit of inquiry was rekindled during the Renaissance that people took a real interest in their environment. The Renaissance began in Italy, although there were forces initiating the spirit of inquiry all through Britain and Europe. As the Church was the political and spiritual power of Rome, when the Aristotelian influence made itself felt, the Church sanctioned a somewhat secular approach to inquiry, and the intellectual and spiritual forces united to rekindle the birth of knowledge.

William Harvey was a Cartesian in outlook, an unusual point of view to be held by a Englishman in a country of staunch empiricists. His Cartesian attitude gave him a mechanistic view of the human body, and it was therefore no small wonder that in seeking to unravel the mysteries of circulation, he compared the heart of a fish to the mechanical device of a water pump, observing the similarities in function, as both draw fluids. Following this mechanistic logic, Harvey examined the human heart and noticed what others had failed to see, that the chambers of the heart served to pump the life-giving fluid of blood throughout the body. He proclaimed to those in his profession his finding that by way of the heart's chambers blood is pumped through the body in a circular manner; it is this pumping which is responsible for its flow. Harvey's discovery was purposeful, for he certainly concerned himself with the problem of the body and the circulation of blood. His discovery of the mechanical relationship between the water pump and the fish's heart led to the testing of the human heart's function as the logical consequence. Because of his mechanistic view and despite the fact that the problem of determining the cause of circulation was not initially his prime concern, Harvey's discovery put to rest the problem that had occupied the medical people for centuries.

The discovery of penicillin is certainly as example of unintentional convergence, and only after the consequences of Sir Alexander Fleming's unusual observation (1929) were drawn out did he make them public and revolutionized medicine. Fleming worked in a hospital in Paddington, London, as a research scientist. This area of London is very busy, so the chances of the events that took place in Fleming's laboratory having occurred at all are astonishingly small. Nevertheless, the penicillium mold spore did blow into the window of his laboratory and land in a culture dish. This unusual event caught the researcher's eye and what was even more astonishing was at the same time Fleming had a cold; as he examined the spore some of the mucus from his nose dripped into the dish. He could have washed the dish, let the matter go at that, and returned to his work. However, the mold spore in the dish aroused his scientific curiosity, and he waited to see the results of this unusual mixture. The penicillium mold had killed the germs in the mucus; and this occurrence turned Fleming from his previous research to the study of penicillin and its perfection as an effective antibodic. Fleming's discovery was therefore unintentional, and his wonder drug was made public only after experimentation conducted on the basis of his discovery.

In both primary and secondary convergence, the element of individual understanding is of extreme importance. Discounting the naive examples of opposites in response to given words and the child withdrawing his or her hand reflexively from a hot stove—the heat transmitted through the nervous system and registered in the conscious level very shortly after—the individual's comprehension is of extreme importance, as illustrated by the example of the detectives. Two detectives of equal training can be confronted with the facts of a crime, its clues, and the people suspected of being involved. One detective can misinterpret these facts and personality traits and hence misread the clues; the other detective can read the message of these facts, avoid all deviations to which the clues may point, and by drawing the proper conclusions, catch the criminal.

Secondary convergence relies on personal understanding and the willingness to try unique approaches. Many medical people before Harvey drew conclusions based less on their research than on the works of others who preceded them. These works were sources of authority indicating that there was no need to look for valves in the heart as the means for pumping blood or to consider the heart's chambers as factors in circulation. Harvey could have taken the comforting position that authority is correct and that there is no need for him to devote his time and efforts to this problem. Fleming's discovery was certainly unusual, and he could have easily ignored the spore or washed the culture dish after the mucus had contaminated it. For convergent creative reasoning the puzzle stands either as given, requiring efforts to solve it, or after the events are observed, in the case of Fleming, stating the problem and formulating its solution. Those who look for meaning and understand the puzzle, taking new paths toward discovery, will most certainly solve it.

THE DIVERGENT APPROACH

In normal thinking, that is, thinking not pertaining to any specific problem, free and unrelated thoughts often enter into our conscious awareness and allow us to wander far from the mundane situations of life. In this sense, creative thinking is not normal, as it relates to problems and the rules of logic which the problems seem to possess. Moreover, convergent thinking tends to regulate reasoning according to the problem, in terms of the restrictions and symbolic manipulations of the problem.

Divergent reasoning also has its rules, whose relevance to the problem in question often relies on clues, both obvious and subliminal. An example of naive divergence is provided by the synonym-response test, where synonyms are required for a given stimulus word. The word "damp" evokes an image of a wet place and the letter "d" together with the image conjures up the word "dank," providing a mental picture of a place both wet and unpleasant. This goes further and leads to the image of "soggy," and from there other associations are reeled off: steamy, saturated, swampy, and so on. The answers provided demonstrate a deviation from the stimulus word, with each answer-word having its own unique nuances; yet each is associated with the stimulus word, possessing common properties that unite them within the context of the problem.

In this naive example, the synonymous words already exist in the vocabulary, and it is a matter of drawing on recollection to produce these words, which, while different in nuances, share the common property evoked by the stimulus word. The nuances and meanings of each word illustrate their divergence from the stimulus word; nevertheless, they are joined, associated, by the common property as determined by the problem. In this example, imagination is allowed and the maneuvering is dictated by the rule of providing a synonym for a stimulus word.

For the problems of the arts and sciences, however, there are no existent answers that, on the basis of their common properties, require fusion with the problem's terminology or content. For the divergent position with respect to the problems of the arts and sciences, the answers must be sought with the use of the associative stimuli provided by the problem's content and linguistic construction. Because of the importance of association in this type of reasoning the terms "divergence" and "association" are often used interchangeably and will be used so here.

Divergent—that is, associative—reasoning takes two forms. One form is the naive associative reasoning discussed above. Another example of naive divergence is that of the detective examining the clues of a crime and combining the evidence of other such crimes in order to find a common property or properties and hence establish the criminal's identity with the assistance of similar detective methods. Moreover, associating the evidence with the suspects' behavior patterns helps to reveal the criminal's identity. Should this method of reasoning fail, it may be due to incomplete evidence, an incomplete suspect list, or perhaps a combination of both.

Another example of divergence in its naive form is that of the laboratory research worker who tests a hypothesis against the experimental facts. These facts yield either the desired results, thereby corroborating the hypothesis, or if not, may result in the formulation of a new hypothesis, which after testing is found to correspond to the results yielded by the experimental data. This is also an example of naive divergence, because while the facts do not fit the original hypothesis, another hypothesis is stated that associates with the experimental results.

Testing for vaccines is a case in point. Underlying such testing is a wealth of knowledge about microbes and their actions as well as the bodily responses to many germ fighters. Slight deviations in preparations to cope with the problem in question illustrate the trial-and-error approach to vaccine formation, which is naive divergence. The processes of imagination, active and stimulated by experiments already conducted and those which have proven successful in the past, bring into play the multilevel associations that assist in constructing the required vaccine. This is a procedure of trial and error, possibly leading to the desired results, usually after many rejections of differing chemical combinations.

The other form of divergence is strict bisociation, in which two (or more) matrices, unrelated in content and purpose, are fused, with the consequences of a new approach being devised. This is divergence because these unrelated matrices merge only when the bisociative act welds them into a viably associative pattern.

This approach is explained by Arthur Koestler. He defines a matrix as a unifying structure in its content so that "all mental habits and skills governed by a fixed set of rules but capable of varied strategies in attacking a problem are contained in the matrix."[2] The matrix includes the "rules of the game," such as the rules for playing chess and the manifold strategies that are allowed as the game develops, and the mundane task of bathing with all the operations allowed by this procedure. The matrices in these examples state the specific rules and purposes for acquiring the desired objectives, for playing and winning in chess and for bathing under the many different circumstances in which these activities can occur. While the rules of the matrices allow for trial and error, the execution of these rules varies with the conditions under which the activities allowed by these rules occur.

Hence, Koestler coined the term "bisociation" to distinguish between the routines of disciplined thinking within a single universe of discourse—that is, within the rules of the matrix —and the creative types of mental activity that always operate on more than one plane or within a single matrix.[3] He provides a very interesting example of bisociation, that of Archimedes and the crown.[4] The king was presented with a finely sculptured crown and was told it was pure gold. Accepting the crown graciously, the king was somewhat skeptical as to its real worth and turned to his friend, the philosopher Archimedes, giving him the problem of determining whether the crown is indeed pure gold or a mixture of precious metals.

Determining the purities of metals according to their specific densities was a process well known to Archimedes, but he had worked with assaying metals of no specific form. To beat down the crown and then measure its water displacement would have certainly provided an answer but at the expense of destroying the crown's intrinsic value. Archimedes pondered the problem for days. One day, he let his thoughts wander, forgetting the difficulty his king had placed before him. Taking a bath, he watched the water rise as he submerged his body in the tub, an observation he had made many times. In an instant, the two matrices merged; specific densities of metals, no matter what shapes or forms they take, give off the same water displacements according to their weights when submerged; should the crown be a mixture its displacement would be different than it would be if it were pure gold. The problem could be solved without destroying the crown's beauty. At the moment of realization, when the solution came to him, such emotion was released that Archimedes leaped from the tub, ran down the street screaming "Eureka! I found it!" The king, after hearing the cries of the naked philosopher, thought that the problem had been too difficult and that Archimedes had snapped under the strain. After he calmed down, he explained to the king that by weighing the crown against an equivalent measure of gold and then determining the specific densities of each, the answer could be found without destroying the crown. Archimedes's solution was sound and according to the specific density, the crown was indeed pure gold.

According to Koestler, Archimedes "fused" or bisociated the hitherto unrelated matrices of bathing and measuring the specific densities of metals into a single matrix having its own rules. This fusion or bisociation occurred at the very moment that Archimedes realized that the crown would behave in the same manner as his body when submerged in water. This fusion of two unrelated matrices occurred when, in an unguarded moment, Archimedes's attention was allowed to wander.

This mental fusion of divergent matrices into a single operative matrix is the associative reasoning process of creativity. It operates in a manner similar to the naive divergent thinking discussed above. The synonym example as well as the detective example are *naive* because they provide no really new knowledge. The synonyms exist to be recalled upon stimulation; the criminal certainly knows who committed the crime, and if the detective is successful, this knowledge will become available to all concerned.

Rigorous divergent thinking, however, does provide new information because of the fusing of matrices unrelated to the problem's linguistic structure, its terms and operators, and the manner by which these can be employed in studying the problem. Rigorous divergence is valid when matrices are fused and allow for the formulation of knowledge hitherto unknown. Both Tycho Brahe and Kepler observed the movement of the planet Mars, yet Tycho computed its movement in a circular orbit and tried to explain the orbit in mathematical language; Kepler fused the planet's orbit with the mathematical form of the ellipse, thereby removing the discrepancies, which his mentor Tycho was unable to do in spite of his sophisticated mathematics and measuring equipment. The new matrix Kepler formed was extended to the motions of all the planets and served as one of the pillars of Newton's three laws of motion—the other pillar being Galileo's earth-physics. Newton fused the two into his own matrix and provided the basis of physics until the latter part of the nineteenth century.[5]

Another example of bisociation is Johannes Gutenberg's invention of moveable type. Seeking a way of making printing an efficient and far less time-consuming process, Gutenberg experimented with all sorts of devices. One day at a winefest, slightly inebriated and letting his thoughts wander, he watched the pressing of grapes and made notes of his observations. The next day, more sober, he read his notes and realized that the principle of the wine press could also serve as the basis for the printing press. The bisociation of the age-old process of pressing the fruit of the vine to obtain its nectar became fused in Gutenberg's mind with the pressing of the letters on paper. These divergent operations, completely unrelated, became inseparable with the fusion of their matrices.

For naive divergent reasoning, no new knowledge is provided but clarification is given for knowledge which already exists; thus divergence in its naive form provides for the expansion of available knowledge through the associative thought processes, generated by the common properties that stimulate the associations. In the situation of strict bisociation, the matrices as they stand are divergent, each covering a specific range of activities and governed by specific rules. Bisociation fuses these matrices, with the point of fusion being common property; the creative mind has made the new matrix original and operable.

A CRITIQUE OF THE MUTUAL EXCLUSIVENESS OF CONVERGENCE AND DIVERGENCE

It will be argued in these pages that the convergence and divergence approaches to creativity, held as mutually exclusive by their respective supporters, are in fact complementary and operative, each in its own way, in the contemporary process of creativity. This has to be demonstrated, but first, the mutual exclusiveness of these positions must be critiqued. By showing that there is no mutual exclusiveness between them, the theory of creativity relevant for our era of knowledge can then be stated.

Consider Koestler's description of the founding of electromagnetism.

> Lodestones—magnets—were known in antiquity as a curiosity of Nature. In the Middle Ages they were used for two purposes: as navigators' compasses and as a means to attract an estranged wife back to her husband. Equally well known were the curious properties of amber which, when rubbed, acquired the virtue of attracting flimsy objects. The Greek word for amber is *elektron*, but the Greeks were not much interested in electricity; nor were the Middle Ages. For nearly two thousand years, electricity and magnetism were considered as separate phenomena, in no way related to each other. In 1820 Hans Christian Oersted discovered that an electric current flowing through a wire deflected a magnetic compass which happened to be lying on his table. At that moment the two concepts began to fuse into one: electro-magnetism, creating a kind of chain which is still continuing and gaining in momentum.[6]

In criticism of Koestler's position in the quoted passage, two points must be made. First, Koestler states that Oersted discovered that the current flowing through the wire deflected the magnetic compass. This discovery was actually a convergence, similar to Fleming's observation of the spore in the culture dish; it was an essential discovery for the two hitherto unrelated frames of electricity and magnetism, for in the absence of discovery the mental fusion, the bisociation, could not have been made. This is the second point: both convergence and divergence were directly involved in forming the new matrix.

The reason for the supposed mutual exclusiveness of these positions is the ease with which the proponents of the two camps move from the naive situations to rigorous reasoning. For example, the proponents of convergence tend to treat discovery as they do the solving of an algebraic equation with one of its values to be determined by symbolic manipulations. That which is to be discovered will be found by the correct manipulations of the problem's terms. This approach is, however, appropriate only for primary convergence, in which the solution to the problem exists and can be found by breaking the problem's code. On the primary level of convergence, ambiguity is nonexistent; the problem is stated and the solution exists and awaits exposure.

It is on the secondary level of convergence, where no solution already exists, that ambiguity sets in and the difficulties of exclusiveness occur. For example, Harvey's discovery of the circulation of the blood is a proper observation corresponding to secondary convergence, in which he observed the heart's functioning in a manner hitherto unknown to the medical profession. However, his discovery could not have been made without the bisociation of the water-pump matrix with that of the fish's heart. It was this mental fusion, requiring observation, that brought Harvey to examine the chambers of the human heart and explore their functions, thereby making his famous contribution.

For issues that bear scientific or artistic significance, there is no single explanation for the comprehension of the nuances of meaning as they merge in the human mind, employing sensitivity and awareness; most certainly convergence cannot adequately explain the act of creativity in these fields of endeavor.

The proponents of the divergent school are just as at ease moving from naive divergence to rigorous bisociation, so that word association, in which divergent meanings are combined because of a common relationship, is treated in the same manner as is the association of separate and distinct matrices into a single working structure. This ease of movement results in the equation of naive divergence with bisociation, and this equation is as erroneous as the fallacy that primary convergence is to be treated in the same way as secondary convergence.

That such a movement is in error can be seen with the example of Harvey. For it was convergence that sustained the divergent reasoning, that of merging the frames of references or matrices of the water pump and its operations with that of the fish's heart and the examination of its operations; without the empirical observation, the merger of matrices comes to nothing. The proponents of each school equate the naive forms with rigorous reasoning, but naive thinking has nothing to do with creativity. It is only rigorous thinking requiring both convergence and divergence that brings about creativity.

However, with primary convergence and naive divergence, the position of mutual exclusiveness is indeed valid. There can be no convergence in word association, where synonyms are required; nor can there be divergence where word opposites are demanded. Naive divergence is inoperable in the process of discovering solutions to mathematical equations, and primary convergence has no place in the solution of the detective's puzzle, where the correct associations to the clues have to be made for the solution to be formed. Both these levels of reasoning, however, have no role in creativity. There is no mutual exclusiveness between secondary convergence and bisociation in creativity, as each operates on its own level in the creative process. Historical examples abound in which ex post facto analysis demonstrated that this mutual exclusiveness is nonexistent. The question is, therefore, why these two camps have remained in opposition.

The answer lies in the reassessment of Western educational systems in the wake of the first Soviet Sputnik. Prior to the satellite's launching, education was strongly oriented toward convergent reasoning: information provided before a test had to be repeated on the tests. Hence, the emphasis was on a problem being given and the answer having to be discovered (recovered) from the student's storehouse of information. With the successful Soviet launching, the entire education system was re-evaluated. Instead of relying primarily on conventional teaching methods emphasizing convergent reasoning, divergence became considered as a form of original and creative thinking. Tests were also devised to analyze students' divergent reasoning ability, and the students with impressive scores, as decided by the testers, were moved to higher classes.

One such test was devised by J. W. Getzels and P. W. Jackson, described in their article, "The Highly Intelligent and Highly Creative Adolescent."[7] The test consists of a picture of a man traveling in an airplane, reclining in his seat, with a contented smile on his face; the object of the test is the interpretation of this picture. To show the contrast between convergent and divergent thinking, two interpretations are provided. The convergent interpretation is:

Mr. Smith is on his way back home from a successful business trip. He is happy and he is thinking about his wonderful family and how glad he will be to see them again. He can picture it, about an hour from now, his plane will be landing at the airport and Mrs. Smith and the three children all there welcoming him home again.

This type of interpretation is somewhat obvious and can easily be derived from the picture. However, contrast this interpretation with the divergent approach:

The man is flying back from Reno where he had just won a divorce from his wife. He couldn't stand to live with her anymore, he told the judge, because she wore so much cold cream on her face at night that her face would skid across the pillow and hit him in the head. He is now contemplating a non-skid face cream.

The convergent interpretation was given by a gifted child with a measured high intelligence quotient. It is convergent because it describes a situation which seems commonplace, an air traveler pleased with the results of his journey and anticipating seeing his family again. The child probed the picture and presented a standard answer according to the problem's terms; her interpretation could be used as an airline advertisement with the traveler relaxing in comfort on this particular carrier. The child's response converges on the standard scenario for this type of picture.

This standard interpretation is exactly what was not being sought by the testers. The divergent interpretation deviates from this standard interpretation by associating different situations and merging them in the pictorial presentation of the relaxed and smiling traveler. The nuances contrivable from this problem of interpreting the picture are as many as this single divergent presentation indicates. The traveler may have found a cure for a rare disease; he may have committed what he thinks to be a successful murder, and so forth. Because this divergent interpretation differs from the one commonly presented, it is considered by the authors to be a unique approach to problem-solving in this context, one that breaks out of the convergence-mold of reasoning and demonstrates a unique approach to thinking and interpreting.

The difficulty with this type of testing is that it praises naive divergent reasoning and rejects primary convergent reasoning and stops there. No further conclusions can be drawn concerning the mental abilities of these students who offered their interpretations, for the problem itself requires no rigorous thought. The projection from this type of naive reasoning to creativity is blatantly false and is as erroneous as praising primary convergent reasoning for its creativity.

The validity of such tests for measuring intelligence and creative ability is certainly debatable. They tend to exclude such factors as each child's home environment, personality, income stratum, state of health, alertness, and state of nervousness as the test is given. Granted, there is a need for classification in the education system, and the Soviet Sputnik certainly influenced the consideration of requirements and testing of education methods and approaches. However, mixing the slow learners with the fast ones tends to reduce social inequality and may indeed improve the learning abilities of those who learn more slowly than others. These measurements of learning ability are certainly not valid and final criteria of a child's creative ability.

The purpose of determining the factors of creativity in school children is to prepare them for the rigors of life in our era of knowledge. Moreover, with the initial Soviet success in space and the importance of maintaining a competitive posture on the military, economic, and social planes, creativity in early education has indeed replaced to a large extent the rote learning system so well established in an earlier era. This, however, is where the difficulty sets in: the creativity involved in education is in response to problems set by the educational boards. Certain types of solutions are acceptable and have been predetermined prior to the problems' presentation. This is certainly not the case with the problems confronted by artists and scientists, by technicians and engineers, in our time. For these problems, pre-established solutions are nonexistent, and the difficulties of acceptance and rejection are far different from those set up by school boards and higher academic institutions.

Hence, the movement from naive and primary thinking required for school testing to secondary and associative reasoning necessary for creativity is invalid. The two different types of reasoning are for two different types of problems; the naive and primary reasoning for problems with established and acceptable answers, the secondary and rigorous reasoning for problems concerning the real issues of creativity. In the chapters to follow, a theory of creativity relevant to our contemporary era of knowledge will be provided, and the issues of acceptance and rejection will be discussed.

6

The Dynamics of Creativity—II

A THEORY OF CREATIVITY IN OUR CONTEMPORARY ERA OF KNOWLEDGE

In 1869 F. Galton published his book, *Hereditary Genius*, in which he sought to describe genius not only as a characteristic that sets those blessed with it apart from the rest of society because of their potential and actual abilities, but also, in a more scientific vein, as a characteristic that could be understood statistically with its frequencies in inheritance to a large extent predictable.[1] This book appeared at a time when there was no great societal interest in developing its intellectual resources; it consequently found an audience among a select number of educators and psychologists.

Renewed interest in Galton's work began in 1957, after the Soviet Union sent up its first satellite. Amid the strenuous competition between the Eastern and Western bloc countries, the news of the successful launching stunned the West, with one important result being the revaluation of the educational system and the search for approaches to education that would stimulate intellectual activity. Methods were sought for testing children to determine which children were gifted and talented; means were searched out for assessing the differences in levels of abilities as affected by subenvironments and subcultural influences and for stimulating creativity within these levels.

While the impact of the Soviet Sputnik was responsible for bringing the search for understanding to the fore, nevertheless, research was undertaken, albeit in a much lower key, prior to 1957. Interesting enough, the pre- and post-1957 scholars reached the same conclusions: that creativity is either convergent or divergent but not both. Moreover, the questions raised then by this mutual exclusion remain. For example, when is discovery creative? Is the creative act the "blinding flash" of understanding that provides the answers to tormenting questions? What, in light of Galton's research and subsequent work in the field, is the relationship between genius and creativity?

Galton argued that genius has the greatest chance of propagation in those families that have achieved social standing, either through the personal efforts of individual members, or through social inheritance and positions of wealth, which enhance prestige. He argued that these families have the necessary resources for securing the best education for their children, thereby ensuring them good stations in life. Their wealth tends to bring them into contact with families of similar situations, often resulting in interbreeding and strengthening the family bloodline. Galton also pointed out that in most of these families there is a decline in the revitalized abilities in the direct descendents, while indirect descendents, in the third and fourth generations, maintain the line of the original families and tend toward genius.

Galton's argument touched on aspects other than biological inheritance of genius: He maintained that eminent people are the offspring of good parental stock and sound marriages. He concluded:

> The best form of civilization in respect to the improvement of the race would be one in which society was not costly; where incomes were chiefly derived from professional sources and not through inheritance; where every lad had a chance of showing his abilities and, if highly gifted, was enabled to receive a first-rate education and entrance into professional life, by the liberal help of the exhibitions and scholarships which he had gained in his early youth; where marriage was held in as high honour as in ancient Jewish times; where the pride of race was encouraged (of course I do not refer to the nonsensical sentiment of the present day that goes under that name), where the weak could find a welcome and a refuge in celibate monasteries or sisterhoods, and lastly, where the better sort of emigrants and refugees from other lands were invited and welcomed, and their descendants naturalized.

While the importance of the psychological dynamics of creativity were considered pre- and post-Sputnik, the sociological dynamics are still very much ignored. The emphasis in all these works is on the individual and his or her convergent and divergent reasoning. The impact of existing systems from which problems are derived and that therefore provide the grounds for creativity, has been ignored. That this is so, is indicated in the conceptions of genius as they have evolved into today's usage of the term. The term has fluctuated from being a biological concept as with the ancient Greek *genos* meaning "race," "stock," "gender," and the Latin derivation of *genius*, which refers to the social collective output, to an individual concept such as the *jinni*, a mischievous character in Middle Eastern folklore that is at the command of the person who possesses it, to the Hebrew *gaon*, the bright illuminary of the holy teachings. The concept of genius in common usage has also reflected the unusual person, the deviant from the social norm who locks himself or herself away and performs great deeds in isolation; the concept thus refers to the brillant person whose work sets new standards in the field of his or her endeavor.

In fact, the contemporary genius, as the term is used here, is one who operates on both the personal and the social levels, for his or her output is necessarily personal, for only the individual creates his or her own work, as well as being social, for he or she operates on problems that are existent in systems or establishes a new system for others to use and to derive problems requiring solutions. Creativity, while being personal, depends on social dynamics, on the groundwork provided by others, on problems being drawn out from existing systems or from issues with which no systems deal and for which a new system has to be established.

Hence, throughout this discussion, the creative individual and the genius (as the term is used here) are one and the same person. It makes no difference to this discussion if a person resolves a difficulty in an existing system, allowing the system's utility to be increased as the source of entropy has been resolved, or whether a new system is established in which new concepts are formulated and new methods of work provided. Both forms of creativity provide social continuity as they rid sources of decline. In the situation where the system's integrity is reinstated, the system's continuity as a working basis is reassured; for the new system, the social dynamics of knowledge are that much more re-enforced as the system provides new operative and area languages, delineates a unique problem area, and sets others' ingenuity as they work within the system. Another issue comes to the fore here, however: if the creative person is the contemporary genius and thereby provides continuity, how can our social era of knowledge come to an end, to be replaced by another, perhaps more productive, but most certainly a different era? This question must wait until the last part of this work. But now, a theory of creativity for our contemporary era of knowledge must be stated.

ON CONTEMPORARY CREATIVITY—THE CREATIVE ACT

The creative act is an individual response to a problem and is the individual's solution which is offered as a resolution of the difficulty. This response is made with respect to two types of problem situations. One is a difficulty within an established system requiring the alteration of either one or both of the languages used within the system. The second problem situation is the construction of an original system, which may either provide competition against existing systems or set a unique system for a well-delineated and originally conceived problem area and provide a basis for working with the system on the problem.[2] In the first situation, information incorporated into the system is a source of entropy to the system, and the creative act is the attempt to resolve this difficulty. For the second situation, information that exists within systems is extrapolated and restructured into a new system, thereby altering the nuances of the information, rendering its meanings unique to the system's construction. This second situation may be considered a limit-case of the first, because only after the information is extracted and reconstructed does the individual present the system for consideration by his or her peers, whereas with the first situation it is not the system in toto which is being presented, but the repairs undertaken to ensure the system's utility. The example of Fleming's discovery of penicillin fits into this limit-case situation, for the existence of the mold and its specific properties were known and also the properties of mucus were well understood. It was only after Fleming's observation and his subsequent work on his findings that the new approach to fighting disease was made known and evaluated by his fellow scientists. Also, Oersted's observation would only be a curiosity in the annals of science had he not researched his observation and drawn out its unique consequences, thereby establishing an early theory of electromagnetism. In both cases, the people involved had to analyze further and experiment with their findings before making their systems public and available for others to consider.

Both primary convergence and naive divergence have been ruled out in creativity; secondary convergence and rigorous divergence indeed have significant roles in the creative act. The individual's concern with a problem within a system of knowledge allows him or her to seek relevant information either from other systems' languages or in the formulation of the information through the creative process, information that is unique and that will serve as a solution to the problem. There are thus two levels of creative activity here, each using secondary convergence and rigorous divergence in the formulation of the solution.

In each level, the information is unstructured. Information extrapolated from existing systems loses its utility, for its utility is obtained only within the system in which it exists and is worked upon. On the first level, removing this information and placing it within a different system requires adaptation so that the information will be able to fit and be worked upon with the maximum utility possible within the system. The entropic elements are thus removed and the new elements placed within the system, so that with the new nuances of the transplanted information, the system's utility is restored.

In the second level, the creative act is quasi-innovative, in the sense that a new system is not being formed, but new information is being developed to fit into the system. This does not mean, of course, that the information in its various stages and elements did not exist previously; it does mean that this information has become crystallized into a new form, with its own unique nuances, which must then be shaped and given utility within the system's structure.

For both levels, the finding and interpreting of this information, unstructured for the system it is intended, is strictly a personal affair and depends on the individual's self-projection as manifested in his or her approach to seeking the information and in the manner of his or her understanding of the information's nuances and significance for the problem. This personal aspect provides the uniqueness of the creative act, and projection is the extension of the individual's personality as expressed in the interpretation of the information. Personality projection determines the approach to the problem and the paths to be taken in the attempt to find the viable solution.

As the individual is unique, so are his or her personality, conceptions, and approaches to problem-solving in the creative act. The processes of becoming receptive to the nuances of information, of comprehending the problem, and of delving into the recesses of mental activity and imagination are certainly unique.[3] But projection not only illustrates the idiosyncracies of the individual engaged in the creative act; it also imposes the individual's character on the solution he or she presents. Occupation with a problem results in a degree of mental tension, which highlights the individual's receptivity to all kinds of information and the possibilities which this information, once restructured, can have as a solution. This tension makes the individual's reflexes and sensitivities responsive, very often at a subliminal level, so that situations which previously had no utility are cast in a new light. Archimedes's bathing, certainly a routine and mundane affair, took on new significance that day when he sat down in his bath and, while watching the water rise, understood the solution to his problem.

Not only is this tension a subjective experience based on personal projection; it is also incorporated into the work. This tension is certainly prevalent in the works of the postwar musicians and artists. The uses of visual disharmonics and musical dissonance are statements of intent to express this tension; they are clashes of emotions expressed within a harmonic unit, expressions of artistic and musical conflicts that the creative person feels in our contemporary era. Information in works of art takes on significance when placed in an artistic content, so that the same information used in different works takes on the nuances of those works, according to the utility assigned to the information, as determined by the artists who adapt this information to portray their messages. Tension as both technique and emotion allows for a swift emotive response to be generated by the perceiver, a reaction that allows the perceiver to interpret the work according to his or her own experiences and emotional development. For contributions in the sciences, personality projection allows for the building of the contribution—be it an alteration of a theory or a theory itself—in a manner unique to its creator; it serves to bring attackers and defenders into the realm of debate and criticism. With the sciences as well as the arts, personality projection and the use of tension help to maintain interest in the works involved.

The creative act must entail both rigorous divergence and secondary convergence. The fallacy of their mutual exclusiveness reduces each of these forms of thought to their lesser forms of naive divergence and primary convergence, which, as was argued above, have no place in the dynamics of creativity. The type of information sought and the merging of this information depends on these factors: the individual's perceptiveness at the time; his or her receptivity to stimuli that seem to others to be ordinary and mundane; the individual's education, training, and sensitivity to unusual things that others may not notice or may dismiss as irrelevant.

This information, as the individual experiences it, can be worked on at a conscious level, as is the case with a purposeful search to meet the problem's requirements; or it may be operating at an unconscious level, when the conscious level of awareness is given the freedom of relief from the problem and the burden of searching. In this latter case, the tension of the search is transformed from the conscious to the unconscious level, sustaining the person, who is often unaware, on a high level of perceptive cognizance.

Divergence remains the sole operating process in the creative act until the actual information data are worked into a single unit. As this is not a transformation of information from one system to another, but a reformulation of the information, providing new information by the combination of several information units, this divergence is made according to the objective interpretations placed on the information as assessed within the system with respect to the utility measurement. However, there must also be a subjective interpretation of this information; otherwise it would not be selected by the divergent reasoning processes. This subjective interpretation depends on the individual's unique personality projection and the tension that he or she seeks to achieve; the information must fit the individualistic requirements as well as the objective utility requirements.

In spite of the conscious and unconscious attempts to bring about an information merger, the newly formed information unit has no utility until it is placed within the context of the problem the individual seeks to solve. Nor is this information entropic because without a system in which it is used it has neither utility nor entropy. Hence, while the information unit may seem convincing to its originator, this is insufficient for the formulation of this information to be termed as a creative act.

Only one part of the creative act has been undertaken by the information construction; the other part, that of placing the information in a setting in which its utility or entropy can be assessed, is the role of secondary convergence. The system in this sense can be seen as a puzzle in which a faulty piece has to be replaced by a piece which fits properly. The creative act requires that the information so constructed meet the requirements of a solution to the problem; if not, then the information constructed remains just that: information with no systematic utility. It is the combination of divergence in the constructing of new information and convergence in placing this information within a working system that constitutes the creative act. Both parts are necessary, for divergence alone results in information without utility, and convergence is merely the finding of something without relevant information content. Harvey's observation of the water pump and the fish's heart would have remained just that, an observation; this merger of information took on utility only when placed within the theoretical context of the circulation of blood. Fleming's observation of the mold spore in the culture dish would have led to nothing had he not merged the results of the action of the spore on the mucus and placed this information in a context of microbiology.

What are the techniques of the creative act concerning an entropic element within a system? Consider the statement $o_d a$, that is, a definitive and delineating relationship between an operational statement and an area statement. For this statement information through merger has been constructed and must be tested. Moreover, in examining the faulty statement it was found that o is affected by a and that the emphasis must be on the area statement in the reconstruction of information. Through searching and finally merging of information, new information is constructed, so that a becomes a'; the newly formed a' has new information particles a_o, a_b, a_c, with the first particle belonging to the original a statement and the others taken from other systems, B and C respectively. As they are reconstructed to serve as a solution, they are joined to the *a* problematic statement and thus formed into a new a'. This alteration requires changes in the operational statement *o* so that it relates accordingly to the new area statement. Hence, a change in one statement requires a corresponding alteration in its paired statement, so that the definitive operation and the utility of the statement in both its parts are retained.

The test of this statement's utility after the corresponding correction of the operator is determined by the statement's probability within the system and is assessed by

$$[P(o_d a'/O) = I^*(O_d A/a')]_t$$

so that if the probability falls within the accepted range as evaluated by the new information, I* brought by the alterations, so that if $o_d a' \rightarrow 1$ within its context of the system, then $S' \rightarrow 1$, that is, its utility is restored because of the alteration.

Of course, the opposite may hold, that the altered statement adds nothing to the system's utility and hence becomes entropic when placed within the system, so that the entire process of the creative act must be undertaken again and will continue to be so until entropy in other statements brings down the system or the system's integrity is finally restored.

In this case the statement's utility has objectively declined, that is, general agreement prevails that the statement in question is faulty. This is objective because it is held by the majority who work with the system and efforts are made to solve the statement's problem. There is, however, the situation in which the statement is considered entropic by a very small number of people working with the system, and this in disagreement with the majority who find no fault at all with the statement. This lack of awareness may be due to personal vested interests in the system, or it may be due to a genuine conflict of opinions as to the validity of the argument for entropy. These issues will be discussed in the next chapter; it must be emphasized here that the individual's unique personality is of great significance when working with a system or engaging in a creative act, as this entails the recognition of a problem within the system which might not be recognized by others. Of course, the rejection of a contribution, be it a reconstructed system statement or a new system itself, may be reasonable if the contribution is invalid, which the creator might not see because he or she is too close to the contribution—but this must wait.

The second problem situation, mentioned earlier as the "limit case," operates unlike the first situation: that is, first convergence is employed and then divergence is used. Convergence is employed in the form of discovery, the unexpected finding of a unique fact that had hitherto been either unnoticed or considered without significance and hence ignored. Oersted noticed the relationship between the current flowing through the wire and its influence on the compass needle. He could have let it go, returned to his own work, and let the matter rest. Instead, he sought to explore the relationship, after which he formulated the basic theory of electromagnetism, which others have expanded and altered significantly.

The relationship had not "mentally fused," (bisociated) in his mind, for what he observed and discovered, was an objective relationship. The current had actually influenced the compass without Oersted's imposing a merging relationship on the event. He discovered this influence as a passive observer and then sought to explain it, to find a suitable theoretical context in which to place his finding. He discovered a relationship, and this was convergence; he formulated a theory of electromagnetism by fusing the observation onto a theory of electricity and hence developed electromagnetic theory. First convergence and then divergence. There may, in cases of innovation such as Oersted's, be a final convergence in seeking to transplant the theory onto an existing body of knowledge, but this is an exception to the limit-case act of creativity.

Another example of this limit case, indeed a variation of the first, is the problem when an individual considers a means of improving a situation. Unlike the Fleming and Oersted examples, where new theories were developed on a background of existing knowledge, theories that were formulated as a result of observing the irregular and unexpected, this limit case refers to a problem being tackled as a way to improve a given situation. This is the case with Gutenberg, who understood the processes of written communication and the tremendous lengths of time it took to write a manuscript and the necessary restrictions on its reproduction.

Gutenberg's finding was most certainly unusual, although he spent considerable time on the problems of mass printing. His somewhat intoxicated observation of the wine press squeezing out the juice from the grape was enough to work on his unconscious and even though he took notes of this observation he did not at the time realize its significance for his problem. Only in the more sobered state did the fusion of his observation into his problem occur; the rest was the development of the device that was not the wine press but the printing press.[4]

This variation of the limit case requires a problem due to personal dissatisfaction with existing systems. The stages of the creative act are, first, observation; second, the realization that what has been observed is of utility; and third, the mental fusion. There is a deliberate search for a solution to this type of problem; often the information observed or received bears no significance at the time. While the conscious levels of awareness have sought relief from the problem temporarily, the unconscious levels are still at work and eventually bring up to the levels of awareness the information to be examined. Had Gutenberg been sober at the time he may or may not have realized the relationship between the wine press and printing; he was astute enough to take notes of his observations and only later did the meaning become clear for his problem.

The examples discussed in this work have been historical events that occurred in other historical periods. Harvey's contribution to the understanding of blood circulation made its impact, but other aspects of medicine were slow to follow. Gutenberg's contribution to printing had a fairly slow impact, but it gathered impetus as the publishing of manuscripts became more common; newspapers and other printed means of communication followed, although slowly. Oersted's contribution was picked up at a quicker rate because the scientific community was still basking in the sunshine of Newtonian physics, although some clouds were beginning to gather. Fleming's contribution made a greater impact more rapidly due to improvements in communications, and better comprehension of bacteria.

Compare, however, the impact which each of these contributions made in their times to corresponding contributions today. Should a cure for cancer be found, it would be news almost immediately, and great resources would be channeled for exploring and developing such a cure. In printing, offset and computer-instructed printing have certainly been far-reaching developments, contributions made in our era of knowledge, so that more books, journals, and newspapers are available for greater audiences. Electromagnetism has certainly come a long way since Oersted's chance observation, with electromagnetic systems moving subatomic particles at extremely high speeds in order to research their behavior when reacting with other such particles. Uses that Oersted and his early successors could not have fathomed are being developed for electromagnetic equipment; the results of such research are multidirectional.

The point about creativity in our era, as opposed to the previous eras, is that while previously such contributions were disseminated, accepted, and explored very slowly, today there is a greater willingness to consider contributions even though the systems that generate the problems are more complex. Where previously, the emphasis on creativity was that of innovation, in our era the greater emphasis is on initiation, the act of creativity within a system.

Hence, our contemporary era of knowledge has a higher rate of creativity, in both forms of innovation and initiation, than any other era in recorded history. Systems are being altered at rates unique to our era and new systems—innovations—are being constructed at a pace that not only reflects the increased growth of knowledge, but indeed generates knowledge. More than ever before, problems are generated within systems and are being solved, bringing to the fore new problems. New theories in the arts and sciences, in philosophy and technology, are being innovated with the subsequent research bringing these theories into unsuspected domains and generating new problems to be solved. These are the dynamics of creativity, unique to our era, generating knowledge at levels and scopes never before conceived. How do these dynamics work? How are problems raised? What effects have their solutions on the general levels of knowledge? How do they, in turn, further the dynamics of creativity?

THE DYNAMICS OF CREATIVITY

There are three kinds of role in the dynamics of creativity, each with its own unique importance and neither more important than the others. Without any one of these there would be no creativity, no generation of ideas, no new contributions. These roles are, in an important sense, the aspirations of contemporary people in their search for the new, in their somewhat uncomfortable feelings with the stable. Change has become an expression of contemporary living; this is manifested in travel, in elections, in the new products of economic entrepreneurial activity. In our era, more so than at any other historical period, humanity seeks to challenge the existing order, not only for the sake of rebellion but also to bring to the fore difficulties with existing systems, to explore them, to find any faults, and to correct these faults. New systems are often met with mixed reactions, expressing willingness to work with them and to criticize them, to bring out their utility in ways not considered by their innovators and to bring them into entropic states and solve the consequent difficulties.

Ours is a restless era, forged in the aftermath of a great war, weaned on the knowledge that we may at any moment be confronted with total destruction due to a grave miscalculation or out of political necessity to stem the tide of a recognized enemy. We place our faith in our political leadership only because we understand that they alone hold the reins of power; yet we retain our skepticism, questioning their judgments and often relying on our own. We often see political decrees not entirely in the light of sound judgment but perhaps as miscalculations, as policies not too well thought out. Because of the abundance of knowledge available at our disposal, we form opinions, based very often on sound reasoning that conflict with the opinions of our chosen leaders or of those who take political power because of their military and industrial base of support.

We seek change because of the abundance of knowledge at our disposal, and we attempt to use this knowledge. We therefore recognize, both historically and in the contemporary sense, that what we know now is most likely to be refuted, cast aside as wrong, in the near future. We have seen the paradigms of knowledge in the sciences fall and understand the relativity and indeterminism with which we must work on the macro and micro physical levels: we hear experts in medicine disagree, and we read of our legal experts in debates that seem unresolvable. Ours is an era of knowledge, and our knowledge has reached an abundance in all fields of inquiry. In order to comprehend our era, the dynamics of creativity must be understood. Contemporary creativity differs from that of the past and must therefore be treated in the context of our contemporary era, for knowledge is derived from the very dynamics of creativity.

The roles involved in the dynamics of creativity are: the imitator, the initiator, and the innovator. A person may at times occupy each of these roles; an imitator at a different time may be an initiator or innovator, bringing system statements into domains of entropy. Indeed, an innovator, having constructed a system, may bring the entire system into a condition of entropy through its exploitation. An artist, for example, having begun a new systemic approach to his or her art may later change styles and develop another system, one which he or she considers still more relevant to his or her problem and to the changing social time. An initiator, having solved a problem within a system and thus having restored its utility, may find another problem with the system; unable to solve it, he or she may leave it for others to work upon. The roles are well defined but are left to people to fulfill them.

Imitation is the working with a system already established and well formulated. It involves using the system's statements for a well-defined problem area, according to the established rules of operation. It is imitation because the system being used is one established by another. This is, of course, not to be meant as demeaning, for imitation is extremely important in the creative process. Through imitation, problems are revealed and difficulties brought into the open, reducing the system's utility. The process of strict imitation reveals no problems, for this is the application of the statements according to the rules of operation and to the area designated within the conditions of the system. This is copying; it is the performance of procedures already performed by others and the execution of operations on areas that have become standard within the system. There is no difficulty here, for with strict imitation no problems can arise. The operative terms and the area language are within the confines allowed by the system and no more; there is no exploration here.

Contrasted to strict imitation is explorative imitation. This is the imitative process that allows for the searching of difficulties. While the system dictates the languages to be used, it does not forbid the introduction of ambiguities within the languages' meanings. Even when such ambiguities are not sought, they often arise and must be dealt with. Explorative imitation is the intentional introduction of such ambiguities so that the operative and area languages take on nuances not strictly allowed within the system's requirements. Such ambiguities may come about as a result of the changes in the meanings of the terms in general use throughout other systems, even though for the system in question these terms are rigorously defined and so delineated. The explorative imitator may transfer some of the nuances into the system to analyze the influences they may have; this may result in the nuances being more effective than the original language. The imitator may not understand how these nuances are to be incorporated into the system, but their being there has brought the statement into an entropic condition because of the lack of repair to make the statement fit. Hence the statement, having become entropic as a result of this intervention, has to be repaired for the system to retain its utility. As the existing statement is inadequate in light of these nuances, the imitator having done his job leaves the repair for the initiator (who, as has been stated, may be the same person).

Another form of explorative imitation is awareness imitation. This is the type of imitation that occurs due to the understanding and comprehension of other, not necessarily competing, systems whose problem areas incorporate segments of the imitator's problem area. As a result of the influence and impact of differing systems on a single area, the area undergoes changes that make the area statements entropic to the degree of change within the segments of the system. While other imitators may not be aware of the alterations within the area, due to the unfamiliarity with the other systems in which part of the area is incorporated, this imitator explores the differences existing between the area statements and the area as it now exists. The imitator brings this to the attention of others, who then comprehend the problem; it is for the initiator to find the solution.

This awareness imitation is also manifested with the nuances of language being altered by other meanings entering into the operative and/or area languages, thereby bringing about de facto shifts in the meanings of these languages, while the area remains stable. The language deviations have to be corrected and must therefore be rephrased. This, again, is the initiator's job, to find the terminology that preserves the system's utility in light of these nuances while maintaining the elements' effectiveness.

However explorative, the imitator's role does not end with the introduction of entropy into the system. Having done this, the explorative imitator reverts to the status of strict imitator, in this case evaluating the initiative contribution. The initiator alters the entropic statement $o_d a$ to $o_d a'$ and leaves it to be evalued by those who work with the system, the imitators. It is not enough to reconstruct an entropic statement with the intention of restoring the system's utility. The statement must indeed fit and have no dynamic entropic effects on other elements within the system. This can be determined over time, as such effects may not be readily prevalent.

Consider, for example, the initiation in response to a linguistic ambiguity. One of a statements elements, say the *a*-statement, has become entropic because of nuances imputed to the term but not considered within the system's construction. The initially corrected *a'* leads to a corrected *o*; as the statement is part of a system, these alterations may generate negative dynamics throughout the system. The *o*-statement may be used in part or completely with other operative terms and its correction for the specific statement may lead to the correction's nuances to be incorporated into other element statements. The difficulty with a knowledge system in our time is that its utility is very often threatened because of increasing knowledge.

Knowledge is not increased in isolation. Indeed, its very structure and content depend on the knowledge system in which it is formulated. Knowledge is not fact, isolated and stated independently of a system, for such statements may reflect the homespun wisdom acquired through living and may be informative, but this is certainly not knowledge; if anything, such statements are grass-roots philosophy, grass-roots because of their not being incorporated into a philosophical system. As we live, we have experiences that educate us, experiences that are not only factual but also informative and of great personal meaning and depth. This remains private information; even if we should pass it on to others, it is not systematic. Therefore it is not at the disposal of others to be worked upon to derive further knowledge through explorative imitation and creative initiation.

Knowledge is increased within systems. It is also decreased within systems, as knowledge statements within systems become entropic and are replaced by other statements through the process of creativity. Knowledge is public to the extent that it is available within the system for those who seek it. The knowledge of physics is available to students and practitioners of physics in its various branches; the knowledge of the problems in the disciplines that constitute the field of physics are also available to these same people.

There is another form of knowledge, however, that is different from the system with changing elements altered by entropy and corrected by initiation. This is innovative knowledge, the construction of a unique system for a set of problems conceived by the innovator (and perhaps independently by a few others) for which no previous system existed. This is strict innovation and must be distinguished from competitive innovation. Strict innovation is the creative act that brings elements of knowledge from other systems into a new and working system for a set of problems that the innovator perceived but that were not accepted generally as problems. New artistic movements, such as pop and op art, expressed messages for which there was no general problematic need; no artistic systems previously existed to express the attitudes of these schools. However, problems existed within society that were made the subjects of these art forms, as delineated by the styles, the subjects, and the points of meaning in each of the paintings and sculptures. In music, jazz for example, the West Coast school developed along with the East Coast school in the early 1950s, independent of the problems of expression and musical interpretation that arose with the deaths of Charlie Parker and the young Clifford Brown. Some musicians, such as Thelonius Monk and Charlie Mingus, defied "coastal" placings and just spread their music as they saw fit. They too were strict innovators, as they formulated styles to express their unique conceptualizations of their art forms and interpretations of their experiences within these forms.

There is a matter of some ambiguity that must be cleared; it concerns strict and competitive innovation. All innovations, once they are accepted, are competitive in the sense that they attract followers from other approaches and thus become alternative systems generating their own dynamics. This, however, is not the point here; strict innovation is creativity for a set of problems hitherto generally recognized as such, while competitive innovation is creativity with respect to established problems and systems dealing with these problems. Strict innovation defines problems and the operative terms that work with the problem area; competitive innovation has the problem already stated and seeks to do a better job of handling the problem, thereby reducing the utility of other such systems and establishing its predominance as the viable and single system.

There is also the case of innovative systems being formulated independently of others that are constructed to deal with specific aspects of a problem area and that are brought into competition by their adherents. This is more often true in the sciences than in the arts, an example being the monetarist versus the neo-Keynesian schools of economic theory, in which those advocating monetary policies for regulating the economy maintain that through the supply of currency and the regulation of interest rates, employment and output can be either increased or decreased accordingly, while the neo-Keynesians maintain that employment and output regulate the interest rates through productivity and rates of turnover, from which monetary policies can therefore be derived and the interest rates regulated according to movements of output in distribution and sales.

However, concerning strict innovation, the problem area is stated by the innovator, whose task is to formulate a corresponding and isomorphic operational language. The innovator must establish the criteria of utility and must therefore determine the utility of each operational-area statement within the context of the utility criteria. Moreover, as the innovation is unique, the case must be put convincingly for its consideration by those whom the innovator wants to work with the system. (Of course, in the case of competitive innovation, this presents no difficulty.) An artist who develops a unique style and message has to approach the critics and persuade them by the works that the innovation has merit. Moreover, the artist's peers must be considered; they will examine the work with a professional feel and instinct, developed over the years of learning and working experience. In the sciences, various journals and conferences are available for presenting the innovation to a discerning and aware audience, which is expected to provide proper evaluation (a topic to be discussed in the next chapter).

For competitive innovation, the problem area is already defined, and the innovative aspects undertaken must be the development of a better formulation or a solution or approach to a problem area which reduces or eliminates the utility of the competing systems. Still, the problem area itself can be the subject of the new system that redefines it and makes it more operable, especially with regard to the corresponding operational language incorporated in the system.

Having stated the various types of creativity, the dynamics of creativity must now be examined. In our era of knowledge, we search for working truths, only to find them problematic. What we have accepted as valid (possessing utility within a system of knowledge at one time) may be entropic and questionable at another time. The explorative imitators bring to the fore the difficulties of our systems and the creative individuals search for their solutions. First with divergence and then convergence, the dynamics of creativity, begun with the processes of explorative imitation, became established and influenced systems not yet touched by entropy.

Systems develop and expand, are altered by their users, according to difficulties encountered with their utilities. Changes in languages are brought about by the influences of other system languages; these in turn are formulations of creative individuals in light of problems developed within their systems or in the formulation through innovation of unique systems.

Great scientific theories and great movements in art are the products of creative minds in light of problems they sought to solve. We have not, in our contemporary era, great sweeping theories in the sciences and schools of art, such as those developed in previous historical eras. Indeed, in our social time adjustments in our systems are small, compared to those systems in other areas, because so much knowledge is available that changes are made rapidly and easily. Thus the utility of these systems remains generally unaffected, and entropy, which could bring them down, is kept at bay.

This does not mean, of course, that our social time is fixed, that this will continue to be the case. Indeed, the types of problems on which the majority of people in the arts and sciences are working are those of imitative status, as this is where the majority of problems due to explorative imitation are found. Social time is determined by the types of problems occurring within a historical era, and our social time is measured largely in terms of initiative creativity.

There is a momentum to social time that carries ideas and knowledge systems over into different domains, into previously unknown problem areas. Our social time is moving us from the difficulties of the postwar period and the complexities of the cold war, to a period of reflection and developing new problem areas. While most of our knowledge systems are well established and creative activity is initiative in nature (repairing these systems to retain their utility), we are moving into another aspect of our era of knowledge. Innovation is becoming more frequent in the arts and the sciences, so that new systems are being established and signs of irreparable entropy are more frequent in the old systems. In computer knowledge, for example, the development of new languages and new concepts pose challenges to the established languages; sophistication in business and the increasing intricacies of transactions require languages of greater depth and power to ease these difficulties. Computers themselves are becoming more sophisticated, entering into the fields of laser technology and increasing their scope and functions. Medicine is undergoing changes to cope with well-known diseases such as cancer and newly developed diseases such as Acquired Immune Deficiency Syndrome (AIDS). The sciences and the arts are exchanging knowledge so that the astronomers searching still for the "harmony of the spheres" are using the most advanced state of the technological arts, and artists are employing the scientific techniques of optics, computer science, and, in contemporary literature, the very feeling of the modern scientific world, to explore their disciplines.

In order to repair the damage in a system, information has to be taken from other systems and altered, changing its collective nuances and adjusting it to fit the system. From information of other systems, therefore, comes new information and a revived utility. This is information adaptation, taking information from other sources and adapting it to the specific problem at hand. This adaptation is the creative activity, first employing divergence and then convergence; divergence to associate the other external information as possible relevant information with the statement in question and the system in general; convergence to adapt the information, altering its nuances to the point where it fits into the system and then evaluating the new statement in terms of its utility. From established information, new information is derived; from entropic information, information of utility is constructed. From one system, the information needed to repair another system is obtained; hence through divergence and convergence, the creative process constructs the new information on the basis of information already established.

Interactions among systems and the use of information from various systems to construct innovative systems are hallmarks of our era of knowledge. This interaction provides information and knowledge to the extent never before generated in the history of mankind. Previously, fairly long periods of gestation were required to bring difficulties to the fore. Paradigmatic systems in the arts and sciences (the prevailing schools of thought and methods of conceptualization) were accepted as being true in the sense of at least being operable. In the seventeenth century, after Newton's great theory of physics, who could have thought that the theory was correct only for a limited realm of the universe? Not only was his theory accepted as the true paradigm of the physical sciences, but mathematics (which Newton helped strengthen through his development of the calculus) was considered the queen of the sciences, ruled only by the king of Newtonian physics. The gestation period was long, some 250 years, before cracks in the strong edifice became noticeable. Moreover, mathematics began to lose its power of certainty with the onset of basing the foundations of mathematics on a logical and rigorous pedestal.

Einsteinian physics, despite its great significance for contemporary problems of space exploration and of atomic physics and subatomic particles moving at velocities approaching that of lightspeed, has also begun to show cracks in its impressive edifice. The black holes in space—super-gravitational fields that are the remnants of imploded stars—may operate according to physical laws not appropriate for our space-time conceptualizations derived from

Einstein's theory. Moreover, white holes, the inverted black holes, are thought to provide time-tunnels, leading to other parts of the universe, parts that may have physical laws of their own. The attempt to understand gravity within terms of a unified field theory have so far been elusive, and the Heisenberg uncertainty principle throws into question the conceptualization of Einsteinian thought.[5]

The point is that since the beginning of our era of knowledge, the rate of knowledge turnover is greater than ever before. Systems exist in greater number, and entropy sets in at a greater pace, bringing problems to the fore through explorative imitation. True knowledge, as determined by the system, soon becomes entropic and subject to the repairs of creative activity. Information is gathered and altered to fit into innovative systems, which stimulate others to join them in imitative fashion: these systems in turn become subject to entropy and repair.

In spite of the great turnover of knowledge and the existence of manifold systems, each system has a period of gestation, a time for imitators to work out the dynamics of their system and for society to accept these dynamics. It is not as if every explorative imitator finds fault with the systems and that they are in constant flux between the states of entropy and utility. Nor is this a psychological condition in which people seek a rest from change and look for a degree of stability. Systems must settle after they are established and after their difficulties are solved; they must be worked upon using strict imitation to determine what they are able to accomplish within their defined and delineated problem areas. Thus, for any period of time, the situation in contemporary society which has entered the era of knowledge will take the form:

$$S_t^* = \Sigma \left[\overset{n}{\underset{l}{S}} (S_e \cup S_u) \right] t$$

where S^* is the society in which the dynamics of knowledge occur, S_e and S_u represent the total knowledge systems, both entropic and of utility, for the time t in question.[6] Some of those systems will be entropic, though previously they were of maximum utility; others will be of utility, though previously they were entropic. Still others may no longer exist, while those not yet formulated will be within the systems of maximum utility. The total number of systems working within S^* may be altered due to the phasing out of some and the introduction of other systems.

There is an exception to this situation in which some systems are entropic and others are not. This exception is when S^* is in a total condition of gestation, usually following after an intensive period of creative activity. One such period occurred during the early 1950s, after the resolution of the Korean conflict. The arts were working out their new ideas, and music was flourishing in its new forms. This period lasted until the latter part of that decade, when the new forms of poetry and music replaced the old, when East Coast Jazz, for example, replaced the West Coast styles that had become almost completely entropic. New art forms appeared somewhat as expressions of protest at the intellectual and artistic "quiet" which prevailed due to the social gestation.

It must be understood that the dynamics of creativity are mostly in motion, which are manifested in established knowledge systems becoming entropic, somewhat "out of date," while other systems are strong and others still being formed. Styles of thought change in light of problems and solutions offered, which attract the interested and informed. Emotions are involved due to vested personal interests in the systems. In cases where new systems provide great attraction, a combination of instinct and emotion is stimulated and brings prospective imitators into the system's realm for consideration of the system's problem area and the possibilities of working with the operational language. The rate at which these dynamics shift depends on several factors. One factor is the readiness of people to explore different systems when society is saturated with systems. Another is the duration of gestation, combined with the impact of new systems on the gestation period as it tapers off and explorative imitation sets in to move the existing systems into entropy.

New systems making their debuts when established systems are enjoying the benefits of being worked out through strict imitation are not very likely to find ready audiences to shift their loyalties and work with them. The gestation period, when system saturation is setting into the social knowledge structure, requires that imitators work out most of the systems' ramifications before explorative imitation takes over. Until this is achieved, innovation is likely to be very slow, as problems are seen to be handled by the prevailing systems, and individual conceptualization of new problems will not readily find an interested audience of potential imitators or even of those who will offer critiques. The exception to this is if the innovation is so profound and the problems with which it deals so elusive for other systems, that its impact, both for followers and critics, is in equal response to its profundity and contribution. This type of innovation comes as a stimulant to explorative imitation in many systems, at a time of gestation when strict imitation prevails.

Another factor determining the shifts in dynamics is the more common situation of various systems being in differing stages of utility and entropy. Ther are situation is when S^* is in gestation, that is, when the totality of knowledge systems is engaged only in strict imitative activity. As was mentioned before, this situation occurs after a burgeoning of creativity, in which many changes in existing systems were undertaken and several innovative systems were introduced. The public is therefore not prepared for further changes, and the emphasis on imitative activity is on working out the systems' ramifications. Should explorative imitation occur, it usually does so because genuine problems have been found, not because of an explorative state of mind or general public restlessness with the status quo of knowledge.

This rare situation places the systems in a state of dynamic equilibrium, in which the activity within the systems is related primarily to strict imitation. These systems are in equilibrium because they are not undergoing alterations due to the problems of resolving entropy. The systems' integrities remain intact. They are in a dynamic state because they are being worked upon, drawing out their nuances and ramifications, in which the consequences of the operational languages on the area languages are being derived. These systems maintain their positions of utility while entropy has made no inroads (again, except for those cases where genuine difficulties have been uncovered).

The usual situation is, however, one of dynamic disequilibrium; on this basis, most contributions to knowledge are made and the significant innovative systems brought to the fore. In this state of dynamic disequilibrium, systems are fluctuating between those in utility and those in entropic conditions. Moreover, as time moves, so do the positions of the systems, so that where entropy prevailed, bringing systems into tenuous positions, the entropy has been removed and the systems, albeit different, have been restored to utility; at the same time, the systems that were in positions of utility may be entropic and worked upon to remove the source of entropy.

Dynamic disequilibrium in general does not rule out gestation periods for knowledge systems. Some systems, especially those newly formed, are being worked on by imitators operating according to the conditions of utility established for each system. These systems are functioning, and the results of their operations conform to those allowed by the utility conditions; there is no explorative imitation being conducted, nor is there yet any need for this activity. Indeed, the fact that some systems are in periods of gestation, while others are entropic and still others are in stages of explorative imitation but high utility, demonstrates the disequilibrium prevailing in societies' knowledge systems.

Thus, for societies having entered the era of knowledge, the S^* of each society is placed between the maximum and minimum values of utility and entropy: $0<S^*<1$ for time t. Can there be a case in which $S^* \rightarrow 0$ in our contemporary era of knowledge? This can exist only if a society, once having entered our era, can no longer perform because of political paralysis or because of a war that requires the diversion of knowledge to military matters. These are short-term situations, however, because in the first instance a society operating in our era of knowledge will already have sufficient internal dynamics to overcome political paralysis, and in the second instance wars are of shorter duration now, and once settled, internal matters and the dynamics of creativity can again be undertaken.[7]

In our era of knowledge, the issues of acceptance and rejection of contributions are of great significance. Determining the viability of contributions, especially in situations of competitive contributions, is of great importance, given the rapid turnover of knowledge. The issues of acceptance and rejection will be discussed in Chapter 7.

7

On Acceptance and Rejection in Our Era of Knowledge

Throughout the ages, when people worked they performed according to set patterns of procedure, deviating from them only when conditions required differing approaches to deal with the issues at hand. These deviations, however, were never radical and were allowed within the context of the work format. In previous historical eras great changes arose when challenges (from nature or from other peoples) posed problems for which the conventional systems could not provide effective answers. Only then did creativity enter, and the problems were solved. These contributions then became pertinent and remained part of the working operations.[1]

Even the arts and sciences responded to social and technical problems. The sciences originally developed in response to problems of navigation and computation that developed from trade. Those early thinkers who had the leisure contemplated the nature of the universe; this was termed "philosophy," the love of wisdom. Ship construction and methods of production, however, evolved over the years in response to the search for knowledge, knowledge on how to control our universe and make it work for us or at least how to live in productive harmony with our given natural and evolved social circumstances.

During the Industrial Revolution, systems of work underwent changes more rapidly than any other previous historical era. The merger of science with technology—of the search for knowledge with the applications of knowledge—provided different and increasingly more efficient methods of production, allowing for greater product-range at reasonable and competitive consumer prices. Systems of production, once established and proved efficient, were readily challenged and overthrown by even better systems. However, with the advancements in science and technology, this situation not only prevailed in the productive economic sphere; it was also the case with established scientific theories and technical advancements.

An outstanding example in science is Einstein's revolution in physics, replacing Newton's theory with his own. Newton incorporated the earth science of Galileo and the astronomy of Kepler into a unified theory of physics. He said that his vision was greater than those before him because he stood on the shoulders of giants, but Einstein stood on Newton's shoulders, as well as those of Hendrik Lorentz, Bernhard Riemann, and Max Planck, to mention a few of the scientists who had the advantage of studying Newton and who made original contributions in their respective branches of science.

In technology, an outstanding example is the assembly line, initiated by Henry Ford, which still serves as the basic method of mass production, now using robotics to an increasingly large extent over manual labor. The assembly line utilized other technological contributions, such as electricity directed toward production, blueprinting techniques, metallurgy, time-cost studies for efficient line modification for the production of different models, labor training, and diversification in labor orientation on the production line according to the needs of labor concentration for specific product requirements.

Hence, during the Industrial Revolution and especially toward its end, with the impending war and the depressed economies of the world, the groundwork was laid to a certain extent for the forthcoming era of knowledge. However, along with the new era came a certain degree of an ambiguous attitude to change, especially when at the beginning of the era, when the changes were introduced more rapidly than ever.

In the aftermath of World War II, when production was changed over from wartime to peacetime goods and the demand for products rose because of demobilization of the forces, there was an initial return to the prewar methods of production and conceptualization. Military regimentation prevailed to some extent, and conformity in industry and society was accepted by people who wanted to return to a peaceful life without the storms of changing ideas and methods. Organizations provided the techniques of wartime production, as they had both the means and the ability to mobilize resources for production, and it was to these organizations that most people turned for employment. These organizations set policies at the upper echelons and sought to reduce deviation within the ranks of their employees. This rigidity was necessary from the organizational perspective, for only by such discipline could they achieve their aims; it was also untenable, for the very dynamics of the new era in which these organizations existed (and which they inherited from contributions made during the war) required a different and unique approach to their problem areas, one based on critical thinking and creativity at lower levels of authority. The strict discipline had to be relaxed as the problems of these organizations were confronted, criticized, and solved, in light of domestic competition and competition from abroad; both the allies and the defeated countries were recovering from the war and sought intellectual and economic supremacy.

There soon became evident in society a serious conflict between the dynamics of knowledge, by which existing knowledge was subjected to intellectual scrutiny and brought down when found faulty, and the psychological condition of many who innovated systems and those who worked loyally with them. Knowledge must be objective in its content and thereby subject to testing and further analysis. Yet knowledge is the result of the efforts of individuals, of their work and imagination, of their solving problems posed by others and—in cases of innovation—of constructing systems out of their own conceptions of problem areas and operational languages. Therefore, people are reluctant to see their work brought into question by others, moved into entropic conditions, with the possibility of being replaced altogether. There has always been resistance to good and new ideas. Great ideas have become outmoded—great contributions in the arts and music have been superseded by other contributions.

In our era, however, the dynamics of knowledge have a new importance, because the interchange of knowledge within systems is more rapid than at any other period of time, and innovations are brought into entropic conditions at a far faster rate. This situation often leads to conflict between the individual who worked on a system and perfected it and society's need for new systems in order to renew and fortify itself, in light of external competition against other societies, on a similar level of intellectual and technological development that seek to undermine it. Renewal is also necessary for the internal requirements of society: industries and academic institutions seek out new systems that can replace those that have become suspect or somewhat entropic, as the case may be.

Ideally, critics of new contributions examine the contributions on their merits, on the claims they are supposedly able to accomplish, on their replacements for entropic elements in a system (in cases of initiation), and on the total contribution according to its claims (in the situation of innovation). Criticism is both necessary and socially healthy, for it tends to filter out from the general body of social knowledge any ideas and theories posited as contributions that have no social merit, those that may add to the entropy of their systems, or those that provide nothing to the realm of knowledge. In this situation, the conflict between the individual and society exists and cannot be avoided. Contributions posited with the best intentions may be shown to be inadequate for their stated problems by people who have no personal or emotional involvement in the issues; this process may be to the advantage of the contributor as it allows him or her to reconsider the position, re-examine the problem, and re-evaluate the contribution in light of criticism.

This does not necessarily eliminate misunderstandings; the critics may not fully comprehend the contribution or the stated problem, or they may even provide unintentionally false criticism, having not fully realized the rigorous reasoning and its nuances regarding the contribution. These are honest errors, in the sense that they are not made from a position of personal involvement, hence dogma. There is no idealistic clash, no professional commitment at stake. Having passed judgment in good faith, should there be errors in judgment, they stand to be investigated by others concerned with the stated problem and the contribution.

This type of objectivity, with its potential tendency to err, is certainly not ideal. Works of painting, music, and literature have been rejected by some critics, only to be accepted by others. Often a certain historical period of social time is required to pass before the work in question can be revalued and reconsidered.

The point must be remembered, however, that total objectivity is impossible and has never been a part of the human condition. Humans are complicated creatures with tastes, opinions, likes, and dislikes varying over time and often determined by irrational emotions, each individual's reasons often unconscious. Even the people entrusted with the evaluation of a contribution cannot negate this aspect of the human condition. No matter how critics try to suppress their own personal considerations in the evaluation of a work, seeking to understand the work for what it is supposed to be and attempting to evaluate it on this basis, such total negation of personal propensities is not possible. There must be a base for criticism; for each individual, this base is the education received, the experiences undergone, and the lessons derived from them; even such a seemingly unimportant factor as personal feeling at the time of review comes into play.

There is such a criticism based on professional objectivity, however, where the honest critic takes into account his or her personal tastes and feelings and therefore either seeks to suppress them to provide as honest a criticism as humanly possible, or if this cannot be done because of the specific nature of the work to be criticized, they only admit the influence of personal biases in the critical process and then allow for an objective review, given the personal constraints.

Criticism has its drawbacks and these are objective. Where one critic honestly and openly rejects a contribution, and another valid critic praises it and recommends its acceptance, the imitative audience for which the contribution is made must themselves assume the role of critic. They must evaluate the contribution according to its claims and probabilistic "fit" (in cases of initiation) or on the claims, the probabilistic structure, yield, and workability (in cases of innovation). These criteria may prove invalid over social time; rejection may be reviewed and the contributions posited again for the same difficulty. These are the chances that must be taken when a work of creativity is submitted for review. It must be understood that neither acceptance nor rejection are permanent unless the work is of such poor quality that it bears no relation to its described problem area or unless it is of such universal appeal that its interpretation varies over social times and historical eras and retains its validity under the impact of change and the variations of existence that occur over the historical eras.

Moreover, a work of such importance, say Adam Smith's *Wealth of Nations,* is surely irrelevant today as a treatise on contemporary economic theory. It retains its value because it was of extreme importance in coping with the economic developments of the Industrial Revolution, and it is important today as a historical document on economic thought, as well as being the foundation stone of modern economics. Hence, this is a work which has since become entropic as far as its original utility is concerned, but it has acquired a different utility in the passing of the historical era of the Industrial Revolution into the new era of knowledge.

Works that are rejected outright may find acceptance by later generations. Vincent Van Gogh's paintings and drawings were certainly not considered great works of art during his lifetime. His prime source of financial support was offered generously and with love by his brother Theo, perhaps one of the few critics who understood Vincent's works and the pathos felt in his struggles for artistic expression and financial security. The lack of concern from those who were supposed to understand led to the rejection of Vincent's works during his life, but his works have since received the highest artistic acclaims, and he has achieved a place in the history of art as one of the truly great.

The difficulty with our era of knowledge, as far as acceptance and rejection are concerned, is that the turnover of knowledge in light of problems through innovative and initiative creativity occurs at a rate never before experienced in a historical era. While people like change, they also require a gestation period to absorb changes that have already occurred. Psychologically, therefore, people tend to resist change and new contributions in light of problems being resolved. This built-in social bias is generally recognized where and when it occurs; it becomes part of the evaluative process, though suppressed as far as possible. This bias is not the main difficulty.

The main difficulty is that often the critics are those who were earlier engaged in creative activity, and the problems that arise are in the realms of their own contributions. Innovations are subject to severe testing and criticism and are accepted only after passing rigorous inspection by others well versed in the area. The critics have most likely made creative contributions, and the work in question has the potential to become a competitor with their own contributions. In cases of initiation, the critics may be jealous because they were unable to solve the difficulty in their capacity of prospective initiators and therefore view askance the contribution in question. Should this be the critic's conduct, to criticize from a genuinely, purposely biased position, others will soon become aware of this bias and revalue the criticism. However, should the bias be unintentional, operating on an unconscious level and brought to the conscious mind in good faith but in error, then this is a difficulty of another dimension. It is this situation which must now be discussed, because with the rapid turnover of knowledge, many critics are having to subject their own works to the test. Their objectivity may be distorted when testing other's works because of their own personal ties to the works they support. They may feel threatened by the competition of another work, one possibly superior in depth and function.

PSYCHOLOGICAL CONSIDERATIONS OF EVALUATION

Systems of knowledge deal not with truth, but with fact. Truth exists and is eternal. It may be regarded in a religious sense or in a philosophical sense, for truth is wisdom and wisdom is enduring. It was a fact that the sun rose in the east and set in the west, until the knowledge system changed and placed the earth in orbit, revolving on its axis as it travels its path around the energizing star of the sun. It is true that the earth exists and that the solar system is kept in a fragile balance as the planets counteract each other's gravity in their positioning with regard to the sun. It was a fact that an object that moved straight up would eventually come down; it is true that "straight up" is relative and that not all objects that rise return, as the properly functioning satellites remaining in orbit so aptly demonstrate.

Truth and fact are unrelated. Truth pertains to the human condition and our existence in the world. It is the greater, metaphysical understanding of life, and it relates to and is directly involved with the interaction of persons and with the impact of humankind on the world. Fact is system-based and theoretically derived; it is the result of the functioning relationships existing between area and operational statements. Facts cannot be false, as false is the opposite of truth; facts must be either valid or invalid, with their status depending on the systems in which they exist. Facts are impartial and impersonal and should be approached as such when considering their status within a knowledge system.

Here, however, there is often difficulty, for evaluation requires objectivity, and this may be lacking. It is not merely enough for people who are unable to be objective to claim that they are fallible and therefore prone to subjectivity when considering a system of knowledge in which they have vested personal interests, either for or against the system. Any vested interests can be taken into account when considering the critic's evaluation. There is a point, however, when such human frailty becomes irrational, and denies the very reason for rational criticism and the existence of other possible contending systems. This point is reached when a system breaks down, becomes entropic, but its entropic condition is not recognized by those who hold onto it. In the dynamics of knowledge, a system is constructed to represent a specific problem area and to offer ways to deal with the area. When the system breaks down and is either challenged or replaced by another, more effective system, there can be no rational reason for holding onto the entropic system, vested interests or no. Indeed, such tenacity is irrational, and the reasons for it must be explored briefly here.

First, the reason for holding with a system of knowledge is that the system is considered viable, of utility, and most effective for dealing with the delineated problem area. There are no serious Aristotelian scientists today, although Aristotle's physics is of great importance in the development of contemporary physical theory. Those who continue working with a discredited system cannot do so because they believe that the system will be once again revived, intact and with full utility; the reason for much belief is the psychological commitment to the system as a means for abolishing anxiety and to achieve a sense of belonging to a worthwhile cause. Again, people who work with a system usually have loyalty to the system and seek to use it to the fullest, exploiting all its advantages and minimizing its drawbacks. Hence, the strict and explorative imitators working with the system realize its potential in the actualization of its functions. This is not the type of loyalty being discussed here, however, for such loyalty is prevalent until the system becomes entropic to the extent that it cannot be salvaged. Indeed, explorative imitators are to a large extent responsible for the penetration of entropy, because they seek to move the system's elements into difficult circumstances in order to challenge them and assay their functions under stress.

The tendency being discussed here is adhering to a system of knowledge after it has been demonstrated to others working with the system that it has become invalidated due to the abundance of entropy. With the dissolution of the system, the tenacious person, the "believer," loses his or her identity. Having worked with the system, this type of person makes an irrational and existential commitment to the system; he or she has found psychological comfort in belonging to those who are identified with the system and thus has gained importance, self-respect, and respect from others who understand the system's merits. There is an erroneous psychological commitment made by this personality type, erroneous because of the mental confusion between fact and truth. This person assumes that because the system has the power to achieve its goals, it must be enduring and hence true. When that power wanes, when entropy sets in, it goes unrecognized; the false association of fact with truth has been fixed in the person's mental make-up. This existential error results in the commitment to the system, no matter how entropic it has become and how much its validity has become discredited with respect to its utility considerations.

The question is, how does such a commitment come about? The answer lies in the dynamics of existential anxiety, the emotions of belonging and of personal importance and being recognized by society in our era of knowledge. This is the social and individual pathology in our era, prevalent among the true believers in systems outmoded by advances in knowledge and the development of other systems.

It is rooted in anxiety, a common existential emotion. It is, however, manifested in the feelings of impotency, of being unable to contribute to the dynamics of knowledge as either an innovator, an initiator, or an imitator. Once a system is discredited, it should be abandoned, for there should be no existential commitment to the system as there is to truth. By its very nature, knowledge is passing in time, and the systems that bind knowledge are also restricted in their validity, according to the duration of their problem areas and of the utility of their elements.

In our era, anxiety and uncertainty of personal recognition is one of the most important individual factors motivating the dynamics of creativity; therefore, it is also one of the most important factors responsible for the holding of biases despite evidence that contradicts the reasons for dogmatically holding such opinions. In our era, anxiety is the psychological motivation for being involved in creativity, whatever the role, because in the process of seeking to overcome anxiety, the person attempts to place himself or herself in the only viable sociological dynamic, that of being part of the creative process, either along mainstream lines, working with established systems that have gained authority, or by deviating and working with new systems that must break through the publicity barrier to gain recognition and attract adherents.

The problem of anxiety is certainly not new, nor restricted to our era. Rollo May has stated that the emotion of anxiety is not an affect among other affects, such as pleasure or sadness. He says that anxiety

> is rather an ontological characteristic of man, rooted in his very existence as such. It is not a peripherial threat which I can take or leave, for example, or a reaction which may be classified beside other reactions; it is always a threat to the foundation, the center of my existence. Anxiety is *the experience of the threat of imminent non-being.*[2]

Søren Kierkegaard called anxiety the sickness unto death;[3] it is an ontological condition of humankind, paradoxical in that the only way to rid oneself of anxiety is to cease to live. As an ontological condition, it is as if anxiety is being carried around with each of us, waiting to explode in us unexpectedly, as is the case with the anxiety attack, which, while perhaps triggered by events outside the personality, is devastating in its consequences. As Ludwig Binswanger stated it, the suddenness of the anxiety attack has enormous significance,

> because suddenness is the time quality which explodes continuity, hacks it to pieces, throws the earlier existence out of its course, exposes it to

the Dreadful, to the naked horror. This is what in psychopathology we term, in a most signifying manner, anxiety attack.[4]

While the approach taken by May and Binswanger is existential, and their method of explaining human behavior is in terms of existential phenomena, their theories do not clash with the argument presented here. In our era of knowledge, the external trigger for the attack of anxiety (in German, *angst*) is the person's position with respect to both the self and society, in terms of his or her contributions. The real lack of contributions, either as imitator or innovator or initiator, or the supposed unawareness of a person's value in the dynamics of knowledge, may trigger the feelings of dread, the sickness unto death, and its devastating awareness. For through systems, through frameworks of contributions, is a person's existence really substantiated, according to the dictates of our contemporary era. Angst is the feeling of noncontribution, the horror of nonexistence in a dynamic and thriving world of working ideas and systems, of ever changing knowledge and the richness of those people active in the generation and perpetuation of knowledge.

In our era of knowledge, the need to contribute, either through the mainstream systems of knowledge or through the unique and original systems of innovation, is extremely demanding. Indeed, patterns of work and employment are system-based, oriented to the frameworks of systems that provide the knowledge for working and output, whether material, artistic, or intellectual. Contributing thus provides the sought after "meaning" to existence, because it provides employment and maintains the dynamics of knowledge through innovation, initiation, and imitation on which contemporary societies are founded.

The commitment to systems is, therefore, very strong. But as these systems provide knowledge and not truth, they are as durable as their utility in their proper probabilistic functionings. Hence to abandon these systems, once the levels of entropy are so high that there is no possibility of salvaging the systems intact, is only rational and reasonable. Other and nonentropic systems require trained imitators; imitators' skills are developed through the working of similar systems and can be altered for unrelated system imitation.

It is irrational and unreasonable, therefore, to cling to systems that are no longer operating. This does not mean that outdated systems, whose only value is historical, cannot be upheld under certain conditions. For a modern physicist to be a Galilean for specific relativistic circumstances, such as considering the relative motions of two ships, using one as a base of measure, is certainly valid; to uphold Galileo's relativity in all cases and thus to deny the validity of Einstein's contribution is irrational and unreasonable. Angst cannot be resolved in this manner in our time, for the turnover of knowledge is so great, compared to other previous historical eras, that such total existential commitment to a system of knowledge cannot be reasonably maintained nor rationally defended. There is an error in these cases, a serious error of existential commitment. Should commitment be a personal value, it should be made to the wisdom of humanity, to truth, and to the search for deeper meaning in truth. As knowledge is shown to be false by new systems and the entropy of existing systems, such total existential commitment is, in reality, a commitment to invalidity, for in time, given the disequilibrium dynamics of our era, all knowledge systems will be overthrown (shown to be invalid), to be replaced by others of utility; these others, as well, are temporary and subject to the same fate. This understanding of the flux of knowledge, the birth of systems, their utility and productiveness and their eventual demise, is perhaps the contribution to wisdom of our contemporary era of knowledge.

There is another type of difficulty with evaluation, also related to anxiety as it is manifested in our era. This is the type of evaluation associated with professional bias, so that an objective evaluation cannot be made. As was mentioned earlier, objectivity is a goal often sought but impossible to obtain because of personal leanings, tastes, and understanding when assessing another's contribution. No matter how unbiased a critic tries to be, his or her personality, education, experiences, and tastes and preferences must influence judgment. Of course, these can be known by those whose works are being evaluated, but with the understanding that the evaluator's integrity is so high that these personal idiosyncrasies are minimized as much as humanly possible and a valid evaluation sought and given. A critic unknown to the person whose work is being evaluated should make his or her biases known or have them made known, so that the subjective element is taken into account and objectivity, to an important extent, achieved.

To whatever extent angst operates in the life of this type of critic, it is certainly not prevalent in the evaluation process. The personal aspects are kept at a minimum, and the criticism is based on the work submitted: whether it achieves its goal, whether the system's elements correspond to the probabilistic rating provided by the innovator, whether the initiative contribution conforms to the system's probabilistic requirements, and whether such a contribution really performs according to the initiator's objectives. This type of critic is balanced in his or her approach, without the ego being involved; the contribution offers no threat and is certainly approached in a manner that demonstrates the critic's noninvolvement in the evaluation. Such evaluations are necessary for the propagation of creativity, for they put contributions, which are numerous in our era of knowledge, into the proper perspective of effectiveness.

Of course, the problem of erroneous evaluation cannot be overlooked. The critic's judgment may be faulty in the evaluation, not because the critic's own position is threatened by the contribution, but because his or her preconceived opinions and considerations prevent the person from relating strongly enough to the work in question. There may be misunderstandings when none are recognized, or the critic may not comprehend the nuances of the contribution and understand merely the probabilistic mechanics involved with the issue of utility. In cases of competing contributions, where each fits the probabilistic requirements, the difficulty is even greater, for it is the contribution's nuances, the potential ramifications, and the possible interest generated in working with the contribution that will bring critical judgment on its side. The critic may not recognize these factors and reject the contribution, or these factors may be misinterpreted and the contribution supported when it should have been rejected. While these situations are not anxiety-based, they are psychologically oriented and can therefore be considered part of the critic's ontological makeup.

Anxiety does, however, enter into consideration in the situation where the critic, respected in the field, condemns all matter not closely related to the field in which the critic operates. This differs from the bias case discussed above, in the sense that bias does not enter into the situation in the form of judgment, but in the form of what is considered valid and invalid material for evaluation. Professional biases in judgment are usually stated or made known through the evaluation, and it is the work itself which is being evaluated. In this particular case, however, it is not the work that comes under scrutiny, but the very material—the field and the problem area—that are dismissed as being uninteresting, irrelevant to the growth of knowledge, or so unimportant that it is a waste of time for someone to have worked on the project or for the work to be presented for evaluation. Hence a respected person in a field employs dogmatic rejection because the new material threatens the critic's self-contained ambience. Cushioned by the prestige gained in his or her field and wary lest the new contribution poses a threat to his or her position, the critic rejects it outright and the field in question as well.

Before discussing the criteria of criticism, another point must be raised concerning the psychology of evaluation. Regardless of their status and the importance of their opinions, critics know that their evaluations may not be permanent and indeed may be contested by others. In those cases where the ontological factors overrule the desire for objectivity, the critical edge is sharpened to an extent that tends to be overhostile and most certainly unfair to the work when objecting to it, and just the reverse—overcomplimentary and too full of praise—when supporting the work. While these responses represent the critic's opinions, they must be viewed by those considering the critical opinions in the light represented; that no matter the standing of the critics and the value of their own works, biases must be isolated from whatever merits are presented in the criticisms.

The human condition is far from static. People's opinions change as they gain in experience and as they deal with their own works and the works of others. The critic who seeks objectivity at one time may be extremely biased at another, while the usually biased critic may display a great degree of objectivity when reviewing a different work. Thus, in the sense of fairness and because future work may shed new light on the criticism and overturn it, those working with a system should take into account the ontological foundations of the critic's evaluations.

THE PROCESS OF EVALUATION

Thus the difficulty with the process of evaluation is the subjective element, which can never be discounted. However, it can be reduced and be kept in check by others who work with the system under consideration.

Evaluation concerns three types of contribution: initiation; strict innovation and competing innovations; and innovative systems in general. For initiation, the contribution must be in accordance with the probabilistic conditions already established for the system. If a statement in *S* becomes entropic and brings the system's utility down so that if $US \rightarrow O$ at time *t*, it must be determined which of the statement's elements is defective. If an operative element is shown to be defective, it must be corrected, and of course the same applies to an area element. How, then, is this to be determined?

First, the defective statement is determined by its declining ability to perform as it has in the past. If, for example, the statement yielded the results prescribed to it in accordance with the system's requirements in time $t - 1$, so that in time *t* these results are not forthcoming as they are supposed to be within the system's context and according to its requirements, then the statement is considered defective and must be corrected. As the statement's utility is assessed with respect to its information yield, and as the information yield is not forthcoming as it should be, then either the operative language has been altered or the area has changed, or perhaps both have occurred. The problem is to find the defective statement, isolate it, correct it, and present the corrected statement for evaluation.

The difficulty with the evaluation process is that, while the initiator may offer a corrected statement for evaluation, presenting it as being corrected within the system's probability rating and information yield, the critic evaluating the statement may not find this to be so. For example, should the operative language with respect to the statement in question become ambiguous, thereby resulting in the statement's decline in utility, correcting the operative language influences the nuances of the statement, so that its import on the area statement will be slightly altered. This new statement changes the system that the initiator presents as having been restored in its utility. The critic may consider that the system's utility has been altered to an unnecessary extent, arguing that, while the new statement may be relevant in itself, its impact on the system in general is too great, and therefore the initiative contribution should be rejected. Another contribution, similar in some respects to the previous one, but different enough so as not to bring about such a major general alteration in the system, may in turn be accepted and the system's entropic condition be removed. Indeed, in cases of competing contributions, where each contribution fulfills the system's probability requirements, the evaluation process acquires a different dimension of difficulty. Each contribution satisfies the system's requirements, so another criterion must be employed to judge them: the assessment of the contribution's impact on the system. This assessment is based on projection, on the possible future ramifications that may occur within the system as a result of one or the other contributions being incorporated. In cases where a conservative approach is accepted, the contribution with the fewest or least dynamic effects is incorporated, thereby attempting to ensure the system's internal stability in the future. In an area of great instability, the choice should be made for the contribution that provides the potential for changes that could be implemented without affecting the system's general utility, so that its forms remain fairly constant over time in spite of the changes. These judgments must be made by the imitators working with the system. If the competition is close, those who have the better persuasive abilities will win the day.

This does not necessarily mean that the rejected contribution will be abandoned and forgotten. Indeed, it may be applied in other cases, altered accordingly to fit the place of a defective statement. A good contribution, although rejected, will not be completely tossed aside but will be remembered by the strict imitators and may be incorporated as another statement to the system, after being altered to give it new shape and import so as not to interfere with the other system statements.

Initiation is perhaps the easiest form of contribution to evaluate. The system's probability criteria are already established and the strict imitators understand the types of contributions which have to be made to replace entropic statements. Not so for innovation, where the system itself is under scrutiny and examination by those critics who may be interested in the system professionally or merely intellectually. The difficulty with innovation with respect to evaluation is that the contribution establishes its own operational language, delineates its own problem area, and sets up its own utility rating. Hence, as these are not already provided for, a renegade statement has to be worked upon and evaluated according to the innovator's criteria. The system in its entirety comes under investigation to determine if it is successful in its area delineation, whether its operational language is effective with respect to the problem, and whether the probabilistic conditions that determine the system's utility are adequate and valid.

How is this evaluation to be undertaken? The system's area may include parts of areas entailed within other systems; the important consideration here is the redefinition of those parts so that they will conform with the system's general program. Moreover, the operational language may include terminology of other systems; these must be redefined to eliminate possible ambiguities that may arise, so that the operational language is strictly isomorphic in relation to the area. The system's statement of its intentions and purposes and of how its area language is to be considered and the corresponding operational language applied provides the basis of evaluation to determine the system's validity. The probabilistic rating thus provides the proper guide for such evaluation. Should the critic illustrate that, according to probabilistic considerations, the system does not fulfill its intentions, then the system will be rejected; should there be only one or a few statements that are not of utility, and if corrections can be made to bring the system up to its own probability rating without altering its stated objectives, then the system should be accepted upon being corrected.

This evaluation, of course, requires a stringent degree of objectivity. Newness in systems, which is what innovation provides, is too often met with a mixture of opinions, reflecting the extremes of "a breath of fresh air in an atmosphere of stagnation" and "an upstart contribution made by a person trying to be different." These opinions are expressed by those who are often too ready for change or (by their very natures, due to their own unique experiences) too willing to look askance at all new contributions. Hence, the very newness of a contribution tends to evoke opinions and criticisms, which in themselves may be persuasive and which may prevent the contribution from standing or falling on its own merits.

There are two forms of innovation. One is the strict form, in which a formulation is constructed that defines a unique problem area with its operational language. Such is the case with new art systems, new approaches to art that have never before been considered. Styles in painting, in sculpture, in music, and in literature represent this innovative form. In jazz, for example, the music of alto saxophonist Charlie Parker set the trend for both East and West Coast musicians, as well as jazz performers and artists throughout the world. Parker's playing, derived primarily from Benny Carter and Johnny Hodges, took on a rhythmic and harmonic style that is still being worked out today. Another example, this time from physics, is that of W. C. Roentgen's development of the X-ray, the uses of which are still being explored and adapted to such diagnostic techniques as the physiological scanners relying on radiation and magnetism for picture generations.

Examples of strict innovation are to be found in every field of inquiry. Roentgen's contribution was met with skepticism and rejected by many of his peers until he demonstrated it convincingly. Parker's style was criticized as being childish, nonsensical, and too much a deviation from the roots of jazz, until people in the field really listened and began to understand his rhythmic conceptualization and harmonic extensions and realized the potential for thought and expression that his style offered. Einstein's theory of relativity was also met at first by many irrational criticisms, until his theory was tested by Eddington's eclipse experiment and found to be valid for the problem area that the theory delineated.

Because of its newness, strict innovation is the most difficult to evaluate. There is no real basis for comparison, and as innovation results from problems perceived by the people working in a special field or by an individual who perceives a problem without the general consensus that it exists, there can be no established format on which to judge the contribution's validity. This evaluation must therefore be conducted with respect to the innovation's ability to perform as is proclaimed; this also requires the determination of the system's probabilistic rating with respect to each of its statements. Had there been contradictions within Einstein's theory, the test could have yielded the desired results, and should other results have been derived, the contradiction would have yielded these as well.[5] Had Parker's contribution been seen as merely an extension of Carter's and Hodges's playing, synthesized into a different style, it would have been rejected as a jazz innovation but might have been accepted as an interesting variation of already established styles. Evaluation must determine if the operational language performs on the area language as stated within the system; this can be assessed with respect to the probabilistic ratings of each statement. In general, if the system works, then it should be accepted; if not, then it should be rejected. The value of an innovation, once accepted, depends on its impact on the domain of ideas and its contribution to our era of knowledge. In this manner, it attracts imitators, but it also sharpens the criticism leveled against it. Hence, an accepted innovation with significant import becomes strengthened by the working of its imitators and by the criticisms of its detractors. This criticism may be valid in part, as some of the system's statements become entropic, or it may be based on the irrationalism motivated by personal angst as the innovation is viewed, perhaps unconsciously, as a threat to the critic's ontology. The validity of the criticism can, of course, be determined within the context of the system's probability and by the imitator's agreement about entropy existing within some of its statements.

The difficulty of evaluation becomes compounded in the case of competitive innovation. For example, consider this situation: two approaches, two systems, are operating on the same problem area. These systems are already established and have their imitators, generating competition between them. Each innovative system must be such that it deals with the problem area and has other properties pertaining to other areas or to a single area. If this were not the case, then the systems would be identical, and there would be no difficulty. The differences attract adherents but pose no contention; the difficulty comes when the common problem area is in question.

In this situation, it must be realized that imitators are attracted to one or the other system because of these differences. Moreover, because of the competition, they seek to bring these differences into the common area in terms of linguistic nuances in either the operative language, the area language, or both, in order to provide greater entropy for the competitive system. The areas of difference provide internal information, already established and of utility; incorporating this information within the area of contention does not alter the system's internal language to the extent that the "foreign" information would, even after its adaptation to the system's probability requirements. The information in the areas of difference is already of utility, according to the probability requirements. To adapt this information to the area of contention would pose no great difficulty, providing that such adaptation can be undertaken. Hence the competition between the systems continues and will cease only when one system or both systems become entropic, either because of shifts in the contended area or because of the decline in utility in the areas of difference.

What then of a third system, an innovation that seeks to take a competitive place in the area of contention and to dominate it? Again, as with strict innovation, it must be evaluated as objectively as possible to determine that it performs as claimed. When this procedure is over and the innovation is accepted, it not only takes a place in the competition; it also seeks to establish its supremacy in the area. This brings into focus the concept of the critical test to determine which of these systems is of greater utility, the validity of each having already been established by its acceptance.

The significance of the critical test lies in its decisiveness as well as its very reason for being undertaken. In the case of two competing systems, such a test is more difficult to construct, unless one or both of the contending parties maintain that such a test can be constructed to be absolutely and finally decisive. In previous eras, such conditions could be established, so that a test of finality could be formulated, as was the case with the spontaneous generation theory of life, which Louis Pasteur refuted in an experimental confrontation with his respected opponents, Joly, Pouchet, and Musset.[6] Other systems, such as the particle versus wave theory of light, were not so easy to decide upon in terms of the critical test—more so now as the information contained within the systems is of greater sophistication, making the construction of a critical test much more complex and hence subject to ambiguity in the test's terms and criteria for resolving the conflict.

In this situation, the main reason for innovation is to resolve the conflict. The other reason, of course, is for strict innovation, that is, constructing a system within the terms of the existing problem area independent of the conflict. This is very rare; when it does occur, the results are the same as if the intention was resolution. The new system must cover the area in question as well as provide sufficient information to differentiate the system from the others, as is the situation with the original competing systems. Innovation in this circumstance is undertaken to resolve the difficulty of determining the effective system operating within the area of similarity. Should the innovative system prove more inclusive, taking into account the dynamics of the other systems and offering its own unique dynamics to the problem area, then the other systems will be abandoned and the new system established.

For example, a system newly innovated to cope with the difficulties of two competing systems must have the properties necessary for working within the area of similarity. Assume that the previous systems have statements ranging from *a, b, . . . n* for S_1 and *a′, b′ . . . n′* for S_2, with the problem area statements varying slightly between the systems so that there is no great discrepancy between the systems in the area of similarity. The statements are equal in number and extremely close in the dynamic impact on the area. The innovative system S_3 will contain the problem area statements *a″, b″, . . . n″, m,* with *m* equal to or greater than one or more statement that can still be contained within the delineated problem area. The contention is that the extra statement (or statements as the case may be) not only fits in the designated area, but also expands it, thereby making the new *S* even more encompassing than its predecessors. This, of course, has to be demonstrated in the process of critical evaluation. But first, how is the system to be constructed?

The concern for the problem area brings the innovation to a position similar to those of the other systems: the statements of similarity differ only in insignificant ways, which allow the system to be competitive with the others. The advantage comes from the extra statements that relate to the area and indeed expand it. The difficulty lies with the delineation established by the other systems. Because of this delineation, the imitators worked with the area as constructed and understood. The additional statement or statements must therefore be probability-coherent with the area's requirements, so that no illogical *m* or working contradiction can be derived. After this requirement is met, the additional statements must really be constructable as extensions of the original problem area. For in reality, problems are not cut off, disconnected from one another. There is a continuum of problems, just as there is a continuum of knowledge and information, which has to be altered and adapted accordingly to obtain utility in the manifold knowledge systems. The imposition of knowledge on areas shapes them. Nevertheless, such delineation must be sharp in order to form a well-constructed area for working. The inclusion of a new aspect of the area in the innovative system must be executed with great skill, or else this will open the possibility for chaos in the form of other systems being introduced with further extensions of the area, bringing the entire network of systems down in entropy, with the problem area dissolved into statements lacking systemic utility. Thus, if possible, such an inclusion must have a closure, indicating that any further extensions of the area will bring about the network's dissolution. This closure must be clear in the system's descriptive language, illustrating the way the sentences perform, the probability criteria for understanding these sentences, and the conditions in which they can become entropic.

The weight of argument for the area's closure must be such that examples are provided that demonstrate the possibilities of other statements in different systems extending the area, showing why they are of no utility. Only later can the new system take its place as a viable challenger to the competing systems and, if found upon evaluation to perform as stated, will take the lead position in the area.

Hence on this basis the innovative system will be evaluated. It must demonstrate its closure of the area and that its statements of similarity provide no significant deviation from those of its competitors. It must portray internal consistency, so that its probability rating is consistent with its statements' utility. The system must operate as described and be subject to repeated use according to its terms without difficulties, until entropy sets in. Once it has passed these tests, it will be accepted as the working system; should it not meet these requirements, it may be accepted as another system competing in the same area, but not as the decisive system its innovator maintained it to be.

Finally, further comments are in order on the critical test. The value of such a test is that it is constructed to be decisive in either/or situations, that is, when there are different approaches to the same problem being submitted for consideration. Either one proposed medical approach will cure a severe illness, or another one will; as these are mutually exclusive, the test is to determine which of these approaches is valid and the conclusion of the test will tell for one side and not the other.[7]

However, in our era the situation is becoming more to the point that competing systems differ significantly only in those areas where they relate to other problems; where they relate to a common problem their similarities are such that whatever differences may exist are of no great consequence. Hence, the difficulty in constructing a critical test is that this situation does not present an either/or mutually exclusive alternative to be decided by the test, but a condition in which competing systems are in close agreement over the area of concern.

For this reason, third and even nth innovations for a specific problem area are generated in society. And this is one important reason that our era is so fruitful in knowledge. A competitive innovation that offers slightly different system statements for the same problem area as other systems operable in the area will not be considered; its evaluation will be relevant as far as the internal consistency is concerned, but as far as its significance for the problem, it will be dismissed out of hand as merely an intellectual exercise, an attempt to do what has already been done.

The critical test assumes relevancy when determining whether the additional information concerning the previously delineated area is valid. If so determined, then the system takes the position of being the sole system for the problem area, while the others become entropic concerning the areas of similarity, to be repaired through creative activity, if possible. The test has to be so constructed to determine the system's internal validity and to assess the validity of the problem area's extension.

There is a caveat, however, which must be stated. Systems competing for the sole authority in a problem area may themselves take on such extensions, and those extra statements constructed within them in order to compete will also bring about an area extension. The problem is the cutting-off point on these extensions, that is, the final determination as to the area's fixed boundaries. Without establishing the area's limits, increasingly further statements added to provide the paradigm system for the area will only serve to weaken the area to the extent that it becomes entropic, bringing the competing systems down with entropy. The point of area delineation provided by a system is to allow the system to operate on the area; as the tendency for area extension sets in, there is a momentum for overextension and hence the decline in utility. This tendency can be halted if the imitators working with the system agree on a cut-off point: that only a certain degree of extension will be tolerated, for all further extension will only bring about entropy. On this basis the systems can be tested critically if an either/or situation can be established; if not, then they will remain competitive until decline sets in and they become irreparably entropic, either in those areas of agreement (which unite the systems in competition), or in the areas of difference (which give the systems their uniqueness), or perhaps in both, for entropy is not discriminating in its presence, as information changes, as systems are brought into question through explorative imitation, as the disequilibrium dynamics of knowledge continue through imitation and creativity.

PART III

THE DYNAMICS OF OUR ERA OF KNOWLEDGE

8

Further Comments on Anti-Realism and Social Time

> There is a growing gap between the right to decide, which is authority, and the power to do, which is specialist ability. . . . The gap is growing because technical change, with resulting specialization, occurs at a faster rate than change in cultural definitions and heirarchical roles. . . . In short the most symptomatic characteristic of modern bureaucracy is the growing imbalance between ability and authority.
>
> Victor Thompson, *Modern Organization*, 1977

"The attempt to establish particular absolute causes of change is misleading," wrote S. Herbert Frankel, "for it misconceives the very nature of the process of change of growth itself."[1] Frankel criticized the notion that change is technical, that technology brings about change, because he maintained that such a view presupposes a kind of mental certainty of the type of change required to bring about a particular consequence in the near or distant future. He argued that basic to this technical approach is the notion that our deliberate actions in the present will necessarily produce determined and demarcated results in the future; his rejection is based on the lack of control of the relevant forces of the future and ways our actions are now affected by those future forces.

Yet ours is an era of knowledge; as knowledge is far from stagnant in our era, it is most certainly an era of technical change. Victor Thompson is correct in saying that technical change with resulting specialization occurs at a rate faster than cultural definitions and hierarchical roles. But is this relevant for contemporary society? His comment that in modern bureaucracy there is a growing imbalance between ability and authority perhaps had significance for an earlier social time in our contemporary era.

Frankel's criticism concerning change being technical is correct; his argument that our actions, according to this viewpoint, will be determined by the future, presupposes a kind of isomorphic influence from the future onto the present, which is most certainly puzzling. People who evoke change can reflect on the various scenarios that may occur in the future as a result of change, but the idea that we control the future or that the future controls the present as change occurs is at best metaphysical pondering and at worst a debilitating influence on the very dynamics of change.

Concerning Victor Thompson's idea that technical change with resulting specialization occurs at a rate faster than cultural definitions and hierarchical roles, the question must be raised as to the significance of this position. In our era, both cultural definitions and hierarchical roles are formulated with respect to change, as knowledge is dynamic and as systems are both formulated and phased out. Cultural definitions are based on the dynamic disequilibrium generated by our era of knowledge; hierarchical roles are flexible with respect to these changes.

Thompson's statement that there is a growing imbalance between ability and authority, however, has no validity in our present social time in our era of knowledge. This sentiment was valid during our era's early years, in the social time of post–World War II reconstruction, when the dynamics of knowledge were being felt throughout the academic, artistic, and business worlds. In the first instance, there was the problem of converting wartime production to meet the pent-up peacetime demand. This was manifested when the skills learned during the war were turned into peaceful uses with the necessary adjustments from the military chain of command, issued by generals and executed by the lower ranks, to the peaceful construction of markets according to the understanding and the facilities at the disposal of the captains of industry. Moreover, with the memories of the post–World War I depression as well as the Great Depression still very fresh in the collective psyche, similar conditions were to be avoided. As governments had some control over their economies, they could avert depressions of the type and intensity that had led to the rise of militarism in Europe and Asia, which had been brought about by distorted market forces.

Still, in the postwar period the change in mentality necessary for the reorientation of societies certainly required time. At the outset of our era, the gap between the skilled industrialists and those workers returning to industry certainly widened. This was due to the fact that industrialists had the skills of their professions, while the work force had to be reoriented to peacetime production. The gap had widened between authority, which was trying to stimulate demand and reinstitute industrial growth, and the workforce, whose abilities had been sharpened during wartime production in producing the materiel of war.

Potential and actual ability are two different aspects of a workforce. Actual ability is manifested in the production programs established by industrial managers. This ability can be measured in terms of output and quality; it is strictly determined by production programs. Potential ability can be neither measured nor determined. It is the awareness, the instinct, the working sense as it were, gained from being in the workforce, having obtained skills and talents for the execution of projects. There can be no growing gap between ability and authority in this aspect, for ability is expressed in the actual sense of carrying out projects set by authority. Potential ability can be converted to actual ability, moreover, by finding employment that provides greater scope for one's talents and allows fuller expression of one's abilities because the task is more challenging.

Our cultural definitions and hierarchical roles have become formulated within the dynamics of our era, changing according to the specific dynamics of social time. These hierarchical roles in society—and industry as a subculture of society—alter as the specific conditions of society respond to the dynamics of the prevailing forms and contents of knowledge. One has only to consider the computer and its impact on social structure, cultural definitions, and hierarchical roles to understand this.

Postwar computers were bulky, and their proficiencies were extremely limited. They performed faster than human minds, which was their main attraction, but they could not construct multidimensional pictures, converse in humanoid languages, or operate assembly lines for efficient and standard mass production. They developed, however, into high technology and big business with the refinement of the silicon chip, which is the machine's "mind." Computers have influenced military planning and political strategy; such diversified fields as the waging of battle and the approach to the subject matter of education have been reoriented due to these marvelous machines. Cultural definitions have been revised to cope with these devices, and hierarchical roles in society have been changed to add the computer as a method of control, planning, and scenario construction.

These cultural definitions and hierarchical roles have to be revised also in terms of the impact made by atomic energy and especially the computerized control of this energy. These factors are far from having been developed in isolation from each other. Second-generation computers have been in the forefront of developing second-generation atomic reactors and weapons; they have influenced space exploration and the ideas of philosophy and psychology.[2] These are some of the manifestations of our era of knowledge and the disequilibrium dynamics generated in this era. Phasing out generations of computers, for example, depends on mechanical and conceptual developments, as manifested in the computers' abilities in terms of program development and expansion. The use of atomic energy plants as a viable means for counteracting the energy crisis has been brought into question because of the problems of leakage, reactor meltdown, and disposal of atomic wastes.[3] Space exploration, once considered vast in possibilities, is being exploited as an extension of earthbound militarism; moreover, the restrictions of our solar system place theoretical and practical restrictions on space as a real open frontier. With gravity not yet explained and the balances that keep our planetary system functioning not understood, the restrictions on space exploration prohibit our conquering our cosmological territory, our moon and our immediate gravitational outyard between earth and moon.

What can be said with a great deal of certainty is that our cultural definitions are becoming oriented to our era of knowledge and that our hierarchical roles are being associated with various knowledge systems, not merely teaching them and working with them, but also exploring the dynamics they generate. Those in social hierarchical roles are either elected or appointed, as is the case with government officials; they are elected or appointed because of their abilities, proved in various fields of inquiry and working systems. Elected officers are placed into office by their constituents on the basis of their known abilities for organization and for assigning the best people for the lower administrative jobs; in those situations where this is demonstrated afterwards not to be the case, the administration is removed in future elections. Where the constituents have become dependent on such an administration—that is, where the corruption has become too entrenched to be removed easily—only a new generation with different attitudes and outlooks will be able to unseat the administration.

Cultural definitions are formulated within the framework of heritage and the social time. Social and cultural inheritance establish the social "myths," the reconstructed histories on which traditions are founded. Social time gives expression to these traditions within the context of the ambience of the current dominant knowledge systems. Thus there are differences between cultures, even though they are tied by the common bond of problems and the search for their solutions.

Hierarchical roles are those which are established by society's development in accordance with the prevailing systems of knowledge. These are the roles of administrator and of teacher of theories and the practice of these theories. These roles are in a sense, then, assigned by the very cultural forces that define the social hierarchy. As these forces are historical (in the form of social inheritance) and present (as delineated by social time), in one sense they are permanent and in another, they are changing. Their permanence comes from their historical basis. Every social body politic has its foundations in its political evolution. Prior to the establishment of the British monarchy, for example, Britain was ruled by chieftains, by local kings whose armies gave credibility to their claims to territory. This type of government is common, as witnessed, for example, by the Chinese warlords over their territories and the Germanic nation-states that existed before their formation into a united country. This period can be termed a pre-inheritance social time, only to be realized as inheritance social time when the divergent and manifold social and political forces come together into a working political structure in which the various dominant aspects in the society have an influence on the running of people's affairs.

It is during this period of transition, often tumultuous and exciting, that the social hierarchical roles are established. The government is formed, the power blocs are represented, and the transition of power is formulated. The hierarchical roles are therefore obtained by those who wield power, both political figureheads and the real controllers, and these are set as part of the nation's collective history. These roles, once established, remain in place as long as the new form of government lasts and its power is transmitted according to the rules.

However, this process is not without its difficulties. It is a historical fact that no country has been formed without internal conflict and strife after its basic foundation has been established. Great Britain, during its period of forging its peoples into a unified country, suffered many internal wars; the political conflicts between England and Scotland and England and Wales are far from being settled permanently. The fall of the great Russian imperialistic regime did not result in stabilization for the newly formed Soviet Union; Josef Stalin, as V. I. Lenin's successor, brought havoc and chaos to his country, and the damage has yet to be repaired. The United States endured a bloody civil war, the scars of which can still be seen in areas of the South; Sherman's march through Georgia and the devastation it brought is still bitterly recalled.

The struggle for power on an established foundation may be part of the human condition, given expression to those who have the ability and the backing to enter the political arena. Thus, political instability can most certainly be present in every newly formed country, reaching back through the annals of history. Even Rome, the city of law and constitution, was ravaged by internal strife, as Tacitus related in his works.[4]

The human condition may be as enduring as mankind, but it is manifested in ways unique to every situation. Hence, the situations of political nation-states today are different from those of previous historical eras. This is not seen so much in those countries established in earlier eras that have weathered their own internal strife to emerge solid and functioning in a lawful manner, according to the principles that have evolved and developed within them. These countries are in a position to exploit the dynamics of knowledge; they can incorporate these dynamics into their own institutions that generate knowledge and thus make their own unique contributions in innovation and initiation. In these countries, political conflict has achieved a level of refinement, so that the conflicts are resolved not by taking to the streets and fighting battles and spilling blood, but by taking the issues of conflict to the respective judicial and legislating bodies of government for their judgments. These countries, of course, are not devoid of politicking—far from it; but the back-room pressure groups exert their influence through persuasion and reason, often trading favors or threatening to raise scandals, rather than reverting to physical confrontation and the force of arms.

This system does not exist to any extent in the newly formed countries because they have no political history of compromise and bargaining. Most of these countries broke from their colonial roots by force of arms, and their politicians often use force to resolve their conflicts, because it is less time-consuming and certainly more decisive.

These newly formed countries are often the victims of instability for two reasons, one related to the human condition and the other as a result of our contemporary era of knowledge. Instability due to the human condition is the age-old factor of seeking power, either for self-aggrandizement or because of the actual realization that a better job of ruling can be done, or for a combination of both. Those people engaged in the power struggle after the formation of the country as a body politic are, in most cases, the same people who forged the country into existence, by either throwing off the colonial yoke or by establishing the political foundations on which the country is to be ruled. Exceptions to this are those people who take over pressure groups after their formation and seek to obtain power on the basis of the groups' strength.

Adding to the instability is the play of the big powers for influence in these countries, so that pressure groups and personalities are supported, either clandestinely or overtly, by supporting one of the streams of political influence, such as those outspoken Marxist socialists or the pro-West faction. Internal stability can be established only within the country; while support may come from outside, it is effective only when applied inside the political and national boundaries of the newly formed country.

Another factor contributing to instability is lacking the actual ability to govern, so that being an able leader on the field of battle or in the halls and chambers of international diplomacy is no guarantee that this ability can be applied to the country's internal situation. Establishing systems of transportation, beginning a viable education system, and providing adequate health institutions are far different than sitting in the diplomatic offices and arguing an abstract case for independence. For once independence is gained, it must be maintained; this depends mostly on the country's internal viability, and this, in turn, depends on the leaders' ability to provide the necessary infrastructure and political savvy for mustering the political forces for development.

Of course, high levels of leadership ability have always been required, regardless of the historical era. In ancient Rome, the demand for leadership ability had reached high levels, so that too few leaders had this ability, a lack that contributed to Rome's eventual downfall. The United States Constitution—a great document that takes into account the problems of political power and the lessons of history and that established the principle of checks and balances of power—was in itself insufficient to prevent the great tear across the Mason-Dixon line that led to the Civil War. The study of history illustrates only too well the opportunities lost by leaders who were unable to rise to the challenges that confronted them and their people.

Our current historical situation is not unique in this point. The leaders of the power blocs have often not acted in accordance with their understanding of the situation confronting mankind now. The threat of total destruction has not been removed, although summit talks and disarmament discussions have perhaps eased this threat somewhat and provide a forum for dialogue when confrontation becomes too active or too hot.

Specifically, however, the leaders of the emerging countries have the greatest challenges to confront. Their countries have not achieved the stability nor the political maturity that the great powers have, due to the differences in time of existence and the maturation gained by having to solve great internal and international difficulties. These emerging countries are trying to become established in the world of nations but are uncertain of the means they have available to accomplish this. Their leaders are all too often in the crossroads of the movements and currents generated by the great powers, and they have not yet gained the skill to navigate. They are tempted to play the powers off against each other on the assumption that their positions as emerging countries provide them with advantages as the great powers vie for their friendship. These leaders are, however, in error when they seek to use the great powers for their advantage, for in reality it is the other way around, that the big powers use them instead. In our era when colonialism has been proclaimed an offensive relationship, it has been replaced by a more subtle form of dominion, that of not actual ruling, not deciding the political fate of these countries, but exerting control indirectly through economic and military means. Providing financial assistance, for example, provides great leverage over the decision-making processes and the direction these decisions take. Providing military assistance also allows for the exertion of great political leverage, especially as an army has to have standardized equipment to be effective, and the single great power source supplying armaments ensures this standardization. No military move can be made without the consent, tacit or explicit, of the great-power supplier and the receiving country must act in some instances as a surrogate, for in war munitions are quickly exhausted, parts are required, and political support must be forthcoming. The exploitation of this one-sided relationship by the great power results in the receiving country being in its control.

The broadest problems confronting these emerging countries in our era are those of establishing cultural values and hierarchical roles. As these countries are formed, they represent the conglomeration of many peoples and subcultures, each representing a unique approach to the world. There may be diversified religious groups that merge into a greater unit for protection. There may be political groups, religiously or non-religiously oriented, that form a country for their mutual benefit and common causes. The difficulty of establishing cultural values within this newly formed unity is that the synergetic overculture must provide for the expressions of the subcultures, as well as allowing a unique culture to emerge, one that will give identification to, and be identified with, the newly formed country.

Of course, all modern countries have subcultures thriving within the frameworks of their overcultures so that they can be governed and contribute to their society. What makes the emerging countries unique is that they are spared the general problems of economic development, which the established countries had to undergo, by the technology and the state of the arts in our contemporary era, as well as the emphasis on the expansion of knowledge. For example, the benefits of agricultural organization and development are available to emerging countries, and these advancements can be adapted to suit cultural and climatic requirements, soil conditions, water availability, and plant life. Construction techniques are advanced, so different materials can be used for countries' unique geographic circumstances. Of course, education can express both the culture of the emerging countries and the benefits of the advanced countries and the contributions being made there, until the emerging countries can become productive and hence act as contributors as well.

Cultural values need not, therefore, be lost in our contemporary era. Indeed, they can flourish, and the amenities available for those who work and acquire them can only lead to a further expansion of those traits that do not clash with the modern world. The traits that do clash will be phased out in the process of development, perhaps to the betterment of society in general.

These cultural values can be maintained within our era of knowledge only on the condition that the hierarchical roles are established and are sufficiently stable to allow for a secure internal development and expansion to proceed without the unsetting dynamics of power struggles and coups d'état. In a sense, however, the very conditions of our era generate unsetting circumstances for these countries. Consider, for example, the economic situation. The developed, Western-oriented countries have achieved extremely advanced levels of living compared to the emerging countries. Moreover, the newly formed countries require some of the goods and services of the developed countries, goods that are in fact luxuries but that are nevertheless necessary for operating the emerging countries' systems in an efficient manner. Computers are an example, although they can be supplanted by more archaic forms of computation, control, and billing. Computers for the emerging countries are more than just status symbols; they are the most efficient aids in planning and directing materiels and people to specific tasks, and at a more sophisticated level, for controlling industry. The operation of computers, however, requires a skilled service force of programmers and technicians to program and maintain the machinery. Also required is a populace sufficiently educated to apply computers to national and local problems and to interpret and apply the data gained from research and computer compilation. In this small yet significant sense, the process of development must be rushed so that able people can be trained and educated to meet the task.

It is plain that rushing the process of development leads to a distortion of the countries' material wealth at first; it is the second reason for instability. Not only is a class of people educated along these lines, but those who receive the education are usually not chosen on the basis of an almost impartial educational system, for this has not been developed yet. Favoritism, the often necessary handmaiden of development, sets in, and on this basis the elite educated class is formed. While favoritism may begin as a way to provide the benefits of education to those most deserving, it often degenerates to political manipulation and becomes an essential part of a corrupt regime. The payment of political and personal obligations is, of course, not limited to emerging countries; since it is practiced to some extent in the developed countries, it seems that the political side of human nature is as universal as are all other aspects. But while the developed countries can absorb this favoritism and while their resources are developed to the extent that there is no great necessity to rely on this form of relationship, in the emerging countries the temptation is strong to use favoritism so that many who truly deserve assistance are deprived and those who obtain assistance only in response to political favors may or may not be worthy. The tendency is thus to magnify this process, as debts pile up in the formation of the country. Favoritism becomes a means for allocating resources—such as they are—as the country is transformed from a conglomeration of subcultures into the overculture of a developing country. But in the dynamics of development, this process will only be detrimental to the country's future and its prospects for political maturity and economic development, as people unworthy of high positions are granted them in the form of payment for political favors.

What can be said of social time for these and the developed countries? How does anti-realism enter in the relationship to social time? Social time is delineated within an era according to the stage in which the era exists. In our era of knowledge, we have undergone great political and economic changes since the end of World War II, when our era was first established. We are now in a period of social time in which the dynamics of knowledge have entered a condition of disequilibrium, in which knowledge systems are influenced by the information of other such systems and in which creativity has been undertaken at levels hitherto unknown in the history of humanity. Moreover, as a consequence of the impact of our era, the issues of colonial dissolution and the consequent formation of emerging countries have come to the fore; the developing countries accepted into the United Nations, present their grievances often without much success due to the power structure within the world community.

For the emerging countries, social time has generated cross-currents of ideas as a result of the disequilibrium of creativity. These countries require stability to become established and viable as economic and political entities, and our social time is far from stable. The realm of ideas, of knowledge systems, is in a state of flux; it seems that only those developed countries whose industrial bases and educational systems can cope with the dynamics of changing knowledge and incorporate these dynamics into new industrial and educational systems can benefit immediately from this instability. Indeed, these countries in our social time thrive on this flux and depend on it for their strength. The emerging countries have different requirements. They require the benefits of the knowledge systems and their phasing out through entropy and their rebuilding through imitation, yet without the disquieting influences of such changes. The great issue facing the leaders of these countries is how to achieve stability while coping with the crosswinds of knowledge.

The demands of these countries are such that real time is of great importance. The leaders try to achieve rapid growth with as few growing pains (in the form of wasted resources) as possible through trial and error and without having to undergo their own industrial revolution. The simplest way of achieving growth has thus been to opt for the ideology of a previous era, to adapt so-called Marxism or capitalism to their countries, and to seek the benefits of the power blocs that give lip service to these ideologies. In fact, however, while this approach may have been effective in the early period of our era, it no longer holds true. For by attaching their fortunes to the big power blocs, these countries are mortgaging their independence, becoming de facto extensions of the great powers, and often are coerced into the role of surrogates in military encounters.

Hence, as a consequence of being in the crosswinds of the disequilibrium dynamics of knowledge, the leaders of these countries are gaining the comprehension, indeed the wisdom, and therefore the truth of their situation, that by being the masters of their fate they can achieve economic growth and cultural development. The hierarchical roles must be established and firmly impressed on these countries so that their political systems are stable. The leaders must then establish the best ways to achieve the two main priorities, that of industrialization and education, for the rest of cultural and social development will readily follow and indeed be developed alongside, once the dynamics of these processes take hold.

The leaders of these countries must not neglect the message of the crosswinds of knowledge, that what is knowledge at one time will fall into disrepute at another time. Both the industrial and educational systems must take this into account and be formed accordingly. This is a consequence of knowledge, that it is temporal, subject to entropy and hence potentially in error. The anti-realism of knowledge must not overwhelm the developers of education and industry, for they should never lose sight of their main and very real objective of bringing their countries into the present social time of our era of knowledge, without sacrificing the independence they worked so hard to achieve. The fashion of knowledge is indeed fickle but the issues of economic growth and the formation of a society that can compete culturally with the developed countries is very real and not subject to the whims of fashionable knowledge systems. Hence, the leaders of these countries are confronted with the realism of their unique situations, both internally and in the international arena, as they seek to build their countries and maneuver among the influences of their surroundings and the forces exerted by the great powers. Knowledge must be acquired and adapted to the countries' situations, but not at the expense of insight into what knowledge is and can accomplish under given circumstances. It is only when the countries' institutions—political, industrial and educational—can adapt to the flow of knowledge and indeed make their own contributions, can they be considered as having broken through the barrier of emergence and have achieved the status of being developed.

There is a very important caveat that must be made clear for our social time, and its relevance is greater for the developed societies than for those emerging. The caveat is the placing of too much significance on knowledge without considering it in its proper perspective. The advances made in the fields of artificial intelligence, for example, tend to overshadow the fact that no matter how analogous computers and their variations can be to humanity, they are neither equals nor replacements. This is just one area where tremendous strides in knowledge have been made; indeed this is a real representative of our era, even though its roots go back to the 1930s with the work of Alan Turing.[5] Other examples are the advancements in the sciences and the beginnings of the conquest of outer space. These accomplishments and the others of our era have a profound impact on our lives. By expanding our ideas, they have enabled us to go further into realms of inquiry hitherto unkown and unconsidered. This is certainly beneficial to humanity. But the caveat is that the works of the practitioners of knowledge, no matter how far these works have taken us, and no matter how intellectually stimulating they are, cannot serve as replacements for the emotions and pathos of humanity. We must not therefore emphasize these great accomplishments to the extent that they become our reasons for existence at the expense of human emotions. We must, however, realize them for what they are, great achievements in the development of mankind, whose ultimate goal is to make our brief lives on this planet as comfortable and as rewarding as possible. The dictum passed throughout our history and stated in the Bible is that by the sweat of our faces shall we eat our bread (Genesis 3:19). We work and labor as imitators, creators, or as people whose occupations are more physical than mental. But even the hard physical labor of old has been supplanted to a large extent by automation and technology, the products of creativity. While we must still work hard for our bread, the type of work has been altered, and the possibilities offered in life have been increased by creative contributions and the disequilibrium dynamics of creativity, as they have become incorporated into our way of living. The caveat is, then, that if we live for our work alone, then we must ultimately consider that our knowledge is true and cling to it dogmatically, holding it despite new knowledge and denying the presence of the entropy that will eventually bring it down. This results in psychosis, which deprives us of the right to enjoy our lives. If, on the other hand, we follow the ancient wisdom of the Bible and eat our bread from the fruits of our labor, if we work to live, then knowledge is for us as it should be, a means of enriching our lives. Its anti-realism then will be appreciated and its temporary state accepted. We will be able, in the full esprit of the meaning, adhere to that other biblical dictum, to choose life (Deuteronomy 30:19) and to make our knowledge work for us.

Our cultural values are those established through the disequilibrium dynamics of creativity, generated by explorative imitation, and brought to fruition through the processess of initiation and innovation. Our hierarchical authorities should be established to allow our political, economic, and educational systems to operate efficiently and to allow the incorporation of the disequilibrium dynamics of creativity deeper into our social structures. This must be so for the developed countries to maintain their positions of strength and for the emerging countries to enter our social time of our contemporary era of knowledge.

9

Some Consequences of Our Era of Knowledge

> Madmen in authority, who hear voices in the air, are distilling their frenzy from some academic sribbler of a few years back. I am sure that the power of vested interests is vastly exaggerated compared with the gradual encroachment of ideas. Not, indeed, immediately, but after a certain interval; for in the field of economic and political philosophy there are not very many who are influenced by new theories after they are twenty-five or thirty years of age, so that the ideas which civil servants and politicians and even agitators apply to current events are not likely to be the newest. But soon or late, it is ideas, not vested interests, which are dangerous for good or evil.
>
> John Maynard Keynes, *The General Theory of Employment, Interest and Money,* 1936

The sentiments that Keynes expressed in the last pages of his book are certainly powerful, but somewhat out of date. True, mad leaders in authority still distill their frenzy from academic scribblers of years back, but they also hear the ideas of our contemporary era of knowledge. Moreover, it is no longer age that limits the influence of new ideas, if it ever did, but healthy minds and bodies, as the professions require that practitioners be informed about the latest contributions in their fields and in the arts and sciences. This is a new era, one that Keynes could not have comprehended when he wrote his famous work in economics, which was published in 1936, during the depths of the Great Depression.

The sentiments that Keynes expressed can be considered a closing statement on an ending era, that of industrialization. Dictators rose up within the cultural centers of Europe and Asia and spoke in shrill tones the ideas of academic scribblers, distorting them to suit their own ends and to work up their listeners into irrational mobs. Instead of explaining the ideas of these thinkers, interpreting them to the requirements of their conditions, they offered hate and war as the solution to the economic crisis that had closed down the era of industrialization. These ideas, warped by the dictators' visions, became the handmaiden for those whose vested interests lay in igniting the fires that led to engulfment of the world in a second global military conflagration.

But from the closing of the industrial era and the ashes of the war (which was waged in part to resolve the conflicts of the ending era) our present era of knowledge arose. Mad leaders still retained their authority to some extent, but their reigns were contained; they were kept localized by the threat of the fresh outbreak of hostilities that they had no chance of surviving. Atomic weapons were soon held by both sides, and both sides were aware that the world's arsenals stocked weapons the likes of which never before existed. Moreover, the deployment and use of atomic weapons on anything resembling a large scale was the ultimate decider, the consequences of their use most certainly unpredictable. It was a world recovering from its second great war and still armed with weapons of vast destructive power when it entered a new era, a new renaissance of knowledge in the sciences and arts, one that had far-reaching consequences in the shaping of the dynamics of our consequent geopolitical and cultural development.

Hence, as well as the ever-increasing sophistication in the knowledge systems for acquiring and developing destructive capacity, another consequence of our era, one that accords with its esprit also exists, which is giving shape to our political and cultural contributions. This is the concept of and the awareness of newness, as it is manifested in our contemporary era of knowledge.

Newness as such is not unique to our era. In the Renaissance, for example, the rebirth of knowledge also gave great force to newness. Not only was this so in the development of the arts and sciences, but also manifested in humanity's natural curiosity concerning our earthly environment. Geographical exploration, conquest, and domination by those who sailed forth also resulted in bringing back to their established countries stories about the newly found peoples and lands and their foods, arts, and crafts. Although these exploring countries sought to impose their cultures on the newly found territories, they were also influenced by them, and this was also a contributing factor in the rebirth of knowledge. Moreover, colonialism, with its mercantilistic and physiocratic ideologies and consequences, expanded as exploration continued only to be further intensified by the need for raw materials. This trend was important in the beginnings of the Industrial Revolution and its development.

It is clear that the Industrial Revolution would not have come about without the generation of knowledge that occurred during the Renaissance. During this period of rebirth, not only were the classical works of Aristotle and other ancient thinkers rediscovered, but contributions were also made in the arts and the physical sciences. The new knowledge was not only significant for that era, but was incorporated in the means of production at the time, so when the breakthroughs in industrialization occurred, the necessary mechanical concepts were available; moreover, the correct mechanical approach existed, as new machinery had to be developed to cope with the worker-machine relationship and to increase production and quality. Galileo's and Newton's formulas not only provided for mechanical computation; their transposition of physical concepts into mathematical symbols allowed engineering to expand and further machinery to be developed, which resulted in the increased work potential of the populace.

As work requirements absorbed the workforce, the great cities developed even more. Not only were they centers of cultural and political life, but they became also centers of industry. This, of course, resulted in the development of a relationship between the entrepreneurs and the workforce that led to the industrial expansion. The banking system became entrenched in society, allowing entrepreneurs to borrow and increase their investments; in turn, their investments and greater involvement in the social fabric resulted in their increased sophistication in finance, enabling them to compete for those assets of populations which were accumulating greater personal wealth than ever before.

Not only did industrialization increase personal wealth; it allowed for the increase in cultural activity. Playhouses expanded not only in the great metropolises but also in the smaller cities and towns, and a greater number of playwrights came on the scene. Music of the masters was no longer the exclusive pleasure of the wealthy classes who entertained the great composers and musicians in their halls, but became also the domain of all who could afford the price of a concert ticket. The same held true for the other arts, for the arts lost their aristocratic exclusiveness, and both observers and artists were to be found among the ranks of the various social strata. The sciences also expanded as industry required more technicians to develop efficient industrial processes and more scientists to improve the existing products and develop new ones in light of competition. Thus, the competition in the economic sphere unleashed by industrialization provided the impetus for cultural developments and the advancements of scientific theorizing and development. With industrialization, the old order of class privileges, which had been maintained in various forms and social structures since the development of civilization, gave way to a more universal and less restrictive awareness of social status and order.

The era of industrialization came to an end with the Great Depression. Financial institutions, which had achieved a high level of sophistication, could not withstand the built-up pressures of the market; they collapsed as the exchanges became far too overheated, and industrialists could no longer obtain the necessary loans for restocking. However, there was an unheeded forewarning of such a collapse in the issues that provoked World War I.

Territorial expansion, that ancient cause for military confrontations, was not the sole issue of that war; acquiring both markets and natural resources were also extremely important factors. These were not achieved through military conflict, however, so that in the aftermath of the war, when economic activity was restored, the uncertainties over resource accumulation and market expansion, together with the desire to obtain ever-increasing wealth, gave rise to stock market speculation to an extent hitherto unexperienced in the process of industrialization. When the markets collapsed and the Depression became entrenched, countries sought to redress their situations by going to war once again to conquer territories for natural resources and markets. War was also considered a practical way for solving the Depression, as men under arms cannot be unemployed. The Great Depression signified the end of the Industrial Revolution, and World War II was an attempt to resolve the difficulties that existed as a result of that era's decline; in the aftermath of that great world conflict, our era of knowledge came into being. The newness, vitalized again by the new renaissance and given renewed impetus by the industrialization of the world, became the watchword of creativity in our era of knowledge.

SOME GEOPOLITICAL CONSEQUENCES

Since the dawning of civilization, historical eras have not been entirely new; their roots are based primarily in the era that precedes each of them. Our historical era began in the aftermath of World War II and had its roots in the processes of industrialization that preceded the war. Two very determinate and clear consequences arose in the early days after the war's end, both of which are very much a part of our geopolitical situation today. One consequence is the formation of great power blocs, enabling the surrogates of each power bloc to engage their opposing surrogates in continuous and prolonged battle. The second consequence is the emergence of new nation-states, newly formed political entities that seek their independence; once it is achieved they attempt to make their own ways and establish their own unique paths in the world.

The first consequence is a unique representation of a process that has existed since the times of the ancient conquests of Babylon, Egypt, and Alexander's Greece and that crystallized in the strength of the Roman Empire. What makes this formation of great power blocs unique in our time is that the means of conquest and the methods of retaining control are of an intensity and completeness not possible in any previous era. The use of communications in the processes of mind-control, the application of sophisticated methods of torture together with the more ancient methods, and the use of weaponry in quelling the spirits of those ensnared in the power bloc certainly strike terror in the hearts and influence the calculations of those who seek release from their oppressive conditions. Such was the case when the Hungarians, the Poles, and the Czechs sought political expression and were met on each occasion with the overwhelming response of the military and the secret police, which brought them back to subjugation. Moreover, unique to our era were the unheeded calls for support from the West, which feared that should such assistance be given, it would result in another world war. The spheres of influence established after the end of World War II were to remain intact, unaltered over time, and not influenced by the policies of the opposing power blocs.

This territorial division pertained at first to only those countries directly involved in the previous areas of conflict, so that countries untouched by the presence of allied troops in combat during the war became fair game for the power bloc struggle. The Korean War, officially recognized as a "police action," became the area in which the power blocs exerted their resolve to engage in conflicts while retaining their regional demarcation. China, with its great history and its vast population, had to stretch its muscles, as it were, and test its abilities in this conflict, which resulted in its entering into a new strategic position and hence on a limited collision course shortly after with its one-time former ally, the Soviet Union. Later, the Vietnam conflict pitted the Soviets and the Chinese against the Americans on Vietnamese territory, with the consequence of both the Chinese and the Soviets testing their resolve against other less powerful opponents. The Chinese, for example, still skirmish periodically with India and have difficulties with their other neighbors, especially Vietnam. The Soviets, for example, are deeply involved in conflict in Afghanistan, with apparently no way out except a complete withdrawal and the loss of face that goes with such a maneuver; the alternative is continuing in that country, with the corresponding fall from grace in the international arena. The United States, after ridding itself of the Vietnamese conflict, is engaged in the strife prevailing in the unstable countries of Latin America.

The second consequence of this territorial division is the newly formed nation-states seeking their own identities and independence. This is a direct result of the dynamics of our contemporary era. Decolonialization is a conception and a process that is reversing the policies of the Renaissance and the Industrial Revolution in their drive for exploration and conquest. Moreover, with the existence of the United Nations, these emerging countries receive status, which before World War II would have been impossible to obtain. Invasion as a means of directing and controlling other nations is being ruled out as the lessons of Vietnam and Afghanistan have aptly demonstrated; instead, the use of political pressures and of financial assistance and trade are employed, requiring greater sophistication on the part of the emerging states and the big power blocs, which vie with each other for the resources and support of these new countries.[1]

In their struggles for independence, many of these countries have not had the time to develop their resources nor to determine the paths they wish to take. Perhaps the most unstable of the regions in which emerging countries are the prevailing influence, where they are joined geographically and where the memories of a glorious past of pride and independence merge with an uncertain present and great unpredictability, is the Middle East, where the glories of Arabia, with its highly developed cultures and mathematical innovations, mix with backwardness and the remnants of feudalism and dictatorial and autocratic monarchies, backed by religion.[2] This is a region in which religion, autocratic rule, and the desire for national reawakening are confronted by the big power blocs, in their attempts to accumulate the natural resources of oil and strategic setting. This is the area in which a staunch Moslem, the leader of Libya, first declared himself an anticommunist to the extreme and hence pro-West, then became a surrogate for Soviet bloc operations and a conductor of its policies. Here the Shah of Iran, who wielded power for so long and had become so entrenched in his country's policies, was overthrown and replaced by a religious leader who has brought his country into a new area in which the darkness of ignorance and intolerance compete with the light of the modern world and the era of knowledge, where the prisons now overflow with the new enemies of the Iranian state and where the old enemies are either freed or executed at the discretion of the religious-cum-political leaders. Here Israel, the Jewish state in the region of Moslem countries, must fight and defend itself, where peace is essential for world stability and where quiet is as uneasy and fragile as the whims of the region's many rulers.

The conditions that existed and developed after World War II are, however, symptomatic of our era of knowledge. Not only were these emerging countries formed and given their independence, but aware of their historical relationships and their indebtedness to the great powers—themselves expanding in their influence and socioeconomic and military capabilities—the great powers were placed in a self-restraining position. They placed themselves in check by the very nature of their strength and to some extent by their acceptance of the limited authority of the United Nations as a forum for hearing out world opinion and international debate. Not that they resigned their sovereignty to the greater cause of the world united, but they could not afford to discount this arena as a means of winning the support of those peoples and countries not yet committed to their own ways. This, in the annals of history, is itself a significant development, for it indicates the direction we have taken since the last war.

The first attempt at peaceful political world union was presented by United States President Woodrow Wilson to the world community after World War I. Ironically, it was accepted by that community but rejected by the Americans because they thought it would compromise their fiercely cherished sovereignty. After World War II, all who were concerned realized the importance of world unity, and recognized that national sovereignty would not be compromised, but that such a union would serve to defuse tensions and thereby reduce the risks of another and final world conflict. With the backing of the wartime allies, the United Nations came into operation and has since served as an instrument, not for curtailing sovereignty, nor for the elimination of small-scale wars, but for localizing conflicts and providing peacekeeping forces in those areas of political conflict that request their intervention. This has resulted in restrictions on the uses of surrogates to wage wars, as world demand for the elimination of conflict areas can result in the United Nations providing either sanctions or troops in disputes that threaten to expand into neutral territories, which want no part in the conflict.

Another consequence of our contemporary era of knowledge, which has developed from the artistic and scientific understanding and results from the dynamic disequilibrium of creativity, is the reduction in the resolve of the superpowers to wage war. This seems like a paradoxical situation because of the massive and constant building up of war preparations and weapons systems, but then again, our era, especially in our present social time, is not without paradoxes. Consider, for example, the Korean conflict. There is no doubt that had the United States employed nuclear weapons, that conflict would have been resolved. There was, of course, a precedent for the use of these weapons in the bombings of Japan; by so doing, the United States and its UN allies would have been victorious in battle in the traditional conception of that term. There would have been less loss of life and of materiels for the allies, but despite all that force the allies pursued a different approach, one of discussion and compromise. After World War II, theories of the uses of atomic power for military purposes were discussed at the highest military and political levels. But given the new esprit of knowledge, the awareness of urban problems, the clouds of the Great Depression still not completely dissipated, and the distaste for war very predominant, the accepted policy became compromise rather than outdated notions of victorious war, negotiation instead of the absolute and total surrender that had ended World War II. What is also significant is that this attitude prevailed at the height of the cold war, when the distrust among the power blocs, perhaps a natural situation given the political alignment after the war, was at its deepest.

It must also be considered that domestic problems rated high on the list of priorities among the power blocs. In the West, the memory of the Great Depression, and in the East, the difficulties of building new governing systems, especially given the great loss of life, as well as attempts to settle the turbulent regions of the satellite countries and to cope with their problems, together with the tremendous awareness of the loss of lives and the devastation of the last global conflict, certainly made another such conflict unwanted. Thus, with the spirit of compromise that prevailed, conflict was kept simmering on a fairly low flame; the cold war, with all its international difficulties and the strains it placed on the home fronts, remained cold instead of becoming desperate and overheated.

Both the superpowers have become introspective to the extent that they realize that national priorities are related to and are manifestations of their foreign policies, especially concerning their relations with one another. For the United States, the problems of urban renewal, race relations, and maintaining social dynamics in the multiracial and highly diversified society rate high on the list to be approached. The people of that country struggle with the subcultural difficulties such as drug abuse, improving local education, and dealing with outmoded values of isolationism, fundamentalism, and patterns of regionalism that prevailed during the previous historical era, without violating the basic rights of the Constitution, such as free speech and freedom of thought. American foreign policy is conducted in the same spirit of liberalism and wariness of the abuses of power, such as subversion of foreign governments to suit its own ends. It is plagued with the awareness that its international policies are manifestations of its domestic policies, and these policies tend to be as diversified as the states themselves and various political outlooks and factions. Governing this country has been shown to be a most difficult task, for not only does the democratic process operate fairly slowly on a national level, but also the same process must be reckoned with in and among the various competing political factions. There is often a difference of opinion, and these differences are integrated by the process of making foreign policy, this by the same people voted into office to make foreign policies based on the country's needs and requirements internationally. In democracies, opinions are initiated by one faction to be contested by another; intrigue, powerbroking, and maneuvering for strategic advantage are all legitimate procedures. Democracy allows uncertainty in the decision making process—the awareness that decisions may be in error but that only results can determine their viability. Foreign policy is conducted with similar indecisiveness, but the realpolitik is too fluid and fluctuating for the establishment of results that are to any extent permanent.

In the Soviet Union, there is far less divergence of political opinion. Foreign policy is formulated and established only with the consent of opposing factions at the highest level, and there is little lower-level dissent. But the Soviet Union is also an unruly country, difficult to control, and the legacy of Stalin—dictatorship with all its sophisticated means of establishing a consensus in theory—has not done so in reality. Thus it has failed to fulfill the country's needs economically, politically, and internationally, as demonstrated by the Afghanistan war and the setbacks in the Middle East. But with the new leadership, there is a thaw of the old restrictions. Their intention is to liberalize the means of production, to reduce involvement in international conflicts, and to concentrate more on providing a viable socioeconomic base for real development. Now there is a tendency for a meeting of the ways between the two great powers, although the division between them still remains very wide. However, this is being narrowed by their mutual interests in our era of knowledge, especially those that can remove sources of international antagonism and improve the lot of their peoples through the diversion of resources from weaponry to peaceful production.

We are, therefore, in our social time in our era of knowledge, experiencing a situation unique in the history of humanity. Superpowers, armed with greater destructive force than ever before, are seeking ways to defuse crises and to reduce their vast arsenals without risk to themselves. They engage each other, each from its strategic position, in serious talks to reduce and perhaps eliminate the threat of nuclear war, presenting worst-case scenarios in which such circumstances for nuclear confrontation could arise. In our era, the potential for the force of arms being employed is no longer a symbol to be respected; the consequence of such force is unthinkable.

Instead of respecting the symbols of military might, we respect developments in the arts and sciences. The old fascination for the military is rapidly fading, while the products of innovation and initiation are gaining in interest. Great prizes are given to contributors to genetic engineering, chemistry, physics, and economics, while the reputations of soldiers are not as respected. There are more pressing problems in the preservation of life, such as treating cancer and finding a cure and a vaccine for AIDS. Ways to restore the fatigued heart and reduce the danger of strokes evoke far greater pride and honor in our era than do contributions made to the ever-increasing sophistication of waging war. The point also has to be considered that in our social time, even those surrogates engaged in the wars that the big powers could not wage are less willing to maintain their surrogate positions, for their own internal problems are now far too pressing to devote their efforts and lives of their people in this manner. The great powers are finding that their internal problems and their international policies are receiving similar priorities in their decision-making processes.

This change has resulted in an increasing awareness that domestic problems can be approached from an international point of view, stressing cooperation rather than conflict, which is an important reason for the increasing overtures between the superpowers to decrease the existing tensions and to engage in mutual economic and cultural programs. The food shortage problem, once restricted to single countries, is no longer so regionally bound. When the United States imposed a grain embargo on the Soviet Union to protest against the Afghanistan invasion, both the Soviet citizens and the American farmers were affected; the Soviet population had their food supplies reduced. The Soviet government's correct intentions of using more efficient agriculture techniques were hampered by its own bureaucracy and lack of the most modern knowledge on agriculture. Moreover, these were long-term policies, but the demand for grain was immediate. The Soviet government's incentives were based on its traditional methods mixed with attempts to emulate American techniques, which might have proved beneficial in the long run, had they not lacked marketing techniques and the high-quality, modern food-processing plants required for operating along strictly economic lines.

The result was that crop yields were far below those required for the population. To meet this deficiency the Soviets turned to other countries with abundant crops; Canada, Australia, and some European countries supplied grain, but not in the quantities sufficient to satisfy Soviet demand. Moreover, with grain in short supply, the prices of other foodstuffs also rose, a situation for which they were unprepared. This rise in food prices also affected those grain-exporting countries, because their own demands were not met due to exporting.

The American farmers were affected because, with the cutback in their production, their revenues declined; their surpluses were purchased by the government but not at a price comparable to the more lucrative Soviet market, as they knew from previous experiences under the Nixon administration. The results of this embargo are still being felt, and the agricultural weapon can be used again; moreover, with profits reduced from increased efficiency and abundant agricultural output, U.S. government purchases have also declined. Many individual farms are failing and their holdings incorporated into big business ventures. While this conglomeration process may have been inevitable, it has been speeded up by the grain embargo, with those farmers caught up in this international situation placed at a serious disadvantage.

This situation demonstrates how issues that divide the powers certainly affect their citizenry negatively. In spite of the disagreement over the Afghan invasion, the denial of grain to the Soviet Union increased hostility and undid to a certain extent the relationship formed by the Nixon détente. Recognizing that the dynamics of knowledge can advance the human condition within the historical process of these great countries, the power blocs in our time are motivated to seek more earnestly than ever before an atmosphere that defuses potential conflicts and eliminates the threat of nuclear war as a means of dealing with international problems. Of course, there is recognition that even in the best-case scenarios, in which the nuclear option has been abolished, conflicts may become so tense that the nuclear option may eventually become reinstated. Thus the abolition of the nuclear option is no guarantee that it will never be used. Hence another scenario has to be established, one that will not require the abolition of world conflict, because the tendency for conflict—be it in sports, economic competition, or the arts and sciences, or expressed by battle or debate—is a permanent irrepressible part of the human condition; it is imbedded in our psyche and genetic make-up and is common to our individual and collective histories.

On the basis of non-military conflict, theories are tested, new approaches in the arts and sciences are formulated, new records set in the arenas of sports competition. A contemporary conflict scenario must form the worst and best cases into a single case that prevents the degeneration of international political conflicts into bloody wars and that eliminates vested interests as a cause of bloody social revolution. Can such an approach be formulated in our contemporary era? Does our era offer an approach that, while not denying our collective and individual tendencies, provides a way to prevent the destruction of civilization and humanity? The answer to these questions lies, indeed, in our dynamics of knowledge, represented by the disequilibrium of which knowledge develops, in which new ideas considered viable within a framework of utility are accepted, and irreparable entropy results in the dissolution of the entropic system.

Knowledge has flourished throughout history, though more intensely during some periods and less so in others. The Dark Ages was one of superstition as knowledge, while the Schoolmen made contributions to another form of knowledge, one more attuned to the spiritual realm. No wonder superstition was so dominant in those times, as the physical world was so little understood. While superstition has never ceased, its decline has been drastic, especially since the post-Newtonian period, when the physical relationships described earlier by Galileo and Kepler were refined by calculus and the Newtonian basis of reasoning.

The benefits of knowledge (accrued as a result of the disequilibrium in our era) are such that even the most repressive dictator seeks this knowledge, not only for convenience in balancing rules in light of competing power factions, but also because the dictator realizes that no dictatorship will endure the ravages of time nor the domestic and international forces of the arts, sciences, and technology. Given the increasing sophistication of a developing world, even a dictator understands that only by applying the tools of knowledge to socioeconomic problems, directing these tools appropriately, and establishing them within the country's infrastructure, can a particular power base remain intact and the country flourish and take its place among the nations—and ensure the dictator's place as rightful and benign ruler, bringing enlightenment to his or her domain.

There is a greater danger to the world's order presented by these dictators who try to hold back the tide of knowledge. By doing so, they are weakened internationally as the enlightened countries tend to shun them, and they become prey to other dictatorships in their geographical regions. This situation brings the great powers into their region, as each competes with the other for the support of the dictators. Where they were once avoided, they become the center of attention as another source of conflict, and a situation that the powers wanted to avoid brings them into collision. With the threat of nuclear confrontation, in these circumstances the support of these countries becomes both overt and covert. Seeking to avoid such a super power confrontation, these great powers are used for the military gain of the dictatorships. Resources are wasted and often lives are lost in the name of realpolitik, in stopping the enemy from gaining a foothold in the sensitive region—all regions are sensitive politically and geographically—and in guarding them from influence of the opposing power. There is another dimension to this type of conflict. Because the powers have more knowledge than these dictatorships, the powers seek to use their knowledge of war against less sophisticated peoples. This warfare is both a great waste of resources and a loss of life, resulting in great frustration for the powers (such as the United States in Vietnam and the Soviet Union in Afghanistan). This frustration may be a motivating factor to seek a peaceful resolution of the conflict and thus bring them to pressure their client countries—when such countries are involved—into discussion and compromise. There is, of course, no guarantee that they will take this path.

It is certain, however, that peaceful coexistence among the nations cannot prevail as long as there are malignant dictatorships keeping their people in darkness. Such countries are prey to others like them, especially when war is used to keep the people's attention diverted from serious domestic issues. Even in our era of knowledge, war, disease, and starvation—the scourges of humanity throughout history—still pose serious threats.

By discussing these problems from the vantage of our contemporary era of knowledge, a new scenario can be formulated, one that negates the destructive aspects of our era and yet is not unrealistic. Such a scenario can be perfectly attainable in our era; perhaps it must be brought about by our era of knowledge.

THE PROMISE OF OUR SOCIAL TIME

In order to explain this scenario, some further comments must be made. Looking at history and the evolution of civilization from prehistory to the present, we can see how humanity has altered social conditions and has, in return, been influenced by them. We can also notice how the basic human behavior patterns have remained unchanged. These patterns are biologically motivated and regulated; both the desire for food and the fear of hunger have always motivated people to search for food, cultivate land, and raise animals for food, though dietary customs have changed from one historical era to another. Vitamin pills and cultivated health foods were unknown in the early social times of the Industrial

Revolution, but they are important sources of nourishment today. Clothing and shelter have also been altered throughout history, but no matter how styles have changed, their basic functions remain the same.

While there have been multivariegated forms and changes throughout our history and development, nevertheless certain constants remain that must be satisfied for humanity to survive and flourish. Just as evolution and the necessities of life are handmaidens of one another, our social time places curbs on our evolutionary patterns.

We must obtain food and water for nourishment, but no longer can we do so without considering the consequences; our use of the soil, of animal sources of food, and of water supplies in our advanced economic conditions have repercussions that must be taken into account. Soil depletion and water pollution are now dangers to our way of life, which were of no consequence in earlier eras. Clothing is now made mostly of synthetics, which make it less expensive, with more styles, limited only by social mores and our imagination; shelter has developed into a highly sophisticated art, in which the lie of the land is considered with respect to the latest in building technology. Yet there remain the basics of clothing and shelter, so that no matter how enlightened and sophisticated we have become, we still share these necessities with our ancestors.

Aggression, which has also served humanity throughout the ages and which we have abused, also must be considered. We are aggressive, but our aggressiveness (which has served us in good stead as a means of self-preservation and hence the preservation of humanity) has also been the source of much destruction. Throughout our history, aggression has aided us in fighting our natural enemies, whether they be peoples of other areas, the elements of nature, or wild beasts. While physicians and psychiatrists understand the chemical reactions in our bodies as defense turns into aggression, they realize the nuances of aggression, accepting that unprovoked aggression is valuable in subduing other peoples whose resources can be conquered, and subservience in all its subtleties can be obtained.

Unprovoked aggression has let to many military conflicts, resulting in two world wars and the military actions that followed the last world war. Even in our social time, these acts of aggression have not subsided, because human nature has evolved very little over our history; in this respect, it leaves a great deal to be desired in light of the demands and requirements of our historical era. Moreover, one difficulty for our social time is that conditions require the abolition of aggression, but this behavior cannot be eliminated totally from our psychological make-up. The question remains as to how aggression can be curbed, given our era of knowledge, and the answer should lie in the scenario that can be worked out in our social time.

Consider the three types of political and social structures that have developed since the beginning of our era and that are the features of our geopolitical map. These are the future-oriented, the present-oriented, and the past-oriented countries. These demarcations are far from arbitrary, for they denote the world's societies in relation to their ability to create and to achieve specified standards of living and to participate in generating the dynamics of our era in our social time.

The future-oriented societies are those that have moved beyond the economic levels of industrialization, as determined at the closing of the Industrial Revolution. These are the postindustrial societies, which have achieved not only product potential, marketing ability, and consumer awareness, but also the ability to develop knowledge within the framework of disequilibrium and exploit this knowledge as technology. These societies are Western in orientation, using Western modes of thinking, while remaining within their own unique historical contexts and traditions.

The concept "Western" is used here because that is the geographical area where the Industrial Revolution began and developed; by "Western," then, is meant those countries that underwent the process of industrialization *and* whose political systems are democratic in our social time. This distinction is important, for not all the countries within this classification were always democratic, nor did each country experience industrialization in the same way the other countries did. One reason for the differences in industrialization is that the sociological characteristics of each country differ from every other. This, of course, results from the traditions and histories of each country, so that the British industrialization, which gave rise to the original industrial impetus, differs from that of France and the United States and even more so radically from the historical processes undergone by the Japanese. This is manifested in the types of products manufactured, the manufacturing processes themselves, and the social work ethic engaged in the approach to industrialization and marketing. Advertising differs among these countries—such as Britain and Japan, for example. Consumer tastes vary, and the product mix is unique to these countries in spite of the equalization process of the multinational companies, as they seek to standardize production and consumer tastes. But this tendency toward equalization is also a consequence of our social time, as industrialization and postindustrialized supply and demand seem to tend toward the same living standards; differences between the countries remain historical and traditional, instead of economic.

The countries' democratic systems of representation also differ, and these differences are also the result of their unique histories. Moreover, two countries in the future-oriented grouping were not always democratic. Germany went through the convulsions of Nazism—with the awakening of its mythological-cum-atavistic past in the form of militarism and racial elitism—and only by being broken in defeat in a bloody war, did the German people achieve democracy. Germany remained within the Western sphere, including France, Britain, and the United States, adapting the democratic process to fit their unique German character.

While the culture of Japan developed far from the conflicts of Europe, it has a history of authoritarian government. Although Japan was divided into factions, the ultimate unity was achieved by the emperor; his rule and authority were accepted to the point of deification. After World War II, the allied forces installed a system of government in which the emperor had to renounce his godhead but retained his title only as a figurehead, and a democratic system of representation was established. It has since taken root in the flexible process of Japanese development.

These societies are future-oriented because they combine the traditions of their past with the state of the art in science and technology and with their creative energies in the arts in a way that enables their initiators, imitators, and innovators to apply their skills most effectively in the ongoing process of creativity. They were very energetic in incorporating their talents in the process of industrialization and remain so in the requirements for the development and expansion of knowledge. They are future-oriented in the important sense that they recognize the strengths and weaknesses of their past histories, but look toward the future in their production processes, their education, and their life-styles. These countries set the trends in product development, in materials to be taught and studied in the schools and universities, and in the fashions and conceptions of the good life.

The second category consists of the nations formed since the end of World War II. These are the new and emerging nations undergoing the processes of economic development, often with the internal conditions of political instability and sometimes turmoil, sometimes with the democratic spirit inherited from their former colonizers, but more often with the menace of arms and insurgency. This category also includes the countries of Latin America; although many existed as countries before World War II, they are now undergoing the industrialization that can bring them into line with the future-oriented countries. These countries never had solid political foundations for stable and enduring forms of government; they have been subjected to coups d'état, dictatorships, and military takeovers, some of which relinquished their power when a degree of stability was achieved to allow the peaceful transition to democracy, while others have maintained their power, becoming more autocratic over time. These conditions are shared with most present-oriented countries; Israel may be the sole exception, for the transfer of political power is conducted entirely within the democratic process set by the Kennesset protocols. The levels of creativity in these countries pertain mostly to the arts, while most of their scientific advancements are based on the works of the future-oriented countries that they have incorporated into their own scientific communities; the main exception is those scientific innovations to meet the countries' specific requirements. Because of their geographical condition—sharing common borders with other present-oriented countries, which are also lacking in historic stability—they have not yet formulated the basis of their existence within a constant and stable political framework from which consensus can be stated and the choices mandated concerning their future directions. They therefore tend to fluctuate in their political alliances between the future- and past-oriented countries, both of which have achieved significant results in the arts and sciences. This fluctuation, however, places them in the position of being client states to these powers, a position that tends to usurp their potential for establishing a unique identity and thus prevents them from becoming minor powers in the dynamics of creativity in their own right. They tend to pursue political goals that will provide them with necessary and immediate short-term benefits, but this, all too often, at the sacrifice of their long-term independence.

The third category, that of the past-oriented countries, base their social, political, economic, and foreign policies on the teachings of the leaders who established their countries. The Soviet Union, Communist China, and the Arab countries fall within this category. The communist countries' constitutions were written in the framework of Marxist-Leninist teachings; their decisions in all matters are made in conformity with these teachings as understood and interpreted by their leaders. This does not mean that these countries have neglected industrialization; indeed, Russia under the last czar (Nicholas II) had achieved a degree of industrialization, which was interrupted by the involvement in World War I and by the disruptions of the October Revolution. China industrialized under the leadership of Chairman Mao, only to have it interrupted during the Cultural Revolution. In both great nations now there is a re-evaluation of economic planning and a move toward liberalization. These are manifestations of moving into harmony with the future-oriented societies to gain their benefits, but not at the cost of relinquishing their unique systems and neglecting their individualistic and rich histories.

The Arab countries are included in this category because of their new-found fundamentalism, which requires that they base their socioeconomic and politicial systems and conduct their foreign affairs on the teachings of the Koran. The problem confronting these countries is that, with the great wealth brought by their abundance of oil, they seek to move into our social time, but their religious leaders established in power refuse to allow deviations from their holy writing and its interpretations. Hence, not only has their industry suffered because religous teachings hinder expansion and commercial practices (such as paying a price for money), but their education systems are past-oriented in the sense that they lack the freedom of thought and inquiry of the future-oriented societies; nor have they the inner dynamism for establishing identities in our social time, as do the present-oriented countries. While they, like the present-oriented countries, rely on the Western nations predominantly for their technological skills and know-how, they seek their strength in their religion. They thus lack the necessary ability to separate their religious devotion from the needs of modern activity; this places them within the pale of orientation toward ancient ideas and practices irrelevant to our contemporary era of knowledge. The dynamics of creativity in the future-oriented societies have not been realized in these countries, and they rely on their wealth to purchase their needs, instead of taking their places in the dynamics of our contemporary era.[3]

Having discussed these three types of country that compose our modern geopolitical world, the scenario can now be stated in which the worst-case conditions of global conflicts have been eliminated and the best case of world peace rejected as unattainable. For we cannot continue on our present path of limited conflicts waged by surrogates, because such conflicts are unwieldy and tend to more global strife, which can bring us to the brink of another world war.

The only viable alternative to those two unreasonable scenarios is to let the dynamics of our era take hold and move us along the line of evolution, merging these three types of society into a future-oriented framework in which the histories of these countries are recognized for what they are—as their foundation, to be studied and appreciated but neither to be negated nor to be relied upon too extensively as the basis of the present policies or future direction.

This, however, is far from a passive position; it is not an argument for some form of "natural" motion of the course of history, in which we are merely passive travelers. If we were passive, we would be complacent, not only politically, but also within the realm of generating knowledge; we would negate the dynamics of creativity that yield us our knowledge and contributions. Needless to say, the dynamics of our era will not allow us to become passive, for the search for knowledge has become too intense and the dynamics of creativity too entrenched in their influences on our lives.

We must bring our creative endeavors to the fore if our social time is to be realized fully. The circles of areas which define and delineate our subjects and disciplines will expand, and new theories will be developed; our knowledge will continue its encroachment on the disciplines, thus providing feedback and new information, increasing the rate of entropy and sparking the drive for imitation and creativity. Our social time must be understood as the result of our own efforts and not merely a process of history. We must become more aware of societies different from our own, and the differences within our societies must help us understand that different societies can be equally constructive in the broad dynamics of creativity. The past- and present-oriented societies, for example, are most certainly capable of making viable contributions, even more so once they move into the future-oriented sphere. Humanity is a hostile breed by nature, as the wars of our collective histories have so aptly demonstrated. The military option must be reduced and our aggressiveness channeled into other competitive forms, be it in national sports or in the endeavors of imitation, initiation, and innovation that are now occurring in the areas of knowledge.

Is this utopian? Is it merely another impractical scenario, with no reason or possibility for its being considered, let alone achieved? It is far from utopian and unrealistic, for with the dynamics of creativity expanding our knowledge, it has the ambience for its realization in our social time. Consider, for example, the three types of society discussed previously. Those societies that are future-oriented are establishing the materialistic living patterns, innovating in the areas of technology, applying the fruits of technology to industry, causing and identifying more problems, and improving the arts and sciences by merging them with technological approaches. These societies are the pioneers in the knowledge fields and set the trends for the other social forms to follow.

In contrast, the past-oriented societies are following the patterns set by the future-oriented societies, because the future-oriented societies generate knowledge and technology. They have also to maintain competitive postures with respect to the future-oriented societies, as they vie for the support of the present-oriented societies and as they compete among themselves for influence in these countries. They have to acquire technology on levels that their systems have been incapable of developing because they are past-orientation and they refuse to consider future conditions that might deviate from their historical foundations. The incorporation of future-oriented technologies into their societies is, moreover, a significant development and one that needs encouragement (as long as these technologies have no military importance). By obtaining such information an internal conflict arises—being currently experienced by Communist China and the Soviet Union—in which the past meets the future in the applications of these technologies. For how can a society that is oriented to the past, that bases its socioeconomic, political, and foreign-policy decisions on the teachings of its past, incorporate technologies developed by societies that (while most certainly respecting the past and celebrating it on national holidays and important anniversaries) look to the future and seek to develop their technology with the future as their orientation? In this inevitable clash of the past with the future, it is the future that will most certainly win, for three important reasons. One reason is the obvious situation that the past, while important, is gone; it holds weight only as a set of circumstances, data, and relationships. It cannot be altered, only better understood as more information is revealed and more relationships are clarified. The second reason, also obvious, is that the future has not yet been realized, and the events of the present will assuredly affect future development. By obtaining future-oriented technology in the present, the future can be better understood, and the relevant changes in society can be implemented to cope with the future-oriented technologies and their implications for both present- and future-oriented societies. The third reason is political in nature. It refers to the international competition existing between the future- and past-oriented societies for the present-oriented societies' alliance and alignment in the ordering of the geopolitical struggle for resources, markets, and military bases. This not only results in greater efforts by the future-oriented societies to continue the expansion and development of knowledge in disequilibrium, but also results in the intensification of the clash between the past and future in the past-oriented societies, as they incorporate future-oriented technologies. These technologies are difficult to incorporate in socioeconomic and political climates in which the past is so heavy that very little consideration is given to the future. Therefore, there must be a degree of adaptation of these technologies so that they can fit and be deployed to work within the society. This requires retraining, rethinking, and reeducating; these cannot be accomplished without loosening the reins on the spirit of inquiry. Thus a thawing-out will occur—and is occurring now—and although there will be continuing conflict between the conservatives (who are reluctant to accept change, considering change a betrayal of the principles, ideologies, and teachings on which the society was and is being formed) and the liberals (who, while being patriots, recognize the need for change with the adoption of new technologies and the dynamics these technologies will generate). It is this clash that is necessary for the re-evaluation of values and for bringing the past-oriented societies into the dynamics of our social time in our contemporary era.

The position of the present-oriented societies in our geopolitial pattern merely demonstrates the unity in diversity of our globe and its demarcation into nation-states. For the most part these countries are undecided in the direction of their alliance, which is one reason why it is tempting for the powers to guide them, either with covert threats or with the carrot of trade and aid. These countries provide a genuine source of competition among the powers, which also helps the past-oriented societies to move into a future-oriented direction. But what of these present-oriented societies with respect to their own direction? How can they maneuver among the various political pressures placed on them by the competing powers? It is in these countries that the disequilibrium dynamics of creativity are the most promising while at the same time most difficult. These countries have very little precedent on which to build; their histories are usually chaotic, and in the case of those countries formed mostly after World War II, mostly with memories of tribal unification and strife—alternating as the case has been between these two conditions—only to be unified once again under colonial rule. They find whatever traditions they may have in the foundations of their previous colonial circumstances upon achieving sovereignty. Hence, these countries are prepared for change, while at the same time they are prepared to honor their traditions and those parts of the past they consider worth honoring. Thus, neither tradition nor the need for future orientation is strong, and these countries find their immediate situations far too pressing. They need economic development, they require the building of a viable infrastructure for expansion within their territorial borders, and they must have a sound and constructive education system in order to maintain their independence from the big powers; these problems are far too pressing to be tied to either the past or the future.

In the future-oriented societies, the dynamics of knowledge are integral and are taken more or less for granted; in the past-oriented societies, the dynamics of knowledge are limited, restricted by their people's abilities to incorporate them and to expand on them; this depends directly on their heritage and the emphasis their leaders have placed and their people have accepted on growth and development. It is to the advantage of these present-oriented societies that neither future nor past orientations have set in to restrict them, for this provides them with the degree of freedom necessary for accepting the knowledge useful for building their own countries, adapting it as required by the countries' unique situations, and allowing the knowledge to be incorporated, worked, and expanded in the domestic atmosphere. These countries can engage in social experimentation by applying the knowledge of the future-oriented societies and the approaches of the past-oriented societies; they can also expand and develop their own unique knowledge systems to meet their countries' requirements and thus get on with business: building their own countries in their own ways, using their characteristics and abilities to compete with other nations in economics, art, and science. Their common and collective goal—to take their places in our era of knowledge as contributors and not merely receivers of the benefits of dynamic creativity—will then be realized. Their technical capabilities will then be ready to cope with the new technologies, as their industries will be modernized. The works of their artists will be accepted by the future-oriented societies, not as curiosities, expressions of different ethnic attitudes and traditions, but as trendsetters in their own right, both enjoyable and educational to Western societies. Another point that must not be neglected is that once these countries become engaged in the dynamics of knowledge, they will devote the greater part of their efforts to expanding these dynamics by building up their industries in competition with other countries and concentrate on their infrastructures and education systems to maintain their competitive stances. Thus, they will spend less time serving as battlegrounds among themselves and as surrogates in the conflict situations of the big powers.

This, then, is the promise of our social time—for the world to be united in peace instead of being divided in the useless causes of war, to struggle in competition instead of fighting and wasting human lives and precious resources. Needless to say, there are other battles to be fought, if true peace as described above is to be achieved; there are other enemies, just as deadly as the bombs, bullets, and missiles that take lives and destroy property. Our world has vast food supplies, yet countries are starving, there are great centers of learning, but too many people are illiterate; while our medical knowledge and services are extremely advanced, disease is still rampant. These are the plagues of our social time. We still devote great resources to the tools of war, the very means of poised destruction that threaten and divide mankind; yet we engage in the development of knowledge necessary to unite humanity. We require our scientists and technicians to improve on weapons already lethal enough, while we require other talented people to confront and end these three scourges. Moreover, pockets of poverty in the future-oriented societies indicate that resources are being used in their infrastructures without complete regard to knowledge, and this is an economic waste. The past-oriented countries, with their policies formulated on the ideals of their leaders, have no excuse either for the hidden unemployment, poverty, disease, and illiteracy that plague them, for these were not in their leaders' scheme of things for their respective countries and should have been prevented at the outset.

It is also necessary to note that poverty, illiteracy, and disease are the most virulent breeding grounds for social and political conflict and often lead to rebellion and war. Because of their inherent instability, with internal power politics threatening the fabric of the present-oriented societies, and because of their high rates of poverty, illiteracy, and disease, they are fertile breeding grounds for the big powers to court their opposition politicians or support the regime in control, as the case may be, as a way to destabilize the situation even further, allowing rebellion and providing the international basis for war. The two conflicting ideologies have so far offered no real assistance in the choice of the path for the present-oriented societies. Marxism-Leninism—past-oriented and therefore offering solutions in slogans, appealing to the already committed and the somewhat unsophisticated—has failed because, when put into practice, it has resulted in the establishment of an elitist form of government: a sort of power elite ostensibly in the name of the people but in practice to maintain the elites' power and control. The capitalist ideology is less subtle about its propaganda and perhaps offers a better deal for the people in the very long run, for it brings with it another type of power elite, that of institutionalized big business in the form of a government based on favoritism to industry or one controlled by industry. While this is not without its difficulties, it does provide employment and eventually the expansion of knowledge, as new technology has to be incorporated into industry, people must be retrained, and are thus reeducated. Still, business people and government officials tend to engage in collusion, keeping the big money at the top and leaving very little comparatively to trickle down to the general population; this merely feeds the flames of dissent and opens the way for the rival Marxist-Leninist opposition to gain a foothold and attempt to usurp power. Many developing countries have become battlegrounds for this reason, with either dictatorship and the loss of freedom or a left-wing takeover with a past-oriented and repressive policy maintaining poverty and alienating all those industrialists who could have established a noncollusive industrial base and provided the beginnings of economic growth.

This is another reason why these present-oriented societies are so important for the well-being of our globe today. Not only are they a serious factor in the present instability, but they offer the greatest promise for stability. In an earlier work, I stated these sentiments:

> The challenge exists and the struggle for growth and independence is in earnest. The leadership in each developing country must come to the fore to work with both internal and international forces in building their countries. The alternative is famine, illiteracy, military and ideological war, reliance on the conscience of the developed countries—in other words, more of the same.[4]

This is surely the case, for dynamics do not operate on their own but rely on the politicians, leaders, and industrialists to implement them. These forces exist in the arts and sciences, in technology, and in industry, which rely on these for development and expansion. There is no mystery to the dynamics of knowledge; they will continue to expand and generate if allowed to operate, and they will stagnate and wither if restricted, so that the countries that do not employ them fully will continue to maintain their client status. The assistance these countries ask for and receive (often in the form of cash and money credit transfers, sometimes as food, clothing, industrial goods, and services) is fairly easily obtained, but this assistance, as well as tying these countries to their benefactors, has other drawbacks. The politicians who negotiate these conditions are enhanced in their positions of power as they have positive, tangible results to their negotiations. The difficulty here is that they are short-term and seriously counterproductive for development and independence; this success prevents or at best restricts the leaders from bringing their countries into our social time, tending to foster further dependence instead of seeking the internal development so necessary for independence and growth. The tendency is real and too often realized for all economic activity to be directed to maintain the client-protector relationship, sometimes encouraged by the providing countries, usually necessary for the support of a political faction against its opponents. The socioeconomic consequences, however, are devastating, for not only do they increase the lack of genuine dynamics in the arts and sciences within their own countries, with the arts remaining "ethnic" and the sciences and technologies borrowed, but they continue a situation that, in the power struggles and competition for markets and political support, is untenable. Either the situation will be rectified so that these countries' leaders bring them into our social time, or they will continue to be the breeding grounds for the client-patron relationship, for oppression and rebellion, and for war. There is no third possibility, no other direction for them to choose; not to resolve their situations is, for these countries, the postponing of the inevitable—postponing, but not for very long in our dynamic world.

This is not to belittle the necessity of economic, political, and military assistance, for each is important in the development process. Economic assistance allows the recipient countries to purchase raw materials lacking in their own countries, or the finished products in which their own raw materials are composites, but which they lack industrial capability to manufacture. However, for the good of the recipient country, it should be the assisting country's intention and the receiving country's motivation that the aid will establish an economic base necessary for moving into the patterns of production and consumption necessary for building a strong domestic economy. As this is all too frequently not the case, economic assistance is used as a bargaining source for both the receiving country and its donor, with the leaders of the receiving countries often corrupt and on the donor's payroll, sometimes with the donor's consent and sometimes through their own political maneuverings. A further consequence is the brain drain: a one-way migration of people who acquired skills and talents and who are unable to express themselves adequately and achieve living standards commensurate with their abilities. The consequence is a loss of important and necessary people in the development of their countries to the benefit of the future-oriented societies to which they move.

Political assistance tends to be granted on a partisan basis; support is offered to those present-oriented countries that opt for the system of the supporting superpower. Because of this, economic and military support are also granted. But the relationship, because of the global dynamics that prevail as the great powers seek their allegiance, is very uneasy. A proven political ally at one time can shift to the opposite power at another. This depends on the type of support given, its intensity and durability as the forces of global strategy are deployed by the big powers and the developing countries. Often, a threat-situation develops: the developing countries threaten to go to the opposite side if their demands are not met. This can be a disquieting game, played with the realization of the great powers (which are prepared to tolerate a degree of such maneuvering), but one that cannot be pushed too far, for the big power engaged in such a game may seek to persuade the country's neighbors into an alliance that may be to that country's disadvantage. Political support is necessary, but it must be kept in proper perspective, according to the countries' needs on both sides, so that the degree of freedom for maneuvering by both sides are made clear and the consequences of their actions are apparent.

Military aid is an extension of both economic and political support. Not only does this aid allow the client country to be strong in face of potential external strife, but also provides inner strength against internal opposition. Thus, this too is a double-edged means of assistance, for it allows for legitimate self-defense in the unstable regions that include the majority of the developing world areas, but also allows for regimes to maintain their power absolutely if the leadership so chooses. However, should policies be adopted not to the liking of the patron countries, they can exert leverage primarily through economic restrictions, such as sanctions, and secondarily through the political support of opposing countries in the region. The mere threat to employ these policies may be sufficient to hold the client country in line.

The combination of economic, political, and military assistance is certainly difficult for the leadership of the present-oriented countries to resist. The availability of massive aid in hard currency can provide the financing for new projects, such as improvements in the health and education systems. New knowledge can be absorbed, and the funding of industries will allow for new technologies to be applied and auxiliary businesses to be established; the client country can compete with other countries in similar situations. This funding greatly alleviates the growing pains of industry, so that these countries receiving these benefits can move fairly swiftly into the era of knowledge in our social time. The leaders of these present-oriented countries need to consider the costs involved to their countries and to their positions. Only the most astute of politicians can maneuver and move between the temptations and pitfalls of receiving aid and becoming either personally corrupt or placing the country in a client situation, thereby losing independence. The opportunities to reach the heights of economic and military power in their countries require that only those leaders of the highest ability and integrity seek office. Human frailties are sufficient to bring them to make poor decisions when the fate of the country is concerned; while this can be understood, it is all too often damaging. The position of these countries is precarious enough, and possibilities for personal corruption are rife. All too many times potentially great leaders have succumbed to megalomania and corruption; in these countries it has been demonstrated all too frequently that people of leadership abilities possessing the necessary high caliber and stature are difficult to come by.

This dual objective of the developing countries seeking entry into our social time and being encouraged and assisted into this transition by the big powers has led too often to neocolonialism, instead of genuine independence. Traditional colonialism has been almost abolished; only a few possessions, conquered before the end of the Industrial Revolution, are in the control of colonizing countries. Another form of colonialism prevails since World War II which is manifested in two ways. There are the power blocs which were demarcated at the end of the war; the Soviet bloc includes much of Eastern Europe, with Rumania and Yugoslavia having special status, while the Western alliance, having granted political independence to West Germany, still maintains large troop contingents on its soil, thereby restricting West Germany's military decision-making. Complete political and military independence has, however, been given to Japan and the other Axis countries. West Germany is a special case, because the German peoples were responsible for two bloody wars and because of the separation of forces that occurred and still exists in the somewhat tense environment in Germany, with the Berlin zone being the focal point of the tension. Moreover, the neocolonialism in the Soviet bloc is uneasy, as there is constant threat to the Soviet government that its satellite countries may break out in revolt, either violently as in Hungary and Poland, or quietly as with the Dubcek regime in Czechoslovakia. These countries are also present-oriented, even though they claim a past-orientation because they belong to the Soviet sphere. The point is, that while there exists a strong Soviet influence, it is tempered by the fiery spirit of independence, which has led to revolt and to the special relationships that exist with Rumania and Yugoslavia. These countries maintain a difficult path with their allegiance to the Soviet way while seeking their own entry into our social time.

Neocolonialism within our social time has its own unique features. Consider, for example, the oil-producing countries and their use of oil to influence the foreign policies of other countries.[5] Prior to the Yom Kippur War in 1973, oil prices were very low, allowing industrial expansion on cheap energy. The rapid and dramatic increase in oil prices brought about recession in the Western countries and resulted in a revamping of energy priorities. Conservation and the use of coal and solar energy took time to develop;

until this was achieved, there was a unique alignment of political forces: the oil-producing countries exerted pressure through the threat of embargo, forcing the consuming countries to conduct their foreign policies in ways that appeased the producers. Moreover, voting in the United Nations against Israel was taken for granted, with only the United States coming to Israel's defence in the international forum. This was not totally a one-sided affair, however, for these very same oil producers needed Western technology and industry as well as weaponry to conduct their military ventures and keep their citizens in line. They had thus to make their own interests coincide with their Western client-cum-benefactors, and those oil ministers who studied the global situation and had sufficient insight into the dynamics of power realized that their windfall would be short-lived and that they had to exploit their advantage to the fullest in the time available until the alternative energy sources took over. While exerting their independence, they were, in turn, still subservient to the Westen countries; although they have since moved partly into our social time, their policies are unstable, and the power they once exerted is greatly depleted.

The second form that neocolonialism takes is unique to our time. The traditional method of territorial occupation has become distasteful since World War II. The new colonialism is economically oriented, as the Western countries have taken over much of the means of production and the ethos of other countries. Of course, this has advantages for the developing countries. They have been unable to create their own industrial revolutions, the retraining of their peoples being such a costly affair and practically impossible without industrial guidance. When the future-oriented countries handle the industries of these countries, skills are taught, employment granted, and education obtained. Moreover, their infrastructures are developed to allow for further industrialization. This shortcut to economic growth, however, is limiting in the area of real independence, for there are never economic ties in this type of relationship without political obligations, affecting relationships with the opposing power blocs and the surrogates of these opposing powers. Moreover, as far as the ethos of the developing countries is concerned, this is far from avoidable. Along with the development of industry and the educational and physical infrastructure that accompany foreign assistance in industrialization, comes the ethos of the future-oriented society; it is a part of the very ideas provided for the developing country. This situation becomes more variegated, if not more complex, if the developing country relies on more than one future-oriented society for its industrial and socioeconomic infrastructure. This does not, however, lead to a mini culture-clash as these differing countries of the future-orientation mix within the developing country. These countries share the common bond of future-orientation also shared by the developing country, which requires the ethos of the future-oriented societies as much as can possibly be incorporated and absorbed.

This is, however, still neocolonialism, for it allows the future-oriented countries to dictate both the internal and foreign policies of the client country. This is unsettling, in spite of its benefits. The relationship is predominatly one-sided and is subject to the fickleness of the future-oriented society's leadership. On the grassroots level, the relationship may be strong and binding, but foreign policy often shifts as the opinions of the benefactor country's leaders shift. A country once favored in its client relationship can be bypassed and relegated to a lower position on the scale of priorities as a counter to a policy shift of the opposing power; still other considerations within the future-oriented society may bring about such a change. For the developing country, this can be very disquieting; it may respond by moving from a single client state to one influenced and supported by several future-oriented societies. In this situation, internal competition develops among the future-oriented societies involved, which can be either exploited to the developing country's benefit by its obtaining the maximum possible support from each of the competing countries, or it can generate hostilities through the blatant exploitation of the situation. In any case, tact and reserve are required, tempering the pressing needs of development. But independence must always be compromised, whether to the single power or to the multitude of countries supplying the resources and industry for development. The leaders of the developing countries must reach their goal of growth and solid infrastructure as swiftly as the conditions allow, and the compromising of their countries' independence must be made with as little loss as possible. For only when the goals of infrastructure and growth are achieved can these countries stand in real partnership with the future-oriented societies and move into the era of knowledge in our social time.

These countries will then be self-sufficient economically, importing as well as exporting, and will make significant contributions in the arts and sciences, the works of which will be incorporated into the general dynamics of knowledge; initiation, imitation, and innovation in the dynamics of creativity will occur as new problems arise and others are solved.

In these developing societies no past- or future-orientation has set in, which gives them freedom for experimentation, taking into account the histories of these societies and the contributions they have already made. As the knowledge systems of the developed countries are adapted to the developing countries' needs, they acquire different dimensions and can be altered to meet the people's requirements. So when experiment and adaptation are undertaken, they will usually result in a new form as original as the people they serve, and they will be the focus of interest for the other societies. This change is itself a source of the creativity needed to make the adaptations; if of sufficient utility, the creative contributions can be adapted to the needs of other countries. This is a step in the generation of knowledge, for such adaptations must be original and hence creative.

How this is accomplished, again, depends on the skills of leadership, the understanding of the people, the time it takes for industrialization take hold in the infrastructure and the educational systems, and the ability of the people to adopt the ethos of their patron country to their own unique culture.

One thing is clear: that the problems of the developing countries are extremely pressing. Famine in Africa, for example, still prevails and is worsened by the wars in that region. Foodstuffs sent to alleviate the famine are often rerouted because of the wars, such as in Ethiopia, where many people starved and many more have gone hungry and are debilitated as a consequence. Disease and illiteracy are not restricted geographically and certainly call for elimination. The Common Market has food in abundance that could be distributed to the needy, and the United States agricultural surpluses could be also employed to remove starvation. Disease and malnutrition too often go hand in hand; with the proper reallocation of foodstuffs and the proper agricultural planning, both the immediate problems of food shortages and related diseases and the long-term problem of removing famine from the earth can be achieved. Proper medical care in both private and public sectors of these countries can keep diseases down to manageable levels, thereby abolishing forever the plagues that ravage these areas. Illiteracy should have been abolished centuries ago, but an uneducated people is easy to keep in subservience. Hence the colonial approach and the poor education in these countries and their need for the future-oriented societies. While long-term approaches to these problems are certainly required, immediate short-term solutions are also called for; these problems, however, have been aggravated by neocolonialist subservience and wars, as witnessed by the conditions in the Middle East, in Asia, and in Africa. Granted their need for assistance, therefore, but in the dynamics of power politics, the developing countries can no longer afford to play off one power against the other to achieve a better deal. The big powers have also become skilled in this game due to the lessons learned over the years, such as Egypt's ouster of the Soviets after receiving their financial and military assistance, and such countries as Honduras and Nicaragua acting hostile at worst and indifferent at best after receiving assistance from the United States.

The leaders of these present-oriented countries must be aware that their mandates depend on how they handle these pressing problems of poverty, illiteracy, and disease. They must move into industrialization as swiftly and efficiently as possible and must aim still further, to the postindustrial status that will grant their countries true sovereignty and independence, enabling them to take their places among the nations in our social time, instead of remaining recipients of aid and pawns in the power game of global maneuvering.

These leaders cannot allow for the slow processes of industrialization, for the pressures on them do not grant them this luxury. They must take existing and continuing contributions and adapt them to their countries' needs and requirements; they must bring to their peoples the will to learn and the desire to be economically productive. They must break the cycles of disease associated with their people's living patterns, so to build healthier societies to cope with the contemporary world. They must bring industries that can aid in the educational processes and mold those (and the auxiliary industries that will arise as a consequence) into patterns unique to their countries, so that new products that invite imitation in other countries will be developed. The clock of history cannot be turned back. We live in a new era with a new promise, but the old ways are still too much with us.

The future- and past-oriented countries have established their paths. There is the possibility, indeed the necessity, that the past- and present-oriented countries, while not rejecting their traditions or turning their backs on their heritage, will nevertheless recognize the past for what it is and leave it in its proper perspective. The postindustrial societies, future-oriented, set the standards in the arts and sciences, in industry and technology; this is recognized by both the past- and the present-oriented societies as they seek the future-oriented societies' assistance and knowledge. Indeed, the past-oriented societies are loosening up their reliance on their pasts, as they seek industrial and scientific assistance of the future-oriented societies. Perhaps the movement to the future-oriented direction has already begun in earnest.

One of the real challenges for the world lies with the present-oriented societies, for they provide experimental grounds for new societies as they benefit from the experiences of the past- and future-oriented societies in their own development. They cannot undergo their own industrial revolutions, for their needs are too pressing, and they lack the time. Moreover, with the advantages of living in our contemporary era of knowledge, these people in these countries can take short-cuts in their development. They are the pivot countries; as they change their customs and life styles that do not fit in with such development, as they discard the realpolitik of the earlier era, the direction they take determines who are their allies. Fickleness on their part, moving from one big power to another to suit their own ends, is also a throwback to an earlier era; with the existing weaponry and subtle methods of subversion, such fickleness will be aptly rewarded with disruption and unrest.

These developing countries have the opportunity to enter into our social time and build new societies that neither deny the past nor belittle their mixed cultural heritage, but that will allow the development of their skills in industry, art, and science. Thus they will gain their own independence of expression and freedom from the forms of neocolonialism that manifest the power politics that developed after World War II and are distinctly characteristic of our historical era of knowledge.

There is certainly much to lament in our historical era. We can look back and see the dictatorships in Haiti, the uprisings in Poland and Hungary, and the crushing of Dubcek's regime in the Prague Spring, which sought to give socialism a new and different face. We can criticize the wars in Algeria, Korea, and Vietnam and the battles in the Middle East and Southeast Asia. We can condemn the onerous apartheid in South Africa, censure Batista's autocratic regime, which fell to Castro, and criticize the Castro regime for not living up to its promise and for establishing another form of dictatorship.

But we have to take notice that the United Nations still functions, despite all its faults. We have to appreciate that in this era the old forms of colonial oppression have almost completely vanished and that many countries have achieved their independence. We must appreciate that we have moved out of the period of industrializaion to the era of knowledge, where the contributions to the arts and sciences have never before been so numerous and so significant. We can condemn those politicians who let their people starve because of internal strife, but we should not forget that we have the ability for the first time in history to free ourselves of nature's whims and abolish famine and drought with the proper approaches. We have walked on the moon, sent our spaceships to the far reaches of our solar system, and have even begun farming seabeds. This is our era, and it seems that there is nothing we cannot accomplish if we direct our efforts and knowledge to the challenge.

The scenario is most certainly possible, in light of our present successes and of the potential held by our future. It can be achieved, for the dynamics of knowledge in our social time are influencing the past- and present-oriented societies and moving them into future orientation. Let there be no mistake, however; this movement will not occur of necessity, for inertia is powerful, creating the indecisiveness of the present-oriented countries with regard to the direction they should take and of the past-oriented countries, which need the future-oriented benefits but are wary and thus reluctant to shed their historical chains. Moreover, many people do not understand our era and the promises it holds. They cling to outmoded ways and neglect the dynamics of creativity, thereby holding onto past and outdated systems; they are reluctant to relinquish their truth-attitudes and methods of working and the ways they think of the world. They maintain their styles of thought and procedure in their own professional niches, often disguising their reluctance to change with the jargon of liberalism, wary of their ideas being altered by the appealing if somewhat chilly winds of creativity.

Theirs is not a realistic attitude, for change is a process of our time, so that outmoded entropic systems, while being valid and of utility at one time, are now historical and bear on the present day only with their historical value. They have missed the important message, which is clear to those who understand our era and the social time in which we now live: that truth is not knowledge, for knowledge is changing and truth is permanent and eternal, that knowlege carries its own seeds of entropy, and truth is on a higher plane, untouchable by the ravages of entropy.

For our social time to be realized to its fullest, conflict should test ideas and contributions and not the integrity of peoples nor of countries. In our time, politicians should govern and seek solutions to the unrelenting problems that affect us, while the dynamics of creativity should provide the tools of our conceptualization and the generation of new ideas. There is no historical mechanism involved, for we have developed to the point that creativity, with its dynamics, is at our disposal. This is the promise that our era and our social time holds for all humanity; we need the wisdom to understand our new era and to eliminate the fears and uncertainties that make us hesitant to partake fully in its promise.

10

Further Remarks

> What we call civilization—the accumulation of knowledge which has come down to us from our forefathers—is the fruit of human thought and toil. It is not the result of labour of ancestors of any separate class of people who exist today and therefore is by right the common heritage of all. Every little child who is born into the world no matter whether he is clever or dull, whether he is physically perfect or lame, or blind, no matter how much he may excel or fall behind his fellows in other respects, in one thing he is at least their equal—he is one of the heirs of all ages that have gone before.
>
> Robert Tressell, *The Ragged Trousered Philanthropists,* 1978

COMMENTS ON HISTORY

It is only natural for all decent people to react to the sentiment stated by Tressell with complete and uncompromising agreement, for in light of the events and deeds in our collective past and recent history, it is certainly repugnant to maintain the priorities and superiority of an elite class of people as the rightful inheritors of our earth; it is equally repugnant and simply not true to maintain that persons unable to compete in one field will also fail in all others. On the contrary, the sentiment Tressell expressed is the very same that has served as the foundation of the great democracies and is the basis of the creative and future-oriented societies, as manifested in their artistic, scientific, and technological output.

All peoples, regardless of their geographical boundaries, their political affiliations, their religions, their occupations, are all inheritors of civilization. We share its artistic and scientific contributions, its disasters and wars, and its energies that have shaped the borders of our nations and contributed to its achievements. We are the inheritors of the knowledge and the wisdom of our collective history; we have come to understand that knowledge considered true in one historical era has been demonstrated to be false in those which followed. We have come to view knowledge in terms of its utility and its entropy; we see that truth and falsity are absolutes and are thus not applicable in dealing and working with knowledge.

Throughout our collective history, we have demonstrated the trait of curiosity, seeking to find meaning and understanding the natural and human forces that control our destinies. Since our earliest awareness of our history we have sought its meaning, looked for patterns that will yield the paths of our past, and tried to understand the movements that will take us to our future.

We have looked at history through the conceptual lenses of our eras, for these dominate all our prespectives. Hence, in the middle stages of the Industrial Revolution, when mechanics were important in the workings of industry, we turned to a mechanical approach for our meaning. Both Darwinism and Hegelianism are mechanistic, and these theories dominated our thinking; it was little wonder, then, that Karl Marx wrote his economic theory in the framework of the Hegelian-cum-Darwinian mechanism, in which the final stage of socioeconomic evolution would be the withering away of the state, to be achieved after industrialization has been completed, all the class barriers eliminated, an egalitarian distribution of the goods and services produced by the classless society guaranteed by social and economic ethics and mores.

In this same mechanistic spirit, Oswald Spengler approached history from the position of historical cycles operating in an evolutionary manner according to the cultural spirit of the time. His approach was open-ended, for he saw no end to history but its further evolution, with great powers rising to exert themselves and eventually falling by the wayside as other nations replaced them in power and influence. For Spengler, history has no end, no final objective to be achieved; it is the dynamics of change, mechanistically operating, that brings the fall and rise of political powers establishing new historical eras.

These approaches seek to find the essence of history, allowing us to gain comprehension of our present time and our past. Nevertheless, the mechanistic approach to history raises an important question. In our comprehension, we realize that we alone hold our fate in our own hands; we have the power to destroy ourselves completely with our sophisticated weaponry, or we may let ourselves enter fully into the dynamics of our time and let our arts and sciences, our technology and our industry, expand through creativity. Therefore, as we view the processes of history—from the dawn of history to our present era—can we find the essence of history, which will enable us to better understand our past, present, and future?

This point was addressed by David Hackett Fischer in his book, *Historian's Fallacies,* in which he considered the notion of essence among the 101 fallacies he discussed. Fischer described the fallacy of essence as the old idea that everything has something deep inside called essence, which is the profound inner core or reality. He stated:

> The most durable of secular superstitions is not susceptible to reasoned refutation. The existence of essences, like the existence of ghosts, cannot be disproved by any rational method. But it *is* possible to demonstrate that a belief in essences, like the belief in ghosts, involves an empiricist in certain difficulties.[1]

Holding to essences may involve an empiricist in certain difficulties; while recognizing the importance of empiricism in science, it too has its difficulties. The theories of Galileo, Kepler, Newton, and Einstein are none of them empirical, although the results of their theories in experimentation can be tested for validity. Each based his theory on metaphysical assumptions, which were most certainly integral to the theory. At the time Galileo wrote, there was no refutation possible for his relativity, on which he transformed his physics into mathematical notation. Kepler's "harmony of the spheres" was not taken seriously (mainly because Galileo ridiculed it); yet that harmony provided the basis for his approach to astronomy and his discovery of the elliptical paths of the planets, on which Newton constructed his theory of astronomy. Furthermore, the author of the topology of Hell, Sir Isaac Newton, also merged Galileo's earth physics and Kepler's astronomy, formulating a new unified theory of physics in which he argued for the "ghost" of gravity as the essence of all physical theory.[2] Moreover, there is no empiricism in Einstein's theory, in which particles move at speeds nearing that of light, lightspeed is the fastest possible motion and reached only by light, and space is curved in a four-dimensional continuum; his theory is the blending of metaphysics with physics in both reality and in the imaginary experiments in the macro and micro cosmos. His metaphysics forms the essence of his physics.

While the works of these scientists are essentialist (maintaining that things and theories have essences), they still remain extremely important and significant in the development of knowledge; they certainly provided and continue to provide their imitators with material to test empirically, a process that requires the exploration of their theories and restructuring of the theoretical statements to bring them into the realm of experimentation. It was this exploration that brought Galileo's and Kepler's work into entropy, because these works could not stand alone in a unified world of physics and were unable to solve problems, which arose consequently and which Newton's theory handled. Newton's theory became entropic because it could not relate to the "black box ideal radiation" experiment devised by Max Planck and solved by Einstein. Einstein's theory is in question because of its difficulties with quantum physics—the clash between Einsteinian determinism and Heisenbergian indeterminism—and because of the unsolved questions pertaining to black holes and white holes in the reaches of outer space.

The physical sciences, considered the epitome of empiricism, are far from being free of essentialism. Should theories of history be disqualified because of essentialism? History does not merely relate facts but seeks to determine their causes and motivations; theories of history explore the dynamics of relationships, ultimately attempting to determine if there are universal laws of history. Historians seek to understand their particular fields of inquiry and to expand the information and relationships formulated into patterns that can be used for understanding both our collective past and the present, as well as providing guides in our projective hypotheses into our future. This method is essentialist and is based on the notion that people tend to be alike, no matter their origins or nationalities, that people's behavior can be understood regardless of the manifold cultural and ethnic differences, and that this behavior can be generalized and formulated into standard patterns that can be considered common to all peoples and thus comprehended. Determining these common patterns and stating them as universals is the goal and the study of history; these are the forces of history at work, in any situations or cultural setting, and it is the task of the historian to comprehend and analyze them, exposing them for further study. Stating these universalities, expressed as laws, may bring historians into differences of opinion, but such disagreements are not unique to the discipline of history but are found in all academic disciplines. These differences account for the various schools of inquiry on the essentialist assumptions about the past and the dynamics of human behavior.

As this work deals with historical eras it is also a comment on history. Eras arise according to the needs of the people working in their specific socioeconomic circumstances, these circumstances being the specific times. Even prehistorical periods, such as the Ice Age, are referred to by their descriptive titles. In historical times, the situations that existed are defined by their outstanding properties; thus the era of the decline of knowledge is referred to as the Dark Ages, for the light of knowledge was mostly certainly dimmed during this long relapse into superstition and mental atrophy.

History is viewed as the beginning and ending of eras, with each era represented by its outstanding features. Eras are understood to arise because of circumstances generated by previous events—the casual and motivational relationships—so that the fall of Rome and later the sacking of the library in Alexandria resulted in the Dark Ages, with all their consequences being a direct result of these events. Our contemporary era of knowledge evolved in the same historical process from the dynamics set in motion in the Industrial Revolution which came to an end when the general processes of industrialization had reached the state of entropy and the Great Depression had set in.

The theory of history set in this work is a theory of evolution and is essentialist, for it is based on the law that a historical era evolves on the dynamics of its predecessors, and while it has its own unique characteristics, it is the consequence of the dynamics and the entropic condition of the previous era. It is not, however, evolutionary in a quasi-organic sense of recurring patterns of the rise and fall of civilizations; nor is this work teleological in the sense that in the future everything will cease after an apocalypse. According to the theory of this present work, powers rise and civilizations thrive because of their creative drive and the universality of the contributions they make. This is very far from an organic evolutionary theory. What characterizes our contemporary era is the existence of knowledge on such universal levels, with the dynamics of creativity generating this knowledge in disequilibrium, so that new knowledge is produced and entropy is induced in those knowledge systems which are no longer adequate, bringing their utility into decline. This situation is unique, and the rate of knowledge being generated and declining is greater now than in any other historical era.

Every historian views history as an intrepretation of events and their relationships as well as the dynamics which generated them. These views cannot help but be laden with value judgments and academic biases, but historians make these clear either explicitly at the beginning of their discourses of implicitly during their works. There is, then, always the risk of interpreting history from a personal view, but such is the case with every intellectual endeavor, and the historian's personal view is well tempered by his or her professional ethos and the educated criticisms of his or her peers, so that the reputable historian's theories will correspond well to the facts and data, instead of the facts and data corresponding to the theories. Personal biases and value judgments cannot be avoided, but when incorporated in theories, these theories are subject to the scrutiny of other historians, so that what is passed for history must be valid within the consideration of those working within the discipline.

What, then, can be said about our historical era from the historian's vantage point? What will determine the conclusion of our era and the beginning of the new era to follow? If we could take a page from the physicist's book and with the ideal experiment project ourselves into the future to look back on ourselves, we would see a period of civilization in which more of humanity than ever before participated in the dynamics of knowledge. We would view our period as that which opened the way toward the exploration of the cosmos, realizing the fantasies of many hundreds of generations, as well as that which penetrated deeply into the secrets of the micro world and its seeming infinity. We would see a period in which new nations were formed and their complexities integrated into the global system and, acting as a restraining force, were able to hold back militaristic adventures and temper great power conflicts. We would see the promise of peace finally given expression in the realization that further war will mean the end of all civilization—a dictum which will hold for all time henceforth. We would witness this period as one in which the greatest and most enduring accomplishments of humanity were made and on which other achievements have been constructed.

We cannot speculate about the future perspective of our era from that of another era without wondering what will bring our present era to its conclusion. Advances into space may bring about the changes necessary to end our era; so may the penetration into micro infinity. But most likely it will be the ever-increasing complications of our social dynamics, so that new approaches will take into account not only foreign relations but the migrations of peoples, urban problems and relationships, demands on natural resources, pressures of population centers, crime, aging, traffic and transportation planning, and medical services, which will have to be tested in the field. There will most likely be a unification of knowledge as it expands and enters, altered, into each discipline, generating interdisciplinary dynamics. Knowledge will then be used extensively to define and solve the social problems, and the knowledge gained from this will be used in other differing problem areas. It will be, perhaps, the historical era of the unification of knowledge, with its social times defined according to the most pressing problems. Whatever history holds for our future we cannot know but can only speculate. One thing is for certain, however, and it is that the seeds of entropy for our era of knowledge will be planted and nourished as our knowledge expands, bringing our era down eventually, from which another era formulated on the basis of our own will be set into motion. This, it is posited here, is the essence of the dynamics of history.

THE CAVEAT

Our historical era of knowledge, especially our social time, has provided us with a sense of a dualistic life style. In one sense we live in a world of technological conveniences because our knowledge is manifested in the production of goods and services for both employment and leisure; the wealthy classes even in those countries in their earliest stages of development possessing to a certain extent the luxuries of modern technology.

Yet, in another sense, we live in a futuristic type of world with developments that only a few decades ago—in another social time—would have seemed highly improbable to achieve. Our basic needs and requirements have remained unchanged throughout history, for these are the fundamentals of the human condition. We require food and shelter; we need to love and to propagate our species; we require employment and the means to be productive. We have had these needs since our appearance as a species, and their fulfillment is in part a guarantee of our continuity as a species. In our futuristic world, we continue to strive for advancement, for a better life both as individuals and as the collective human race. Hence, we rely on our present, working within it, while looking toward the future and striving for its accomplishments. We may view the past with nostalgia, but this serves to give us comfort in our present. Our main direction is toward the future, and this has been so since the dawning of humanity; now, however, we have the tools and the imaginations to bring into reality techniques for production and products which once seemed so futuristic as to be fantasies, techniques for bettering our conditions and preventing the beginning of political conflict situations. We live in a social time of realism, for to deny our reality is to function inadequately; yet ours is a period of anti-realism, for we understand that our knowledge is unreal, fleeting as the dissolution of our knowledge systems brought about by entropy.

The readers of Thomas More's *Utopia* could be amazed by his foresight, yet they shake their heads at how far he was from the then-futuristic mark when considering the nowhere world he constructed in his imagination. Even in our day we have not yet developed trees from which to pluck the chickens born and prepared for eating, nor the finished fine wines from the vines. But we have technological devices that More was unable to imagine, as the very notions of their futuristic existence were far too removed from St. Thomas More's time.

Modern futuristic writers have, however, the futuristic foresight to construct imaginary utopias, and they comprehend the possible difficulties that exist in them. They have given us their ideas about utopias but have also given us their apprehensions, which serve as a warning, a caveat, as to the possible abuses of technology and knowledge.

Such a work was George Orwell's *1984,* which has become necessary reading for all concerned with our present and future societies and for comprehending the negative trends of our social time. Another work, less familiar, is Anthony Burgess's *1985,* in which he criticizes Orwell's book, not because of its prophesies, but as a work of despair. Orwell's book is not to be taken as an overreaction to the possibilities the future holds for humanity, but as a work of individual despair of not being able to love. Love was excluded in Orwell's future world, and when its first indications were made manifest, they were stamped out ruthlessly by the inquisitor O'Brien, who destroyed its last vestiges with the epitome of mental torture. Burgess wrote:

> Orwell has, in *Nineteen-Eighty-Four,* opened a gap that cannot exist, and in that gap he has built his impossible tyranny. It rests on air, like a castle in Spain. We are so fascinated by it that we will not use the dissolving power of disbelief and send it silently crashing. *1984* is not going to be like that at all.[3]

Of course, the date Orwell chose is of little significance; what is important is the conditions he described. The real question is, what will our societies be like in the next social time?

Burgess discussed the various types of topias or places. Sir Thomas More's title for his book, *Utopia,* means nowhere or no place. Eutopia, however, means a pleasant place, while dystopia stands in opposition to eutopia and means an unpleasant place. Burgess described as Orwell's work as cacotopia, with the prefix "caco" from the Greek for harsh, disharmonious, jarring, or distorted.[4] However, Burgess's *1985* shares the same difficulty as Orwell's work and Aldous Huxley's *Brave New World,* in that he posited an extremely advanced society in Britain that had the same problems as modern society: high unemployment and heavy union and government control; moreover, in *1985* the dynamics of creativity have ceased, leaving a stagnant and stationary society. The fascination which these dystopian societies hold for us is enhanced by learning what each writer gains from his predecessors, which provides the material for the smooth transition into these imaginary hellish societies.

Burgess's work is distinguished from that of Orwell and Huxley in that Burgess relies on circumstances that, given the right conditions, could possibly exist in a future social time in the decline of our historical era. He assumed a society in which egalitarianism was taken to its extreme form of levelling downward, with achievement and merit being based on seniority and influence. It is a society in which unions have eliminated the creative spark; where knowlege is no longer pragmatic but statistical and dull; where the people still have the creative drive, but when they seek to express it, they are considered social outcasts, living on the fringes of society, and if too presistent with this idiosyncrasy, they are incarcerated or driven insane. Insanity is defined as social deviation, and in Burgess's work the norm is conformity, union-determined and governmentally and socially enforced.

While this is a social distortion, it is not that far removed from scenarios that we can imagine happening now. For example, in Burgess's society, strikes are rampant and called unexpectedly, inflation is very high, and the persistent demand for ever-increasing wages only adds fuel to the stagnant economy's inflationary fires. Social outcasts are tolerated, so long as they do not step too far out of line. Thugs rob, beating victims for the thrill of it (much like Burgess's *A Clockwork Orange*), and punishment for all types of crime is being cast out of the system entirely; repentance for committing crime is made within the mainstream of unionized living. Burgess has his equivalent to Orwell's "Room 101," the supreme form of deprivation of self and torture; for Burgess, it is an institution of detention "at His Majesty's pleasure," but one in which personal creativity can be expressed. The punishment is subtle but severe nonetheless: it is that the intellectual and artistic endeavors will remain forever outside the mainstream of society. Detention is for life until death by natural causes, or by one's own hand as was the case with Burgess's hero, Bev Jones.

These projections into our possible future—with Burgess's perhaps being the most realistic and the likeliest—are warnings about how societies may exist if we fail to maintain our awareness of the possibilities of unchecked control over our physical and natural resources. In our technological time, societies must have checks and balances to maintain their viability; if one single social factor becomes dominant—for Burgess it was the unions—our future will be a cacotopia. If control of knowledge is at the sole disposal of the ruling political power and given the temptations of power to rule absolutely, without checks and balances and with the aid of modern technology, those who rule will seek out and destroy our individuality and freedom of expression and will subvert our behavior patterns, as complex and as diverse as they are, in order to mold them into a single pattern of conformity. It is a mistake to term this projected social possibility as one of harmony, for a uniform society, in which there exists no serious differences of thought and practice and where disagreement is not acceptable, is extremely disquieting to any thinking person.

The caveat in our time is that we should not take our situation for granted. Our sciences and arts continue expanding and our technology improving, providing us with more goods and services. But we cannot rely on a social mechanism to keep these processes functioning, and the benefits we gain have been achieved by the result of hard work and ingenuity. We cannot allow the dynamics of creativity to cease; we must maintain our vigil to see that these are not suppressed for some political cause backed by slogans. We must make sure that creativity is not politically channeled nor intellectually compromised in any way. We have managed to maintain our historically high levels of creativity because art, science, and technology have been sanctioned by our society, as this is the era in which we live. This era and its social time cannot be taken for granted, for dangers such as those posited by the modern cacotopian writers do exist. With each personality-altering drug entering the market, be it a tranquilizer or a subcultural hallucinogen, the danger to our society with its creativity and reliance on the individual becomes greater; every time there is an improvement in the techniques of mass and individual persuasion, the danger of individualism being eroded and the imposition of ideas on the majority of people becomes greater, bringing the existence of a cacotopic rule that much closer. We have today organizations that seek power and wealth by conditioning individuals' thought processes, but in Western countries these are not governmental; those who are not interested or are strong enough to break away, once entrapped, maintain their freedom and individuality.

The modern writers on cacotopia posited stationary states, which is perhaps an accurate description of how the future totalitarian society would be, should it ever come about. While the type of stationary state differs for each modern writer, each writer shares with the others the conditions of the cessation of creativity; the separation of technology from knowledge and the dissolution of the necessary interrelationships among the arts, sciences, and industry. With the cessation of dynamics generated by imitation, initiation, and innovation, the functions of society will be diverted solely to the government, to be supplied and distributed by an unimaginative and self-assured bureaucracy.

It must be understood, however, that the dynamics of our era of knowledge are very firmly entrenched in our socioeconomic systems, and that there is no consensus whatsoever to curb the advancements made in the arts and sciences. The lone radical voice may be heard calling for such restrictions, but let that voice ring out, for this too is necessary in an open and dynamic society. It would take a crisis of severe proportions for a cacotopic state to come into being. Perhaps the mobilization due to the threat of war, in which dissent would be greatly curtailed, or a natural catastrophe requiring the mustering of all available resources and the imposition of the "cause" mentality, which a clever manipulator could use to usurp the people's support and obtain power, would be sufficient enough to bring down our era and begin a cacotopic governmental rule. As long as the dynamics of our era of knowlege continue to be viable, as long as the future-oriented societies operate in a dynamic disequilibrium and the past- and present-oriented societies function within their perspectives, perhaps seeking to move into a future-oriented framework, our era will not decline into a condition of cacotopia. Indeed, should there be movement by the past- and present-oriented societies toward the future-oriented dynamics, our era of knowledge will be strengthened.

There is, however, another aspect of the caveat which must be considered, one of great subtlety and much more likely to occur in our social time. This is the equation of knowledge with truth, considering it as permanent, unchanging, unyielding as truth. This would place knowledge on the same level of truth and the contributors to knowledge as people of a higher order in society. As knowledge will then be truth and as truth is unchanging, then knowledge will be revered for its permanence, placing in on the level of religion, not to be critically reviewed or debunked, but to be worshiped. This would certainly destroy the very dynamics of change, thereby eliminating creativity and bringing about the stagnation of cacotopia. Knowledge would become the sacred possession of the ruling class, and freedom of inquiry, of creativity, would be prohibited. This social system would have to maintain itself by repressing the contemporary human spirit of critical imitative and original thinking. Such a society would certainly be comparable to those expressed by the futuristic cacotopic writers.

We, in our contemporary era of knowledge, have come to realize that for all its importance and utility, knowledge is temporal, hence not "true," and will decline in value over time. Its validity depends on the knowledge systems and their durability and it is as frail as its inability to withstand the entropy that eventually brings it down. For our contemporary era of knowledge to flourish, we must not lose sight that knowledge, being temporal, is thus unstable and that it is truth, contrary to knowledge, that is permanent: the viability of our era depends on this recognition, and the understanding of knowledge as being temporal will enable us to maintain our persistence in challenging the working systems in which it is contained and in which we live. We have been fortunate to have had such brilliant writers as Orwell, Huxley, and Burgess, for they have enabled us to step back for a fleeting moment to look at our present era and its future possibilities. We have been given some understanding as to what knowledge without entropy can bring about. But so long as we remain curious about the growth of systems, about the deficiencies in knowledge statements, so long as we can see the weaknesses of knowledge statements and seek to correct this weakness, will we be able to continue reading their works and to respect them for their excursions into the imaginative scenarios of a future, works that are interesting and possibly enlightening, but lacking in validity in our contemporary era of knowledge.

FURTHER COMMENTS ON GENIUS

Auguste Comte was most likely correct in his attitude that scientific inquiry is to the benefit of humanity.[5] Scientific inquiry is, however, not restricted to the physical and biological sciences, but is useful for disciplines involving human interrelationships, including history, economics, and all other disciplines that require theories, quantification, and testing in both abstract and realistic terms. This inquiring spirit assists us in our awareness of and actions against chemical pollution and enables us to comprehend scenarios of human folly that could possibly bring the world to the brink of nuclear war. Because we possess this spirit, we are able to understand our situations and when necessary we are prepared to band together in a directed voice against policies we consider dangerous to ourselves and our world.

We live on many levels and develop our understanding as we experience life. There is, moreover, a biological level, which explains our behavior for survival as individuals and in the collective sense of humanity. As humans, we are the individual and collective receptacles of genes that evolved and developed over time and through the calamities of history, and we exhibit the preservation motivation encoded in our collective and personal genetic constructions. This has provided us with the will to survive and to overcome the natural and man-made disasters that have befallen us. We are learning to read the genetic code and have gained understanding about its messages; through our science and technology, we are now working to use the genetic code to correct birth defects and to provide industrial uses for genetic engineering in improving our lives and to make our world a better place.[6]

Our physical continuity is determined by our genetic make-up; our cultural continuity is dependent on our genius as it is manifested in our creative endeavors. Our tests for determining potential creative activity have not yet been demonstrated as being reliable and since they are lacking in the correlation between genius and creative activity, talents at the level of Wolfgang Amadeus Mozart and Einstein would probably make poor showings on them. The tests have the problem that the answers depend on the orientations of their originators; some tests require convergent answers, while others rely strictly on divergent reasoning. It has been argued in this work that creativity requires both convergent and divergent reasoning, each with its respective functions. Thus, a test requiring both convergence and divergence would allow the creative process to operate within the confines of a given test-problem situation; the solution provided would have to meet with the problem's assigned utility requirements. This would necessitate the establishment of parameters of acceptability, comparable to those of the utility requirements of a knowledge system. The object of such a test would be to approximate as closely as possible the schematic of a system and to provide the challenge of developing a suitable solution that meets these requirements. Such a test would provide better understanding of creative ability in light of problem situations.

Genius, as discussed in this work, is the source of intellectual activity with which social continuity is maintained. It is also the force that maintains the viability of the historical era; but paradoxically, it is the very same force that brings the historical era to its conclusion. For each era can only be exploited so far and its consequences brought into entropy only to a limited extent, after which the era ends and another begins. We could look at each era of history to evaluate this, but it is not necessary to go so far back in time. Consider, then, the Renaissance in which the revitalization of knowledge gave rise to the modern conceptions of the arts and sciences. It is not with hindsight that we ask just how far this rebirth could have continued if its fruits—its science and technology and artistic conceptualizations—did not withstand the social demands for its dynamics, those very dynamics that burst forth into the Industrial Revolution.

The era of the Industrial Revolution pertained not only to the development of industry but also to artistic conceptualizations. We only have to trace the development of industry and see the corresponding changes in the arts to understand the relationship. Though the Dada movement and Surrealism had their beginnings before our era of knowledge, they bear the resurgent influences of our era in their post–World War I contributions, as the later works of Janco Dada and Salvador Dali testify. Consider the transition from expressionism to the modern painters who stated their works after World War II; not only painters, but also writers, poets, sculptors, and musicians have elements of the expressionist movement in their works. Those students who study the dynamics of society can see the relationship of society—with its industrial development—to the arts and sciences. The relationship is symbiotic in the sense that the artists, scientists, and scholars provide the information that the various strata of society require; these strata, in turn, consume the products of the arts, sciences, and scholarly research, both in industrial output and in the original works as they stand.

This symbiotic relationship is, moreover, still more abstract, for as social time in a historical era is delineated by the emphasized aspects of that era, this emphasis is the genius (or spirit) of the social time, and it is this genius that, as it is manifested in art, science, industry, and technology, determines the social time and with its entropy brings the social time to its conclusion, thereby leading to a new social time. In the final sense, it is genius that establishes a new historical era from the knowledge and entropy of the old and thus shapes society and its emphasis, its very dynamics and conceptions, which in turn are the material on which genius develops and expands. Our society would be far different without the scientific and technological advances we have made, without the artistic, medical, and technical advances of our social time. How it would look is subject to speculation and need not be of concern here. We would certainly not have the conveniences of travel and telecommunications, the miracles of medical techniques, and the scientific and artistic achievements on which we are improving and expanding.

Looking back into history and viewing our own historical era, we can see that Robert Tressell's idea is correct, for we, as the collective human race, are indeed the inheritors of all ages that have gone before, and this heritage is an important binding force for us now. We realize that art and science have no geographical barriers, no cultural restrictions. We understand that by virtue of this inheritance we are all equal; we appreciate that the recognition of this equality is one of the important factors for us today in our relations within our own societies and with peoples of other societies.

Now, in our historical era and its social time, we have a special quality which sets us apart from all past generations: the contribution we will make in the continuum of historical time. We, in our era of knowledge, are obligated as no other people before us to use our talents in ways that will prevent the mistakes and blunders of our past from being repeated in our modern situation; we are further obliged to use our talents for our own works of value and significance, works that contribute to the continuity of our social time, for as they are the fruitions of genius, they will maintain the genius of our time until entropy sets in. We must recognize that by our own unique contributions will our historical era of knowledge and our social time be judged in the future.

11

Coda

In days of old, in the city of Haran, lived Terach and his young son Abram. Terach was an idol maker whose craftsmanship and skill were widely known and respected. His reputation in his trade won renown throughout many countries.

One day Terach had to leave home to travel and put his young son in charge of the idols so that competitors, noticing his absence, would not take advantage and steal or destroy them.

The boy alone began to think: "These are idols, of wood and stone; yet they are worshiped as gods, as the powers of the universe. What would happen if I pushed one?" He did, and it fell to the ground and shattered. Realizing what he had done, Abram then placed a hammer in the arms of the biggest idol, sparing this idol while destroying all others.

His father was shocked upon his return to find his work lying on the ground shattered and destroyed. He questioned Abram excitedly, who answered that in his father's absence the idols began to quarrel among themselves as to who was the most powerful. A fight ensued and the victor was the strongest and most powerful because of his size. Terach, not accepting his son's explanation, suspected foul play on Abram's part and punished the boy severely. The young iconoclast grew into manhood, becoming Abraham, founder of the first great monolithic religion.[1]

In the aftermath of the Peloponnesian War, Sparta established a puppet government in Athens with the Thirty Tyrants serving as its administrators. These tyrants used their authority arbitrarily to oppress the Athenian citizens. When democracy in Athens was finally restored, the citizens demanded an investigation into the causes of the dictatorship. It was found that some of the tyrants would listen to Socrates in the market place; the politician Antyus, the poet Meletus, and the rhetorician Lycon—acting as spokesmen for the people—charged Socrates with atheism and corrupting the city's youth.

In his defense Socrates argued that his purpose in life was to seek the truth, maintaining that others were far more successful than he in this pursuit. His discussions in the market place were conducted in order to find wise men from whom he could learn. He bore no responsibility for those who listened during the debates, as their judgments and opinions were strictly their own. Citing his military service to Athens, for his heroism was known, he argued that as a senator he nevertheless held no desire for politics. His task was finding the truth, nothing more; he sought to corrupt no one and his belief in the gods was unwavering and enduring, for from these supreme forces, from the gods, comes truth.

His arguments were unconvincing to a court seeking causes for the dictatorship that suspected anyone different in any way from the others. Socrates certainly presented an unusual appearance; he was unkempt, and his pursuit of the truth was highly unorthodox—that of holding debates with all who would talk and listen, in the market place, which was the center of commerce.

He was convicted of corruption and atheism and sentenced to die. His friends and students begged him to escape, offered to give bribes for his safety, asked to take whatever action necessary to save his life. Socrates refused, arguing that he lived by Athenian law, and if this law saw fit to have him executed, so be it. In his death he became a martyr, the example of a true thinker, a seeker of the truth and justice. His influence on Plato's thinking and teachings is very marked, and the wisdom of Socrates is incorporated in the philosophical and scientific spirit of inquiry. He was an iconoclast seeking to destroy false notions and prodding those who were smug and sure in their opinions to revalue them in a critical light. As the gadfly of Athens, his success was measured by the loyalty of his adherents, those who stood with him in his time of crisis and mourned for his death.[2]

In 1543, when Copernicus was on his deathbed, he was presented with a copy of his work, *On the Revolutions of the Heavenly Spheres*. In this work he sought to resolve the problems of the Ptolemaic system of astronomy, which had been discovered over the system's use in time. To accomplish this, Copernicus posited a heliocentric system, contrary to Ptolemy's geocentric system; on the basis of mathematical computation, he corrected many errors that had become apparent in the Ptolemaic system. Copernicus posited his system as an alternative approach, one considered more accurate, but not one that was true, for this would go against Church doctrine. As a loyal member of the Church, Canon Copernicus sought not to generate conflict within the Church but merely to offer an alternative system, a different hypothesis, for explaining astronomy's events.

Twenty-two years after the Canon's death Galileo was born. He was to take up the Copernican heliocentric system and teach it as the true representative of the motion of the heavenly spheres. The conflict that Copernicus sought to avoid was brought into the open by Galileo, as he preached the Canon's system and flouted the Church's authority.

Galileo was warned of the crime of teaching this system as true but ignored the warnings, only to be brought before the Inquisition, forced to retract his teaching, and warned sternly never to discuss the matter again. The authority of the Church committee was too strong for the mathematician and after soul-searching, he yielded.

Only later did he write his greatest work, *The Dialogue Concerning Two New Sciences,* using the Socratic method comparing the Church-supported Aristotelian system of a physics animated by spirits and teleological causes to a physics based on mathematics and relative motions. In one sense Galileo yielded to Church authorities, for according to the historians, he never debated the issue of the heliocentric system versus the geocentric system after accepting the Church's decree. In another way, however, he fought the Church authorities and won, for it was this work, Galileo's greatest, on which Newton built his physics, combining Kepler's astronomy with Galileo's mathematical relativity, and constructed a unified theory of earth-bound and planetary physics. When the iconoclast Galileo died he was buried appropriately between Machiavelli and Michelangelo.[3]

Throughout the great civilizations of history, there has been a paradox of culture. In one sense there has been culture looking into itself, with artistic and scientific contributors developing ideas and working within the culture to acquire fame and to provide cultural identity through their contributions. In another sense, there has been culture looking outward, with the contributions of other cultures being incorporated and altered to fit into the adapting culture's conceptualizations. This process did not begin with the great ancient civilizations. The earliest of tribes had exchanges of ideas with other tribes, when not at war with them. In this way these tribes expanded into civilizations.[4]

This paradox is expressed further in the uniqueness of each culture, but this uniqueness is due in part to the adaptation of concepts not only of the culture itself but of other cultures. There is, therefore, uniqueness only if there is intermingling.

This idea is central to this work, and it is certainly not new. It was expressed by the young Abram, who, with many dimensions of awareness, took the concept of *one,* of *unity,* abstracted it from the material world to a level that is comprehensible in the material world but all-powerful on the spiritual level, and interpreted this as the Supreme Almighty. It was also expressed by Socrates, who stopped young people in the Athenian market place and sought out their ideas and this brought about an expansion of his ideas and understanding, sharpening his reasoning abilities still further. It was expressed by Galileo, who took the mathematics refined by the ancient Greek thinkers and merged it with physics, initiating the dawn of a new physical world and carrying the Copernican spirit of scientific revolution one giant step further.

This is certainly true for our historical era as knowledge from other systems is altered and incorporated into different systems, replacing entropic statements and strengthening systems. There have been great thinkers throughout history and their contributions have been outstanding. Our historical era is distinguished by great thinkers, people in all fields of inquiry and expression who have made significant contributions to knowledge. It is the very existence of manifold knowledge systems, however, that gives the dynamism and disequilibrium, as systems with entropy are corrected by the introduction of adapted knowledge from other systems, knowledge that is then tested for its utility or lack of it within the system. Hence, while creativity has been the expression of our thinkers throughout history, our unique historical era, with its manifold knowledge systems, with their utility and entropy generating dynamic disequilibrium, has been the subject of this work.

Notes

CHAPTER 1

1. Of course, emotion is always involved. The scientist who formulates and develops a theory is personally involved in working out the theory. He or she invests time and energy and stakes his or her reputation on the theory and, on a different level, is wrapped in the beauty of the theory. Scientists who accept a theory are emotionally obligated to the theory by their acceptance; should the theory be abandoned, it is only when a theory of greater intellectual power and emotional satisfaction replaces it. Nevertheless, there is much validity in the argument that old theories, old positions held, die with their holders. Science as a discipline is objective; its practitioners are as human as the rest of mankind.

2. See the discussion on Bernhard Riemann in E. T. Bell, *Men of Mathematics* (New York: Touchstone Books, 1986), pp. 484-510. For discussions on J. Bolyai, see Philip J. Davis and Ruben Hersh, *The Mathematical Experience* (Boston: Houghton Mifflin, 1981), p. 220; Morris Kline, *Mathematics* (New York: Oxford, 1982), pp. 83, 86, 88, 164, 181-182. See Roger Penrose's essay, "The Geometry of the Universe" with the comment on Bolyai on p. 84 of Lynn Arthur Steen, ed., *Mathematics Today* (New York: Vintage Books, 1980).

3. See Michael Dummet, "Realism," from his collected essays in *Truth and Other Enigmas* (Cambridge, Mass.: Harvard University Press, 1980), pp. 145-146.

CHAPTER 2

1. This refers to competing goods and services. If a unique product is in demand and production does not meet the demand, the product's price will be high in the short run until competition of close substitutes reduces the price. Should production of the original product increase, the price will be reduced that much further. See my book, *Contemporary Economics: A Unifying Approach* (New York: Praeger, 1986), pp. 90-109, 120-145.

2. See the discussion on this in Emmanuel Farjoun and Moshe Machover, *Laws of Chaos* (London: Verso, 1983), especially the Introduction. This is a book which should be of interest to all people engaged in economics, although there are many points with which this present writer takes issue.

3. In this context, the use of the word "age" refers to a specific conceptualization within the era, making it synonymous with social time. Hence, our computer age is a social-time concept within our era of knowledge. In this sense, "age" differs from the broad concept such as Stone Age, or Bronze Age, each of which can be considered as a historical era.

4. See Arthur Koestler, *The Case of the Midwife Toad* (London: Hutchinson, 1971).

5. A. C. Pigou, *The Economics of Welfare,* 1920; 4th ed. (London: Macmillan, 1960).

CHAPTER 3

1. There should be no doubt that the U.S. could have won the Vietnam conflict if it had taken the action of bombing the enemy out of existence. The consequence of this approach to war, as well as the necessity of allocating funds to those institutions dealing with social problems and to the space program (resulting in such great contributions as walking on the moon), proved to be sufficient constraints that, when taken together with the ultimate humanistic consideration, prevented such drastic action from being undertaken. No doubt the Soviet Union is constrained by its own social programs and humanistic considerations from opting for a drastic solution to the Afghanistan problem.

2. See Douglas R. Hofstadter, *Gödel, Escher, Bach: An Eternal Golden Band* (New York: Vintage Books, 1980).

CHAPTER 4

1. Or neoclassical, as it may be argued that the ancient Greeks were the first classical composers. The origins of music, its compositions and

harmonies, is certainly one of the obscure aspects of human history. The classical composers referred to here are, of course, those who brought together the great musical harmonies and melded them into symphonies, concertos, and operas. These musicians include such composers as Bach, Beethoven, Vivaldi, Mozart, and others of this conceptual period; their works form the basis of all further concert compositions.

Some people argue that Mozart was not a classical composer but a Romantic, because of the passion and feeling, the emotional color tones, and the expression of his music. In that case, then all accepted classical composers were Romantic composers for the very same reasons. Bach and Beethoven and the others composed music with expression, color tones, and great emotional feeling. The term "classical" is used here to denote only style and nothing more.

The musical form of jazz is also a serious art form and owes much of its development to the neoclassical composers. This is evidenced by the harmonics of musicians such as Buddy Bolden and Joe King Oliver, influenced by the New Orleans tradition, where the strains of American musical expression came together with the Latin and French influences into the jazz form. The history of the music, now accepted throughout the world as a valid art form, is as unique as the history of the United States itself.

2. See E. W. Hayden, *Technology Transfer to East Europe: U.S. Corporate Exerience* (New York: Praeger, 1976); S. Herskovic, *The Import and Export of Technological Know How Through Licensing Agreements in Israel, 1966–1974* (Jerusalem: Office of the Prime Minister, National Council for Research and Development, 1976).

3. See Nevin S. Scrimshaw's essay, "Food: Past, Present and Future," Claire Cassidy's comments, and the discussion which followed, in Dan Ortner, ed., *How Humans Adapt* (Washington, D.C.: Smithsonian Institute Press, 1983), pp. 227-262.

CHAPTER 5

1. Poe's *The Gold Bug* certainly provides an interesting example of convergent reasoning. The problem is how to decipher the code revealing the treasure's hiding place. One of the recurring signs in the code is a baby goat, a kid, which is taken correctly to mean Kidd, the famous pirate. The analysis of the frequency of the letters reveals the letter "e," and from this the frequencies of the other notations reveal words, thereby breaking the code and leading to the treasure.

Poe's approach to deciphering was applied by one of the most famous fictional characters of all time, Sir Arthur Conan Doyle's detective Sherlock Holmes. In "The Dancing Men" the message decoded by the sleuth was portrayed by figures of dancing men, with each figure representing a letter in the English alphabet. Holmes found the character representing the letter "e" and the frequencies of the other figures juxtaposed to "e" revealed the coded letters and the message.

2. Arthur Koestler, *The Ghost in the Machine* (London: Pan Books, 1967), p. 212.

3. Arthur Koestler, *Janus: A Summing Up* (New York: Vintage Books, 1976), p. 113.

4. This was first stated in Koestler's *Insight and Outlook* (New York: St. Martin's Press, 1949) and later in his long-awaited second volume of this work, *The Act of Creation* (London: Hutchinson, 1964). The Archimedes example serves to illustrate the second part of his creativity-triptych, the "Ha!" effect.

5. However, see David C. Stove's brief but interesting discussion on Newton's laws in relation to Kepler's law of planetary motion in his book, *Popper and After: Four Modern Irrationalists* (London: Pergamon Press, 1982). In light of the interest in the philosophy of science, this is a fascinating work.

6. Koestler, *The Ghost in the Machine,* p. 214.

7. J. W. Getzels and P. W. Jackson, "The Highly Intelligent and Highly Creative Adolescent: A Summary of Some Research Findings," in C. W. Taylor and F. Barron, eds., *Scientific Creativity: Its Recognition and Development* (New York: John Wiley, 1963), pp. 161-172. Quoted here from P. E. Vernon, ed., *Creativity* (Middlesex: Penguin, 1970), p. 198.

Other examples in this essay (pp. 189-193) contrast high-measured I.Q. and divergent thinking, expressing the authors' bias toward divergent thinking in creativity. The point of contention here is that the testing provided by Getzels and Jackson, as well as by others, lays down rules and criteria for assesssing validity that do not allow the deviant factors that make up for strong creative potential. These factors, such as personal attitudes and independent points of view, must receive proper recognition by the compilers of such tests before the issues of validity can be dealt with. These factors allow for the combination of convergence and divergence. To proclaim the validity of tests in which either convergence or divergence is ruled out is to support tests that deny the de facto properties necessary for measuring creative potential.

CHAPTER 6

1. Francis Galton, *Hereditary Genius* (London: Macmillan, 1869); the quote is taken from the last page, p. 390.

2. The terms "innovation" and "initiation" are used in this work to

refer to the type of creativity that forms a new system or changes an existing system, respectively. The examples of Harvey, Gutenberg, Oersted and Fleming are of innovative creativity, as was most of the creativity prior to our unique contemporary era of knowledge.

3. Hence Archimedes allowed his thoughts to wander far from the crown problem, a recess that let him perceive the solution. Other creative people, such as Balzac, drink many cups of black coffee; others, still, resort to alcohol or narcotics to stimulate the imagination. These techniques are strictly personal and depend on the personality of the creative individual.

4. The first printing press is attributed to the Chinese alchemist, Pi Sheng, when he applied characters to movable devises for printing. Gutenberg was the first European to have developed such a device, casting individual letters in mold. Pi Sheng's work is said to have been approximately A.D. 1040-1050, while Gutenberg's invention was in 1438. See *Reader's Digest Book of Facts,* Pleasantville, New York: The Reader's Digest Association Inc., pp. 49, 324. The Chinese invention used wood for printing blocs; Gutenberg used metal. Arthur Koestler, *The Ghost in the Machine*, New York: Macmillan, 1968, p. 185.

5. See Werner Heisenberg, *The Physical Principles of the Quantum Theory* (New York: Dover, 1949), trans. Carl Eckart and F. C. Hoyt. If gravity results from the interaction of force fields, these fields are generated by the wave motions of particles. According to Heisenberg, we can determine a particle's position or its momentum, but not both, for such an interaction of observation on the particle will exert an influence and alter one or both of these factors. A force-field theory of gravity depends on particles to generate the force field; to understand how these particles operate they must be analyzed, thereby exerting an unavoidable influence on them due to the interaction of observation. Moreover, no matter what the theory is for explaining gravity, it must be tested, so that such influences on the particle cannot be avoided. Is this difficulty really insurmountable? It is certainly a challenge for innovative physicists.

6. A period of time, social time, being determined by the number and quality of knowledge systems, in their various stages and dynamics.

7. The underdeveloped societies and many of those in various stages of development have not yet entered into this era. They are experiencing their own unique conditions and cannot take advantage to the fullest of the contributions made by those societies in the era of knowledge; they are just not equipped to handle these contributions.

CHAPTER 7

1. See R. Buckminster Fuller, *Critical Path* (New York: St. Martin's Press, 1981), especially Part I.

2. Rollo May, ed., with Ernest Angel and Henri F. Ellenberger, contributing eds., *Existence,* (New York: Simon and Schuster/Clarion Books, 1960). From Rollo May's article, "Contributions to Existential Philosophy," p. 50.

3. See Søren Kierkegaard's *The Sickness Unto Death,* (New York: Doubleday & Co., 1954); trans. Walter Lowrie.

4. Ludwig Binswanger, "The Existential Analysis School of Thought," trans. Ernest Angel, in *Existence,* p. 24.

5. Systems have logical structures from which imitators can work. They must be consistent when first constructed so that no contradictions are derivable. According to the rules of formal and mathematical logic, from a statement and its contradiction all statements are derivable and valid. While this type of situation is to be avoided, such contradictions may indeed be derived through explorative imitation.

6. See the discussion on Pasteur and the debate on spontaneous generation in Paul de Kruif's fascinating book, *Microbe Hunters* (New York: Pocket Books, 1943), pp. 60-115.

7. While such either/or situations are ideal, they are most difficult to construct, especially in our era of knowledge with its manifold and variegated systems, which, when in close proximity and in competition, have nuances of differences so slight and yet so important.

A medical example: a remedy that works for one person may be ineffective or even detrimental for another, so that prescriptions have their limitations and warnings are included. This also points out the dynamics of our era, for universal knowledge, be it in medicine or in other fields of inquiry, exists, but not in an absolute form. The exceptions to the rule allow differences and new systems to be constructed to deal with these differences. The dynamics of knowledge are neither restricted by social time nor are they equilibrium, but are changing in orientation, in disequilibrium.

CHAPTER 8

1. S. Herbert Frankel, "Some Aspects of Technical Change," in *The Economic Impact on Under-Developed Societies* (Oxford: Basil Blackwell, 1959), p. 23.

2. See Daniel C. Dennet, *Brainstorms* (Cambridge, Mass.: M.I.T. Press, 1981), especially Essay 5, "Why the Law of Effect Will Not Go Away." In discussing creativity in this essay, he fails to consider one of the important factors in the creative process, that is, its reason: problem solving.

3. See I. C. Bupp, "Nuclear Power: The Promise Melts Away," in Robert Stobauch and Daniel Yergin, eds., *Energy Future* (New York: Vintage

Books, 1983), pp. 134-172. This is an important collection of essays on energy and the problems of finding, controlling, and implementing it, as well as developing alternative sources. This essay somewhat prophetically points to the types of disasters of atomic energy plants, even though it is pre-Chernobyl.

4. For an interesting tour through the history of ancient Rome, its struggles against the world and within itself, see Tacitus' works published by Random House: *The Complete Works of Tacitus* (New York: Modern Library, 1942), trans. A. J. Church and W. J. Broadribb. An enlightening introduction is provided by Moses Hadas.

5. Alan Turing, "Computing Machinery and Intelligence," reprinted in *Minds and Machines*, ed. Alan Ross Anderson (Englewood Cliffs, N.J.: Prentice-Hall, 1964).

CHAPTER 9

1. Because we fear the development of circumstances that could lead to another world war, we have devised unique approaches to small-scale military operations. We have partaken in similar expeditions in the name of territorial integrity, and we have withdrawn when the aims of the operations have been achieved. We have also fought wars internally, not as invaders in the traditional sense, but as guerilla movements, fighting for whatever noble cause is justifying our actions. Sometimes these actions are covert, such as supplying foreign troops with logistics, equipment, and intelligence; sometimes they are overt, such as the Falkland (Malvinas) and the Vietnam wars.

Of course, there is no guarantee that this approach will be successful, nor that it will not be turned against the invader as propaganda, bringing pressure from the international community for withdrawal. While the Vietnamese war was protrayed as a fight for liberty by the United States, it was portrayed as a defensive war against a big power bloc invader by the North's side; its propaganda was far more effective, and the United States succumbed to pressure and evacuated its forces from the country. The issue of that war's justice or injustice is not of concern here. The new techniques for military engagement and the techniques for opposing it are unique to our time and are not restricted to a single political side in conflicts.

2. The influence of religion in that region is so strong that even though the dynamics of knowledge have made some impact, they have been softened by the religious fervor that holds this region isolated to some extent from time. Much of the modernization of the region has been in terms of military equipment, while some steps have been taken to align education

and industry to Western standards. But because the religious hold is so strong and intense, the Middle East is in a mixed historical time reference: in the social time of our era while also being in another, earlier social time, in which the religious leaders worked with the politicians to keep the people in ignorance and subservience.

3. While the price of oil is on the decline, due in part to the developing of energy substitutes and in part to surplus supplies, the oil-producing countries may yet come to realize that they must make basic conceptual changes to enter fully into our era of knowledge so that they can avoid the economic chaos they foisted on the world and not become so entirely dependent on foreign, mainly Western, sources for technology and knowledge, which are becoming more expensive and therefore less affordable.

4. See my work, *Contemporary Economics: A Unifying Approach* (New York: Praeger, 1986), p. 186.

5. See Daniel Yergin and Martin Hillenbrand, eds., *Global Insecurity* (New York: Penguin, 1983). In an essay in this work, Daniel Yergin compares America's and Japan's reactions to the oil crisis. In light of the competition between these two countries today his remarks hold special significance:

> Both the American and Japanese society go about converting the same kind of energy sources with the same kind of technology. Yet Japanese society has proceeded with an assumption of scarcity and insecurity of supply conditioned by its history and position. Recent events have only confirmed this assumption, so there has been a far less divisive debate in Japan about whether there is a problem and, if so, what it is and what to do about it. In contrast, it has been much more difficult to arrive at a consensus in the United States, where society begins with the assumption of abundance. Many Americans simply rejected the idea that a group of foreign oil producers could effectively set domestic oil prices—even though America's reliance on imports had clearly grown to the point where it was the largest buyer of oil in the world market. Here was a view that would deny reality—that the OPEC countries were the source, not only of the marginal barrel, but of many millions of barrels a day (p. 120).

It must be clear that with the Watergate difficulties and the other problems confronting America at that time, there was certainly room for skepticism. This has been dissipated to a large extent by the development of alternative energy sources and with the surplus oil stocks resulting in vast price reductions. In all fairness, then, the Americans acted rationally once the full weight of the problem was realized.

This book is a valuable source of information and references concerning the energy situation and the possible scenarios for the future. Unfortunately it did not foresee a tragedy of the scope of Chernobyl.

CHAPTER 10

1. David Hackett Fischer, *Historians' Fallacies* (New York: Harper, 1970), p. 69.
2. A. D'Abro, *The Rise of the New Physics,* 2 vols. (N.Y.: Dover, 1956).
3. Anthony Burgess, *1985* (London: Hutchinson, 1978), p. 102.
4. Burgess, *1985,* p. 53.
5. Concerning Comte, Ernst Cassirer wrote:

> Of all human idols, the political idols, the idola fori, are the most dangerous and enduring. Since the time of Plato all the great thinkers have made the greatest efforts to find a rational theory of politics. The nineteenth century was convinced that it had at least found the right path. In 1830 Auguste Comte published the first volume of his *Cours de Philosophie Positive.* He began with analyzing the structure of natural science; he went from astronomy to physics, from physics to chemistry, from chemistry to biology. His real aim and highest ambition was to become the founder of a new social science and to introduce into this science the same exact way of reasoning, the same inductive and deductive method as we find in physics or chemistry.

Cassirer goes on to say that Comte and his students failed in their attempt. This was certainly an ambitious task and the social sciences are the better for it.

See Ernst Cassirer, *The Myth of the State* (New Haven: Yale University Press, 1975), pp. 294–295. See also, Harriet Martineau's translation of Comte's work in the 1855 edition, published as a reprint by AMS Press, New York.

6. See Robert Cooke, *Improving on Nature* (New York: Quadrangle York: Quadrangle Books, 1977).

CHAPTER 11

1. See Abraham, Yoma 28b; Kid. 4:14. Also, see Pessachim, 118a.
2. Grabe, G. M., trans., *The Trial and Death of Socrates* (New York: Hatchett Books, 1975).
3. See Stanley L. Jaki's essay on Galileo in *Encyclopedia of World Biography* (New York: McGraw-Hill Inc., 1973), pp. 289-292.
4. There are pyramids in Egypt and the Americas, representing two great ancient civilizations; the pyramids in the Americas differ from those in Egypt by their architectural designs. The Egyptians probably learned their mathematics from the Mesopotamians, whereas the peoples in the Americas learned their mathematics from sources unknown to us. Each civilization made significant and unique contributions to architecture and mathematics. This illustrates how knowledge can be possessed by two

seemingly unrelated civilizations. What can be said for those civilizations in close geographical proximity? Imagine how they developed their knowledge through cultural intermingling. Perhaps it was the dynamic situation in the cultures that prevented their forming knowledge systems and engaging in creativity as we understand it. This is an interesting point for historical research.

Selected Bibliography

Arendt, Hannah. *The Human Condition.* New York: Doubleday Anchor Books, 1959.

———. *The Origins of Totalitarianism.* London: George Allen and Unwin, 1958.

———. *Totalitarianism.* New York: Harvest/HBJ, 1965.

Boorstin, Daniel J. *The Discoverers.* New York: Vintage Books, 1985.

Bragg, Sir William. *Concerning the Nature of Things.* New York: Dover, 1948.

Cassirer, Ernst. *An Essay on Man.* New Haven: Yale University Press, 1962.

———. *The Problem of Knowledge.* New Haven: Yale University Press, 1974.

Clark, Kenneth B. *Pathos of Power.* New York: Harper, 1975.

Crosson, Frederick and Kenneth M. Sayre. *Philosophy and Cybernetics.* New York: Clarion Books, 1967.

D'Abro, A. *The Rise of the New Physics.* 2 vols. New York: Dover, 1952.

Demski, Joel S. *Information Analysis.* Redding, Mass.: Addison-Wesley, 1972.

Dennet, Daniel C., and Douglas R. Hofstadter, eds. *The Mind's I.* New York: Bantam Books, 1982.

Einstein, Albert. *The Meaning of Relativity.* Princeton: Princeton University Press, 1974.

Feinberg, Gerald. *What Is the World Made Of?* New York: Doubleday Anchor Press, 1975.

Fraser, J. T., ed. *The Voices of Time.* 2nd. ed. Amherst, Mass.: The University of Massachusetts Press, 1981.

Fuller, R. Buckminster. *Synergetics.* New York: Macmillian, 1975, especially the chapter on Numerology, pp. 727-785.

Georgescu-Rogen, Nicholas. *The Entropy Law and Economic Process.* Cambridge, Mass.: Harvard University Press, 1981.

Gribbon, John. *White Holes.* New York: Delta Books, 1977.

Hausman, Daniel M. *The Philosophy of Economics.* New York: Cambridge University Press, 1985, especially the Introduction, which deals with scientific method.

Heilbroner, Robert L. *The Human Prospect.* New York: W. W. Norton & Co., 1980.

Hofstadter, Douglas R. *Metamagical Themas.* New York: Bantam Books, 1986.

Hollinger, Robert, ed. *Hermeneutics and Praxis.* Notre Dame: Notre Dame University Press, 1985.

Jastrow, Robert. *Red Giants and White Dwarfs.* New York: Warner Books, 1980.

Kahn, Herman. *The Emerging Japanese Superstate.* Englewood Cliffs: Prentice-Hall, 1971.

Kahn, Herman, William Brown and Leon Martel. *The Next 200 Years.* New York: William Morrow and Co., 1976.

Kissinger, Henry A. *American Foreign Policy.* New York: W. W. Norton & Co., 1969.

———. *A World Restored.* Boston: Houghton Mifflin Co., 1973.

Koestler, Arthur. *Drinkers of Infinity.* London: Hutchinson, 1968.

———. *The Sleepwalkers.* London: Hutchinson, 1959.

Langer, Susanne K. *Mind: An Essay on Feeling.* 2 vols. Baltimore: Johns Hopkins University Press, 1978.

Levi-Strauss, Claude. *The Savage Mind.* Chicago: The University of Chicago Press, 1966.

Lonergan, Bernard J. F. *Insight.* New York: Harper, 1978.

Loux, Michael J., ed. *The Possible and the Actual.* Ithaca: Cornell University Press, 1979.

Lyttelton, Humphrey. *The Best of Jazz.* Harmondsworth, England: Penguin Books, 1980. Covering the period from 1917 to 1930.

Meier, Richard L. *Science and Economic Development.* Cambridge, Mass.: M.I.T. Press, 1967.

Merleau-Ponty, Maurice. *Sense and Nonsense.* Evanston: Northwestern, Ill.: University Press, 1964.

Monod, Jacques. *Choice and Necessity.* New York: Vintage Books, 1972.

Nietzsche, Friedrich. *The Portable Nietzsche.* Walter Kaufman, ed. New York: Viking Portable Library, 1963.

Nozick, Robert. *Philosophical Explanations.* Cambridge, Mass.: Harvard University Press, 1981.

Pólya, George. *How To Solve It.* Princeton: Princeton University Press, 1945.

Prigogne, Ilya, and Isabelle Stengers. *Order Out of Chaos.* New York: Bantam Books, 1984.

Ricoeur, Paul. *Freedom and Nature.* Evanston, Ill.: Northwestern University Press, 1966.

Sabine, George H. *A History of Political Theory.* 3d ed. London: Harrap, 1964.

Schopenhauer, Arthur. *Die Welt als Wille und Vorstellung,* in *Sämtliche Werke* (Wünchen: R. Piper & Co., 1911); in English, *The World as Will and Ideas,* R. B. Haldane and J. Kemp, trans. (London: Kegan Paul, Trench, Truber & Co., 7th edition). This is a 3 volume translation.

Smith, Charles W. *A Critique of Sociological Reasoning.* Oxford: Blackwell, 1979.

Soloveitchik, Joseph B. *The Halakhic Mind.* New York: Free Press/Seth, 1986.

Sowell, Thomas. *Knowledge and Decisions.* New York: Basic Books, 1980.

Spanier, John. *Games Nations Play.* New York: Praeger, 1974.

Taylor, Gordon Rattay. *Rethink.* Harmondsworth, England: Pelican Books, 1974.

Weinberg, Steven. *The First Three Minutes.* New York: Basic Books, 1977.

Whyte, William H. *The Organization Man.* Middlesex, England: Penguin Books, 1960.

Zukov, Gary. *The Dancing Wu Li Masters.* New York: Morrow Quill, 1979.

Index

Abraham the Patriarch, 203, 206, 217 n.1
Acceptance, 47, 77, 103, 105, 109, 110
Afghanistan, 152, 153, 156, 158, 161, 210 n.1
Alexandria Library, 30, 31, 189
Anti-Realism, 15, 142, 143, 145, 192
Anxiety *(Angst)*, 112-117, 123
Archimedes, 69, 70, 84, 213 n.3
Area Language, 50, 53, 57-59, 93, 102, 121, 123
Aristarchus, 9, 20
Aristotle, 20, 112
Association, 68, 73. *See also* Bisociation

Bach, J. S., 211 n.1
Balzac, Honoré de, 213 n.3
Barron, F., and C. W. Taylor, 212 n.7
Beethoven, Ludwig von, 211 n.1
Bell, E. T., 209, n.2
Berkeley, George, 10, 11
Bessemer Process, 29, 31, 32
Binswanger, Ludwig, 114, 115, 214 n.4
Bisociation, 68-74
Burgess, Anthony, 193-195
Britain (Great Britain), 11, 35, 64, 135, 136, 164, 194
Brown, Clifford, 95

Cacotopia, 194-196
Carnot, S., 61
Carter, Benny, 122-123
Cassidy, Claire, 211 n.3
China, 152, 156, 169
Chronological time, 19, 21, 22
Church, the, 8, 64, 205
Churchill, Winston, 35
Clausius, Rudolph, 61
Cooke, Robert, 217 n.6
Comte, Auguste, 198, 217 n.5
Convergence, 62, 63, 72-74, 86, 88, 97, 99, 199; primary, 63, 73, 74, 83, 85; purposeful, 64, 66; secondary, 64, 66, 73, 83; unintentional, 64-66
Copernicus, Nicholaus, 20, 49, 205
Creative activity, 50, 127
Creativity, 47-50, 53, 63; and bisociation, 70, 72-74; and genius, 79-82; and innovation, imita-

Creativity (*continued*)
tion, and initiation, 90-92; and knowledge systems (social) 101, 103, 105, 109, 110, 114, 117, 127, 141, 145, 154; for school children, 73, 74, 76; and social development, 164, 166-168, 170, 194-196, 199, 212 n.7
Critical test, 124, 126, 127

Dark Ages, 8, 20, 24, 25, 64, 160, 189
Darwin, Charles, 9
Darwinian evolution, 8, 32
Darwinism, 186
Da Vinci, Leonardo, 50
Davis, Philip J., and Ruben Hersh, 209, n.2
Democritus, 12
Dennet, Daniel C., 214 n.2
Descartes, René, 11
Divergence, 63, 67, 68, 72, 74, 85, 86, 88, 97, 99, 109; naive, 67, 68, 73, 74, 85; rigorous, 83, 85
Dummet, Michael, 207 n.3
Duns Scotus, John, 24

Eddington, Arthur S., 122
Einstein, Albert, 34, 53, 99, 106, 116, 122, 187, 188, 199
Entropy, 46, 53; as measurement, 59-62, 82, 86, 87, 92, 94, 95, 97, 98, 108, 113, 116, 126, 127, 143, 145, 168, 184, 185, 188; and history, 190-192, 197, 200, 201
Era of Knowledge: and anxiety, 113, 115-117, 132, 134, 137, 140, 142, 145, 151, 152, 154, 157; and the developing countries, 181-183, 191, 192, 196-198, 201, 206, 213 n.7; historical, 41-44, 54, 57, 82, 90, 92, 97, 99, 100, 103, 106; introduced, 15-17, 19; post–World War II, 36-38; and the promise of our social time, 161-163, 167, 171, 176, 181
Era time, 24
Euclid's fifth axiom of parallels, 13
Existentialism, 14

Farjoun, Emmanuel, and Moshe Machover, *Laws of Chaos,* 210 n.2
Fischer, David Hackett, 187, 217 n.1
Fleming, Sir Alexander, 65, 66, 72, 82, 88, 89, 213 n.2
Ford, Henry, 106
France, 7, 11, 164
Frankel, S. Herbert, 131, 132, 214 n.2
Freud, S., 9
Freudian, 8
Future-oriented society (country, grouping) 46, 163, 165-169, 174, 175, 179-181, 185, 196

Galen, 64
Galileo, 6, 8, 9, 71, 106, 160, 187, 188, 205, 206
Galilean-Newtonian relativity, 9
Galilean revolution, 10
Galton, Sir Francis, 61, 79, 80, 212 n.1
Genius, 79-82, 198-200
Germany, 7, 11, 14, 33, 164, 177
Getzels, J. W., and P. W. Jackson, "The Highly Intelligent and Highly Creative Adolescent," 74, 212 n.7
Great Depression, 29, 34, 46, 132, 147, 150, 151, 155

Guillen, Michael, 47
Gutenberg, Johannes, 71, 88, 89, 213 n.3

Harvey, William, 64-66, 73, 86, 89, 213 n.2
Heisenberg, Werner, 53, 100, 213 n.5
Historical time, 19, 21
Hodges, Johnny, 122, 123
Hume, David, 11
Huxley, Aldous, 194, 197

Imitation, 92, 115, 127, 142, 168, 180, 182, 186; explorative, 93, 97, 98, 100-103, 145, and awareness, 93; strict, 92, 100-102
Industrial Revolution, 23-25, 27, 29; post–World War I, 32-36, 39, 41, 105, 106, 110, 149, 162, 163, 172, 186, 189, 200
Information, 59-61; and the creative act, 82-86, 87; (I*), 98, 99, 110, 124, 126, 127
Initiation, 49, 50, 90, 97; contrasted with innovation, 95, 109, 110, 119, 120, 145, 180, 196, 212 n.2
Innovation, 49, 50, 54, 88, 90; competitive, 95, 96, 119, 123, 137; and the process of evaluation, 119-125, 137, 145, 158, 168, 180, 196, 212 n.2; strict, 95, 96, 119, 122, 124; and systems, 95-97, 101, 102, 108-110
Israel, 152, 165, 178

Japan, 155, 164, 177, 216 n.5

Kant, Immanuel, 32
Kepler, Johannes, 50, 70, 71, 106, 160, 187, 188, 206
Keynes, J. M., 27, 35, 147
Keynesian reasoning, 15
Kierkegaard, Sören, 114, 214 n.3
Knowledge systems, 49, 51, 54, 55, 57, 94, 97, 98, 102, 103, 112, 113, 116, 126, 134, 135, 142, 148, 171, 180, 190, 199, 202, 213 n.6
Koestler, Arthur, 69, 70, 72, 212 nn. 2, 3, 4, 6

Latin America, 152, 165
League of Nations, 15, 32, 43
Le Bon, Gustave, 29
Leibniz, G. W., 12, 34
Lucretius, 12
Lorentz, H. A., 106
Lysenko, T. D., 32

Marx, Karl, 28, 187
May, Rollo, 114, 115, 214 n.2
Middle Ages, 8, 26, 64, 72
Middle East, 153, 156, 181, 183, 216 n.2
Mingus, Charlie, 95
Monk, Thelonius, 95
More, Sir Thomas, 192, 193
Mozart, W. A., 199, 211 n.1

Newton, Sir Isaac, 6, 12, 28, 50, 71, 99, 106, 187, 188, 206
Nietzsche, Friedrich, 10, 11, 57
Nixon, Richard M., 158-159

Oersted, Hans Christian, 72, 82, 88-90, 213 n.2
Oliver, Joe King, 211 n.1
Orwell, George, 193, 194, 197

Parker, Charlie, 95, 122, 123
Past-oriented societies (countries), 46, 163, 165, 168-171, 180-183, 190

Pasteur, Louis, 124, 214 n.5
Pigou, A. C., 33, 35
Planck, Max, 106, 188
Plato, 20, 204
Poe, Edgar Allan, 63, 211 n.1
Present-oriented societies (countries), 46, 163, 165, 166, 168, 169, 171, 172, 175, 176, 181-183, 196

Rejection, 47, 77, 103, 105, 109, 110, 118
Renaissance, 11, 20, 26, 30, 36, 42, 48, 64, 148, 149, 152, 200
Ricardo, David, 28
Riemann, Bernhard, 13, 106,
Roentgen, W. K., 122

Santayana, George, 31
Say, J.-B., 28
Schopenhauer, A., 10-11
Smith, Adam, 28, 29, 110
Social time, 15, 17, 21; defined, 28-32, 38, 42, 92, 97, 98, 108, 110, 132, 133, 135, 142, 144, 148, 157, 163; past-, present-, future-oriented societies, 166-168, 170, 178, 180; and our historical era, 182-184, 191-194, 196, 200, 201, 210 n.5
Socrates, 20, 204, 206
Soviet Union (Russia), 7, 32, 36, 79, 136, 152, 154, 158, 159, 161, 169

Tacitus, 136, 215 n.4
Thomas Aquinas, St., 8, 9, 11
Thompson, Victor, 131, 132
Thompson, William, 28
Tressell, Robert, 185, 200
Truth, 3, 15, 16, 17, 21, 111, 113, 116, 184, 185, 197; absolute, 4; anti-realism and, 16, 17; realistic theory of, 16; religious, 4, 17; universal, 13
Turing, Alan, 144, 215 n.5
Tycho Brache, 70

United Nations, 15, 152, 154, 155, 178, 183
United States (America), 7, 11, 25, 34, 36, 155, 156, 158, 161, 164, 178, 180, 181, 215 n.1, 216 n.5
Utility, 46, 48, 53, 57; and its assessment, 58-60, 86, 87, 89; and creativity, 91-94, 96, 99, 102, 103, 110-112, 115, 117, 119, 120, 121, 124, 125, 140, 180, 184, 185, 190, 197, 207

Van Gogh, Vincent, 110
Vietnam, 152, 153, 161, 183, 215 n.1

Weber, Max, 28
Whitehead, A. N., 3, 4
Wilson, Woodrow, 154
World War I, 7, 14, 33, 132, 150, 154, 200
World War II, 7, 15, 29, 34, 106, 132, 142, 151-155, 164, 165, 170, 177, 178, 183, 200

Yergin, Daniel, 216 n.5

About the Author

DAVID Z. RICH, an economic consultant to business firms and multinational corporations, is the author of *Contemporary Economics: A Unifying Approach*.

www.ingramcontent.com/pod-product-compliance
Ingram Content Group UK Ltd.
Pitfield, Milton Keynes, MK11 3LW, UK
UKHW020206290926
15470UKWH00001B/35

9 780313 2610